IT'S ABOUT TIME

It's About Time

Following Jesus through the
Seasons of the Church Year

Brook A. Thelander

Foreword by Don Hughes

WIPF & STOCK · Eugene, Oregon

Wipf & Stock
An Imprint of Wipf and Stock Publishers
199 W. 8th Ave., Suite 3
Eugene, OR 97401

www.wipfandstock.com

PAPERBACK ISBN: 978-1-6667-7365-1
HARDCOVER ISBN: 978-1-6667-7366-8
EBOOK ISBN: 978-1-6667-7367-5

06/07/23

For Connie, Emily, and Davis—the family God has given me to love and enjoy through all the seasons of life; and for my mother, Barbara, who passed away while this book was being written

Contents

Lent-Easter-Pentecost: The Cycle of Life | 99

Foreword

IF YOU ARE READING this foreword, the title has already done its work. "It's about time" is a common expression of relief from some aggravation. So, at first glance, you may be wondering if there is some wisdom to be found here for such occasions. Or, if you have read the subtitle, you may be wondering what time has to do with following Jesus. *It's About Time* has plenty to say about time with Jesus, and in the end, peace for what troubles us.

Time is God's gift to us and it matters how we use it. What is it about time that causes so much consternation—too much time for this, too little time for that. Do you suppose time can be our friend? Whether it flies by or drags on, time moves in a steady cadence of one tick and tock at a time. When we complain there is not enough time, *the preacher* says, *"There is a time for every matter under heaven."* When we are impatient because things are not happening quickly enough, *the psalmist* advises, *"Be still before the Lord and wait patiently for him"* (Eccl 3:1; Ps 37:7)

Imagine my surprise when I discovered there was more to time than minutes and hours, days and weeks, months and years. As a cradle Christian raised in a preacher's home, I somehow escaped learning that it was a good thing to number my days according to the rhythms of the church year. I did not know there was such a year and that it had a distinct inner logic. I came to the liturgical life late, but not too late for it to set me on a very different path. In time I retired from my thirty-three-year career, enrolled in seminary, was ordained and called to a parish.

Early in my quest, Dr. Thelander was called to be the rector of the church that introduced me to liturgy and its concepts and practices. From his first sermon, I knew I had found my mentor. Dr. Thelander is a skilled communicator. With an economy of words, he is able to make the complex easy to understand. I believe you will discover these qualities for yourself as you read *It's About Time*. Do not skip the introduction. The main text will have more impact if you learn whereof and why he speaks.

It's About Time is not only a theological treatise on the church year, it is also a source that will direct you beyond mere observance and ritual to "specific opportunities for growth and celebration that arise in the lives of those who would follow Jesus." Dr. Thelander writes for everyone wherever they are on their walk with Jesus.

I found my Christian home in the liturgy of the church year. Dr. Thelander was patient with my questions and helped me grasp the nuances of liturgical time which came to enrich my life and faith. It was an unexpected privilege to be asked to write the foreword, and it is with tremendous pleasure I commend *It's About Time*.

Fr. Don Hughes
Rector Emeritus, St. John's Anglican Church
Boerne, TX

Acknowledgments

WRITING THIS BOOK WOULD not have been possible without the help and support of the following people: Caleb Shupe, Donna Fletcher Crow, Amanda Patchin, Rod Thelander, Brady Thelander, Brian Jenkerson, Don Hughes, and Bryan Vanshur. I am especially indebted to my wife, Connie, for her encouragement and patience.

Abbreviations

RSV   Revised Standard Version
MSG   The Message
NLT   New Living Translation

Introduction

In the world's great religious traditions, praise of God is
centered around the disciplined use of time.

—DAVID STENDALL RAST

A LITTLE GIRL WAS once overheard praying: "God, where did yesterday go—do you have it?" Now that I am older, I find myself in a similar situation as that inquisitive little girl. But I'm not merely curious about yesterday. For me, the question is: "God, where did all the *years* of my life go?"

Both my lived experience and the collective wisdom of the ages remind me that life is short. The psalmist, writing in sacred Scripture, acknowledges this reality when he states, "My entire lifetime is just a moment to you; at best, each of us is but a breath."[1]

Many years ago country music artist Kenny Chesney recorded a song entitled, "Don't Blink." The song offers both commentary and a caution: Time passes quickly, and tomorrow cannot be taken for granted. My life on this earth is like a mist, a vapor that vanishes almost as quickly as it arrives.[2]

We know deep in our bones that life is short. What isn't always as obvious is how to make the most of the life that we've been given. The dilemma isn't original with us. Psalm 90, attributed to Moses, states that we are fortunate to enjoy seventy or eighty years on this earth. Given this realization, Moses makes this humble request of God: "Teach us to number our days, that we may get a heart of wisdom."[3]

1. Ps 39:4–5 NLT.
2. Jas 4:14 RSV.
3. Ps 90:12 RSV.

1

Moses has far more than time management in view. He asks for grace not merely to live *efficiently*, but to live *wisely*. Obviously, making good use of the time we are given is a good thing. But behind Moses's request lies the truth that the hours, days, weeks, months, and years that comprise our lives are more than just marks on a calendar. Our time on this earth is a gift to be received, not merely a commodity to be managed.

Perhaps Moses anticipated the words of Jesus, who centuries later said, "I came that they may have life, and have it abundantly."[4] I believe that a universal hunger exists in every human being for abundant life. People may differ in their understandings of what constitutes that life, but it is my belief that the desire for abundant life is ultimately a hunger deep within us for transcendence, for meaning and purpose beyond ourselves. Ministering to people from all walks of life for more than twenty-five years, one underlying truth surfaced again and again: the realization that no earthly thing can satisfy an unearthly ache. The experience of many with whom I interact today is that our modern materialistic culture is asphyxiating.[5] Experience teaches us that there must be more to life than the passing of our days on a calendar.

This book is my attempt to discover what is involved in learning to number our days by exploring a deeper significance which pervades them. It seeks to answer a perennial question common to the human condition, namely, How do I make the most of the life I've been given? What is involved in living abundantly and authentically?

I write from the perspective of one whose primary vocation has been the study of the sacred Scriptures of Christianity and the lived experience of people of faith. Many of the answers that I have discovered to the above questions might seem counterintuitive at first glance. But perhaps this is the nature of true wisdom. It is not always readily apparent on the surface of things, and it often comes at the price of the refining fire of experience.[6]

My primary source material for exploring the above questions is the experience gained through more than twenty-five years of pastoral ministry, walking with people and sharing their lives and their struggles. This book is not an exhaustive or academic study, but rather the fruit of almost three decades of personal reflection and pulpit proclamation. Rejoicing with those who rejoice and weeping with those who weep afforded me numerous opportunities to ask what it looks like to number our days and to grow wise through the seasons of life. I've discovered along the way that wisdom does not consist in how much we know, but in how well we *live* what we know.

4. John 10:10 RSV.

5. Snell and George, *Mind, Heart, and Soul,* 79.

6. This characteristic feature of wisdom can be found in the Wisdom Literature of the Old Testament, including the Proverbs, Ecclesiastes, and the book of Job.

A major premise underlying this book is that the Creator God, who stands outside of time and space, entered time and space in the person of Jesus Christ. The eternal God became a human being and moved into the neighborhood. He pitched his tent into the midst of this broken-down, refugee-camp world. The incarnation—God becoming a human being—reveals to us not merely the earthiness and materiality of Christianity, but also the reality that Christianity involves experiencing life at the intersection of time and eternity.[7]

Subsequent to the publication of his novel *A Message in a Bottle*, novelist Walker Percy gave a lecture entitled "Another Message in a Bottle." He observed that in every part of the world where novels have been written and read, the presiding ethos involves the salient truth of life being found in the teaching of a great philosopher or the enlightenment of a great sage. By way of contrast, Percy observes,

> The one great difference of Christianity is its claim—outrageous claim, many would say—that God actually entered historic time, first through His covenant with the Jews and then through the Incarnation.[8]

Christianity asserts that God has revealed himself to us and encounters us *in* time. Christianity is a thoroughly historical religion. The salvation that Christianity proclaims is not salvation *from* the world and its history but the salvation *of* the world itself and its history.[9] This distinguishes Christianity from other religions. God writes not merely with words or ideas, but in and through events, places, and persons. The life and ministry of Jesus has a pronounced historical particularity to it, and the fact that Jesus was a real historical figure is of central importance to Christianity. As a result, the seasons of Jesus's life provide a clue as we attempt to discover what abundant life might look like for us. The seasons of Jesus's life become a lens through which we can learn to see differently, to "number our days" and to gain a heart of wisdom.

One important but neglected reason for this is because the seasons of Jesus's earthly life involved more than mere chronological time. Because God was acting in Jesus for the salvation of the world, the seasons of Jesus's life were marked by a special kind of time, what New Testament writers call *kairos* time. In the New Testament, *kairos* time is infused with life-altering significance. *Kairos* moments are pivotal moments around which lives and

7. Stookey, *Calendar*, 17.

8. Percy, *Signposts*, 65.

9. Driscoll, *What Happens at Mass*, 97.

destinies may change. They often produce serendipitous insight that leads to transformation and new ways of living.

An example of this is found in the opening chapter of Mark's Gospel, where Jesus begins his public ministry by saying: "The time (*kairos*) is fulfilled, and the kingdom of God is at hand; repent, and believe the gospel."[10] In this simple sentence, Jesus is not merely speaking general spiritual truth, nor is he merely calling on persons to make a decision for God. Rather, he is announcing that God is calling all people into a new way of being and living in the world and summoning them to align themselves to this new reality.[11]

We live our lives in time that has a seasonal shape to it. But within the chronological flow of our lives there also exists the possibility of experiencing *kairos* time, moments when we find our lives suddenly and unexpectedly illumined and altered by the life and words of Jesus. This should not surprise us, for he claimed to come into the world to bring persons abundant life. He did this not only by what he taught but by how he lived in time. His claim to bring abundant life is thus a compelling reason to look more closely at the narrative seasons of his life, to discover how God was uniquely at work in him to bring persons to life-altering experience.

Looking more closely at Jesus's life, we discover that when Jesus invited people to follow him, he did not do so merely by inviting them to believe certain propositional truths, although those truths are not unimportant. Jesus literally invited people to *follow* him, to share in his life, and in some mysterious way to share in his death. The apostle Paul captures the paradox when he says: "I have been crucified with Christ; it is no longer I who live, but Christ who lives in me."[12]

The wisdom offered in Christianity, then, involves so much more than believing certain truths. The wisdom offered in Christianity is *lived* experience at the intersection of time and eternity. It involves living, dying, and rising again with Jesus. It is nothing less than the life of Jesus being manifested and reproduced in us. In this book, I will argue that a primary way that Jesus's life is reproduced in us involves learning to be attentive to *kairos* moments of divine grace in the chronological seasons of our life.[13]

---

10. Mark 1:15 RSV.

11. In the Scriptures, *kairos* time is often infused with such significance that the entire cosmos is summoned to respond. As such, *kairos* time is thick with power and meaning. Cf. Whalen, *Seasons and Feasts*, 4.

12. Gal 2:20 RSV.

13. Saint Augustine viewed *kairos* as concrete, personal, lived time which is measured in souls, not bodies; time that is measured by meaning and purpose, not by spatial motion. Cf. Kreeft, *I Burned for Your Peace*, 358.

Doing this requires us to discover a seasonal quality involved in learning to number our days and becoming wise. Just as there are seasons and rhythms to the natural order (*chronos*), so there are seasons and rhythms to the spiritual order (*kairos*) and to the seasonal pattern of Jesus's life. There are rhythms of preparation and realization, promise and fulfillment, sowing and reaping, fasts and feasts.

From its earliest days, the church recognized the reality that time and eternity continually intersect. But it also recognized an irony inherent in this reality, namely, that time can obscure the very eternity it is designed to reveal. As a result, the church found it necessary to mark time in special ways that call to mind God's work in Jesus for our salvation. The church has always understood that Christ's saving actions in the past cannot be relegated to the past but must be brought forward into the present if they are to impact persons in a meaningful way. Similarly, Christ's saving actions that still lie in the future must also be brought to bear on our present experience.

Understanding this may require us to rethink how we view time with our typical categories of past, present, and future. It may be more helpful if we understand time as a continuum where the present is but the moving edge between the past and the future. For example, in a moment you will read a word set in all capital letters. Your reading of that word is currently a future event. BUT now your reading of the word is a past event. In this understanding of time, the past is far more than prologue, and the future far more than a distant dream. The present cannot be conceived in isolation, as if it had a life of its own. The past, present, and future are always of a piece.[14]

The language that theologians use to describe how both past events and future events intersect our present experience is found in two Greek words: *anamnesis* and *prolepsis*. Anamnesis is a rich term that means "the drawing near of memory" whereby the past becomes present through an active kind of remembering.[15] Usually, when Scripture uses the terms "remember" and "remembrance," it denotes not a mental process, but a *ritual* process. Remembering involves engaging in ritual action, not taking a mental photograph. When Jesus instructs his disciples, "Do this in remembrance of me," he is not instructing them to think quietly about him, but to *do* what he does: take the bread and cup, give thanks, break the bread and give the cup to those who seek to follow him. Anamnesis is remembrance by *doing* rather than *cognition*. It involves ritual action whereby the observance of past events brings them into the present moment. When we "remember"

14. Stookey, *Calendar*, 20.

15. L'Engle, *Irrational Season*, 17, defines *anamnesis* as "against amnesia." She observes that where *anamnesis* is truly present the mighty acts of God are present. In such moments we are in *kairos* time.

events in Jesus's life and ministry, we do not reenact them. Rather, we celebrate what Christ has done and what he continues to do for us now.[16]

This understanding of *anamnesis*, however, does not mean that history is cyclical. Events we refer to in the present are not happening again and again as we observe them. Instead, events that occurred only once become contemporaneous with us because the risen Christ holds all time in unity. Consider, for example, Isaac Watts's "When I Survey the Wondrous Cross":

> When I survey the wondrous cross on which the Prince of Glory died,
> My richest gain I count but loss, and pour contempt on all my pride.
> See, from His head, His hands, His feet, sorrow and love flow mingled down.
> Did e'er such love and sorrow meet, or thorns compose so rich a crown.[17]

Although Jesus suffered on the cross only once, Watts shows that the reality of that agony comes into our experience repeatedly. Because past and present are not sealed in boxes, completed historical action intersects our time with the force of reality that we truly experience.

Where *anamnesis* involves bringing past events into the present, *prolepsis* involves the intersection of future reality with the present. The word prolepsis means "to take beforehand." In terms of our discussion, it involves the bringing of God's future into our present.

While this may seem strange and our rational minds may reject it as impossible, the language of the church's hymns is replete with this reality. Consider Charles Wesley's hymn, "Lo, He Comes with Clouds Descending":

> Lo! He comes with clouds descending, once for favored sinners slain;
> Thousand thousand saints attending, swell the triumph of His train.
> Every eye shall now behold Him, robed in dreadful majesty;
> Those who set at naught and sold Him, Pierced and nailed Him to the tree.
> Now redemption, long expected, see in solemn pomp appear.[18]

Here, Jesus's second coming in the future impinges on present reality. Paying attention to the seasons of Jesus's life through *anamnesis* and *prolepsis* helps us to celebrate in our present experience both what has occurred in the past and what we believe—by faith—will occur in the future. This involves Jesus's birth, ministry, suffering, death, resurrection, ascension, his return in glory, and the final sovereignty of God over all things in a world made new. The celebration of these events becomes a sort of time machine

---

16. See also Moore, *Earth Unites with Heaven*, 12.

17. Isaac Watts, "When I Survey the Wondrous Cross," public domain.

18. Charles Wesley, "Lo! He Comes with Clouds Descending," public domain.

whereby we are mystically connected to both the past and the future. They form an intersection of time and eternity.

That Christians should find it necessary to observe seasons, days, and hours in ways that make evident the eternal in our midst may seem strange to some. But consider how essential timekeeping is in organizing our human experience. Try to navigate your way through life without access to a clock or calendar and before long you will find yourself completely disoriented. Further, we invest specific calendar days with significance because of their impact upon us. Birthdays, weddings, graduations, and anniversaries are laden with positive connotations, while traumatic experiences negatively affect us. In both cases, these days are no longer ordinary because of how we experience them. This is equally true in the spiritual life. Thomas Howard observes:

> We mortals live by hours, days, and weeks, so this marking and remembering [the life of Jesus] must take on some actual, temporal form for us. . . . It is not enough to suppose that having assented once upon a time to a doctrine is sufficient. . . . We need to keep coming back around and putting our minds to the Nativity, the Resurrection, and so forth.[19]

Howard is affirming the insight that the church, throughout history, has sought to help us live in time in a way that invests all things with meaning. Through its distinctive way of marking time the church teaches us how to contextualize life, to read the temporal in light of the eternal. Calendar time is taken up into *kairos* time such that each moment of life becomes sacred. In this way the church trains our eyes to see our lives in the light of sacred Scripture and the stories of Christ and the saints who've gone before us.[20]

Learning about the church's sanctification of time through its participation in the seasons of Jesus's life was a *kairos* and life-changing moment for me more than thirty years ago.[21] I came to see that the days of my life are not defined by the civil calendar but by how my life has been caught up in the events of Jesus's life and ministry. My personal story is caught up in the larger story of how God is at work to bring healing to this broken-down world. The seasons of my life have been taken up and transformed by the seasons of Jesus's life. My *chronos* time has been caught up in God's *kairos* time. Jesus's promise of abundant life leads me into ever-deepening insight

---

19. Howard, *Evangelical Is Not Enough*, 132.

20. See Heady, *Numbering My Days*, 112; See also Whalen, *Seasons and Feasts*, 3.

21. It was Dom Gregory Dix who used the phrase "sanctification of time" to describe the church's growing development of historically commemorating the events of Christ's life. See Dix, *Shape of the Liturgy*.

and transformation precisely as I participate in the seasonal rhythms of his life. My personal story finds its deepest meaning in relation to God's purposes for me and for the world. Numbering my days—and gaining a heart of wisdom—involves submitting to Jesus and consciously stepping into his story. It involves having the shape and purpose of my life conformed to the shape and purpose of his.[22]

In the chapters that follow, we will explore how the seasons of Jesus's life and ministry can be a path to abundant life for us. Specifically, the seasons of Jesus's life and ministry are experienced in the distinctive way the church lives in time known as the liturgical year, or the Christian year.[23] The liturgical year allows the saving events of Jesus's life to be brought forward into our present experience as we seek not merely to know more about Jesus but to *follow* him as authentic disciples.[24] I hope to show how the seasons of the liturgical year provide concrete opportunities to deepen our life of faith and to grow as disciples of Jesus. Those opportunities come in the form of both challenges and joys. The church year—and life itself—involves navigating the challenges of life as well as celebrating its joys in ways that transform us.

This book is not a comprehensive history or theology of the church year.[25] It is, rather, a look at specific opportunities for growth and celebration that arise in the lives of those who would follow Jesus, challenges and joys that are engendered and illuminated in navigating the seasons of the Christian year. It attempts to shine the spotlight on specific opportunities for growth in Christlikeness common to all those who desire to number their days and thereby gain a heart of wisdom. Many of these opportunities are linked to particular seasons of the church year, though they need not exclusively be so. As we shall see, maturing in the life of faith involves far more than accumulating information. It involves *transformation* through sharing in Jesus's life and becoming partakers of the divine nature.[26] We

22. Gross, *Living the Christian Year*, 135.

23. In this book I use the terms "liturgical year," "Christian year," and "church year" synonymously.

24. See Howard, *Evangelical Is Not Enough*, 133, where the author observes that the liturgical year is nothing more than the church's "walking through the Gospel with our Lord."

25. Others have undertaken such studies. See, for example, Talley, *Origins of the Liturgical Year*; Whalen, *Seasons and Feasts*; Bradshaw and Johnson, *Origins of Feasts*; Adam, *Liturgical Year*; Campbell, *Feasts of Christendom*; Stookey, *Calendar*; Chittister, *Liturgical Year*. Other helpful studies include Webber, *Ancient-Future Time*; see also Webber, *Complete Library of Christian Worship*; Schall, *Reason for the Seasons*; Moore, *Earth Unites with Heaven*; Ireton, *Circle of Seasons*; Biffi, *Introduction to the Liturgical Year*.

26. 2 Pet 1:4.

shall discover that the gospel is not merely a message of what we are saved *from*; the gospel is a message of what we are saved *for*, which involves our adoption as God's sons and daughters who are refashioned in the image of Christ. This is God's desire for all of us.

It is my hope that in the pages that follow, you will find yourself beginning your own journey of transformation as you discover how God's saving activity has been concealed in time, and how eternity continues to intersect time through the means of grace that is the church year. The liturgical year is not mere recollection or ritual. It is the movement through calendar time of Jesus and the development of Christian community. The church year moves with measured rhythm in order to knit Jesus's life and vision into our own personal journeys through time.

For those who are not familiar with the liturgical year, I hope this book will become a helpful tool and means of grace for your faith journey, an open door through which you might travel further to explore previously unseen possibilities. For those who do have experience with liturgical rhythms, my hope is that you will find fresh insight and inspiration. The liturgical year is a wonderful and life-changing means of grace to help us experience God's *kairos* in the midst of our ordinary calendar days. It is a vehicle in which eternity continues to intersect time, bringing God's saving activity to concrete expression in our lives. The liturgical year helps us to align ourselves with God's gracious purposes. It immerses us ever more deeply into our encounter with Christ. Through it we discover not merely God's design for our individual lives, but also what it means to be the church, the body of Christ, in the world. The liturgical year is the daily immersion of the Christian community in the illuminating life of Jesus.[27]

Although the purpose of this book is not to set forth a comprehensive history or theology of the church year, I do attempt to sketch a brief historical background to the seasons in the introductory chapters to each season. Each chapter of the book also begins with suggested Scripture readings appropriate to the season and to the particular emphases of that chapter. It should also be noted that the sequence of the book follows the liturgical year as we observe it theologically, not its chronological development.

---

27. Chittister, *Liturgical Year*, 13–14.

Advent-Christmas-Epiphany
The Cycle of Light

EVEN THOUGH ATTENTION WILL be given to them separately, the celebrations of Advent, Christmas, and Epiphany are a unity comprising what is typically known as the Cycle of Light. Seeing these celebrations as a unity is necessary because the cycle is often collapsed into the celebration of the birth of the baby Jesus two thousand years ago in Bethlehem. But the Advent-Christmas-Epiphany cycle is first and foremost a celebration of the paschal mystery, i.e., the death and resurrection of Jesus. It reminds the Christian community that it is an adult Christ in his life, death, and resurrection who is celebrated even during the Advent-Christmas-Epiphany cycle.[1]

At the same time, the Advent-Christmas-Epiphany cycle also focuses on the incarnation, the Word of God becoming human in Jesus Christ. A wonderful exchange has taken place. The eternal Word has taken on our humanity. Christ is our brother in the flesh; we are the offspring of God. This is a profound mystery. The whole Advent-Christmas-Epiphany cycle seeks to draw us into this mystery of God's coming to us in Christ. This means that it is inadequate to view Advent as a time when we are living in the past before the birth of Jesus. And Christmas is not reduced to the retelling of the events surrounding Jesus's birth, a mere "birthday" celebration.

A further consideration: Though it is common to speak of Advent as the beginning of the church year, there is no beginning or ending of the liturgical year in an absolute sense. It is more accurate to speak about the church year as composed of various cycles and days which flow into one another each year. It is difficult to pinpoint one beginning and one end. It might be more helpful to speak of the liturgical year as having several different beginnings

---

1. Whalen, *Seasons and Feasts*, 110. One example of this involves the presence of John the Baptist in many of the Advent texts, whose focus is on the adult Jesus as he begins his earthly ministry.

and endings, none of which can be too precisely designated. There is a merging of themes and images which takes place rather than some sort of "beginning" or "ending." Some prominent themes in the Cycle of Light include: light/darkness, patience, waiting, promise, hope, peace, justice, Mary, John the Baptizer, and judgment. In summary, the full meaning of the Advent-Christmas-Epiphany cycle cannot be reduced to any single component. To do so robs it of its power to evoke and to transform us.[2]

ADVENT

The word "Advent" means "coming" or "arrival." It describes an action in progress, an act not yet fully accomplished. But the Latin word *adventus*, from which the word "Advent" comes, has a plurality of meanings. It means not merely "coming" or "arrival," but also "develop," "set in," and "arise." The word *adventus* itself can also mean an "invasion, ripening, incursion, and appearance."[3] In ancient Rome, *adventus* was used to describe the entry of a victorious emperor into his city following a military victory.

Advent is thus a fitting term to describe the period prior to Christmas, because we are preparing to celebrate the arrival of a King. While for many the focus of the season involves preparation to celebrate the birth of Jesus in Bethlehem, Advent is far too rich in meaning to be reduced to that single event. The liturgical year does not begin with Advent because Christmas is coming; the liturgical year begins with Advent to remind us why Jesus was born in the first place.

As such, the beginning of the church year focuses our attention on the *end* of things. The term "end" here means not merely the end of time, but the central purpose or goal of creation. History is not random. It is important to begin the liturgical year with this important truth in mind. Without this understanding, the story of Jesus which the church year rehearses (his birth, life, death, and resurrection) is robbed of its power because it fails to see Jesus's story as the fulfillment of God's will through the framework of historical events.

The fact that God's ultimate purpose for creation is accomplished through historical events partly explains why the arrangement of the Advent season is puzzling to many. The season begins with a focus on the coming reign of God and the call to prepare for the final judgment. The season ends with a celebration of a past event, the Savior's birth. Throughout the season

---

2. Whalen, *Seasons and Feasts*, 118–19.

3. Beale, "Deeper Meaning of Advent," para. 3.

both notes are sounded, with the focus on Jesus's birth occupying greater attention closer to Christmas.

Advent is thus characterized by anticipation. Through the Scripture readings that come to us in the season, we identify with the ancient Jews in their longing for the Messiah as foretold by the prophets and by John the Baptist who was the forerunner to Jesus. With them, we open our eyes again to the darkness around us and lament the suffering in the world. We cry out for God to come and put the world right. We also identify with the Virgin Mary, expecting a child and waiting for her deliverance. While the world around us is swimming in frenetic activity, we seek to be quiet and to wait for the coming of Christ.[4]

In addition to the celebration of Jesus's birth and the anticipation of his return in glory, the Advent season also invites us to be attentive to Christ's coming to us now through the sacraments of the church and our lived experience:

> Jesus knocks at the door of our hearts every day, but Advent makes us particularly attentive to his continuous visits. It helps us remember that He will come again in the splendor of glory and will call us to enter into his promised kingdom. During the season of Advent, while we wait for Jesus' birth at Christmas, our waiting for the final and definitive coming of Jesus is re-awakened and strengthened.[5]

Although the season of Advent inaugurates the Christian year, it is not the oldest season. Determining the precise origin and development of the season is difficult because observances varied among local churches, and regional differences in the celebration between East and West also existed.[6] In Spain and Italy there were places where the season lasted six weeks, indicating a possible correlation with the preparatory season of Lent prior to Easter. In Spain and Gaul (France), an emphasis on Jesus's second coming in judgment gave the season a penitential character, which was reflected in the liturgy by the omission of the *Gloria* and the use of purple vestments. Some of this penitential flavor of the season later influenced the Roman liturgy in the twelfth century, although Advent was not formally regarded as a penitential time.

The earliest record of Advent observance dates to the late fifth century, in the instructions of Bishop Perpetuus of Tours. In Rome, the beginnings

---

4. Gross, *Living the Christian Year*, 218.

5. Biffi, *Introduction to the Liturgical Year*, 14–15.

6. Bradshaw and Johnson, *Origins of Feasts*, 157–68. See also Adam, *Liturgical Year*, 130–38; and Whalen, *Seasons and Feasts*, 102–5.

of Advent liturgies appear in the mid sixth century. Definitive changes begin to emerge under Pope Gregory the Great (590–604), who shortened the season from six weeks to four. Under Gregory, the focus on Christ's incarnation balanced the earlier emphasis on Christ's second coming, because the incarnation was the historical event that marked the beginning of our salvation. The focus on the incarnation also revealed that the Advent season is defined more by joy than penitence.

In time, the features of Advent made prominent by Pope Gregory came to dominate in the Western Church. Advent begins on the Sunday closest to November 30 and includes four Sundays prior to Christmas Eve. The prominent theme of the season is that of *coming*. St. Bernard of Clairvaux (d. 1153) captures this focus vividly:

> We know that there are three comings of the Lord. The third lies between the other two. It is invisible, while the other two are visible. In the first coming he was seen on earth, dwelling among men. . .In the final coming all flesh will see the salvation of our God, and they will look on him whom they pierced. The intermediate coming is a hidden one; in it only the elect see the Lord within their own selves, and they are saved. In his first coming our Lord came in our flesh and in our weakness; in this middle coming he comes in spirit and in power; in the final coming he will be seen in glory and majesty. . .Because this [middle] coming lies between the other two, it is like a road on which we travel from the first coming to the last. In the first, Christ was our redemption; in the last, he will appear as our life; in this middle coming, he is our rest and consolation.[7]

These three comings of Christ—past, present, and future—all live together in one long sigh of the soul during Advent. This reality leads to a secondary theme of the season, namely, that of *waiting*. During Advent God's people wait patiently and actively for what God promises. More importantly, we learn how to live while we wait.

CHRISTMAS

The original context of the Feast of the Nativity is the incarnation, the manifestation in the flesh of the Son of God. The historical origin of the celebration has been difficult to determine with any precision, though it is apparent

---

7. Bernard of Clairvaux, "Sermon 5," 1:169.

that Christ's birthday on December 25 was already being celebrated in the early fourth century (AD 336) in Rome.[8]

In the East, the celebration of Christmas occurred on January 6. Part of the reason for this involves the use of different calendars, particularly the use of the Julian calendar in the East. Both of these dates for Christmas have been absorbed into the respective Western and Eastern calendars, though for different reasons and in different ways.[9] In one sense, it is a matter of emphasis. In the West, the focus of Christmas is on Jesus's appearance as God in the flesh. In the East, the focus is on Jesus's baptism and his manifestation as the Son of God. This leads one scholar to conclude that Christmas and Epiphany can be seen as two aspects of the one Feast of Christmas rather than as two distinctly different feasts.[10] As a result, the church celebrates four manifestations of Christ at Christmas: as the heavenly Son of God, as King of the nations, as Lord of Creation, and as human child.

In the West, a tradition developed in the sixth century involving three liturgical celebrations on Christmas: a service at midnight, a service at dawn, and a service during the day. At the heart of these three celebrations was a belief in what some mystics saw as the threefold birth of the Lord. The first and supreme birth occurs when the heavenly Father bears his only-begotten Son as one with himself in essence yet also as a distinct Person. The second birth, which we celebrate on Christmas, involves Jesus's birth from his mother the Virgin Mary. The third birth is the birth of God in faithful souls as the result of grace.

In addition to Easter, Christmas is celebrated liturgically as an *octave* (Latin for "eight"), i.e., a week of feasting beginning on December 25 and ending on January 1, where the celebration of Jesus's nativity is prolonged for eight days. Each day of the octave is treated the same as the original feast day celebration. The Christmas *season* includes twelve days from December 25 to January 6. In some traditions other minor feasts are observed during this time, such as the Feast of the Holy Innocents on December 28, the Feast of the Holy Family, and the Feast of Mary, the Mother of God.

The Christmas season has the potential to put a glow into our souls if we are willing to see it as a whole rather than an isolated day or event. We

---

8. Adam, *Liturgical Year*, 122. The dating of Christmas to December 25 has been vigorously debated by scholars for decades, with two primary schools of thought. One school is known as the History of Religions approach, the other is known as the Calculation Hypothesis. See Chittister, *Liturgical Year*, 76–80; see also Bradshaw and Johnson, *Origins of Feasts*, 122–30.

9. See the discussion from footnote 8 above for a more detailed discussion of the differences of the respective dates for Christmas.

10. Chittister, *Liturgical Year*, 81.

then develop the capacity to see in the manger the meaning of the empty tomb. The light of Christmas within us takes us beyond any kind of fairy-tale reduction of the great truths of our faith to a lived understanding of what all the dark days of life are about.[11]

EPIPHANY

In Barrow, Alaska, a small town on the Northern tip of the state on the Arctic Sea, when the sun sets on or around November 18, it takes a holiday. Darkness envelops Barrow for approximately sixty-five days, and the sun does not appear again until near the 24th of January. When the light finally does reappear, the people of Barrow gather and enjoy a public celebration of its return.

During winter, I often get the "winter blues," and long for more sunshine and blue skies. But I cannot imagine living for two full months in darkness. It is very difficult for me to imagine what it would be like to greet the light after being without it for that long.

Many centuries ago, the prophet Isaiah spoke about a similar lack of light. It was a moral and spiritual darkness that had surrounded the people for many years. It was a period when God often seemed absent or silent. Into that dark period Isaiah finally announced, "Arise, shine; for your light has come, and the glory of the LORD has risen upon you."[12]

The word "epiphany" means "manifestation" or "openly showing forth." The word was sometimes used in antiquity to describe the official visit of a king or emperor to a city or region of his kingdom. Occasions like this were rather rare, so when they happened the king would usually appear publicly in all of his dazzling splendor.

The pre-Christian Syrian ruler Antiochus, impressed with his own power, at one point assumed the name Antiochus Epiphanes as a declaration that he was the appearance of a god on earth. The Gospel writer Matthew, however, has a different take on things. The religious and secular culture of Matthew's day contained many stories to the effect that a great ruler would be born, and his birth would be accompanied by celestial signs. The text from Isaiah 60 was part of that lore, where the prophet announces that the nations would come to Jerusalem to worship Israel's God.

In terms of how Matthew narrates the story, the Epiphany involves the manifestation of the star above Bethlehem subsequent to Jesus's birth. Interestingly, Matthew is the only Gospel writer to record the story of the Magi and their journey, but the story continues to fascinate us to this day.

11. Chittister, *Liturgical Year*, 88.

12. Isa 60:1 RSV.

It is the story not only of a guiding star, but also a dream of warning, a paranoid and bloodthirsty king, and an intricate itinerary. It reveals to us that the world into which the Light of God came was a partly receptive, but mostly hostile, world.

The Feast of Epiphany occurs on January 6, commemorating the coming of Jesus as the Light of the world and the journey of the Magi to worship him. The season after Epiphany and before Ash Wednesday is known as Epiphanytide, or in some traditions as Ordinary Time or the Season after Epiphany. The Feast of Epiphany, and the weeks following it, are a time when we focus on the appearance or manifestation of Christ to the nations. It is also known as "gentile Christmas" because the wise men from the East who followed the Star were gentiles, most likely from Persia.

If Christmas sees the Light of God rekindled in the world, Epiphany shows that Light coming into full view, being seen by others, and casting its brightness upon all people. Indeed, at the heart of Epiphany is the celebration that in Jesus, God shows himself not just to the Jews, but to all people of the world. Epiphany makes explicit the truth that God chose the children of Israel and blessed them precisely so that they might be a witness to all peoples of the earth and help to bring all nations into covenant relationship with him through Jesus.

Historically, the Feast of Epiphany probably developed in the church at Rome after the establishment of the Feast of the Nativity on December 25. But it was being celebrated in Gaul and Spain before this. This makes sense because Epiphany is an Eastern feast in origin and both Spain and Gaul were influenced by Eastern liturgies. It was during the fourth century that Epiphany was established in Rome.[13]

In terms of marking time through the liturgical year, Epiphany demonstrates that things are moving at a rapid pace. Matthew gives us clues that as the Magi arrive from the East, Jesus is no longer an infant. This is understandable, as the Magi would have traveled more than a thousand miles to reach Jerusalem and Bethlehem. Additionally, when the wise men do arrive, Matthew tells us that Jesus, with Mary, is "in the house" and not in the manger.[14] And still further, paranoid king Herod issues the order to kill all children two years old and under in his attempt to destroy the new king. All of this is to say that Matthew's shepherds and Luke's shepherds do not arrive at the same time, and we should not confuse Matthew's account with Luke's.

---

13. Whalen, *Seasons and Feasts*, 104.

14. Matt 2:11 RSV. See the discussion from chapter 6 about the arrangement of Jewish homes.

It is obvious, though, that from the perspective of the church year we are moving forward rapidly to the beginning of Jesus's adult life. The first Sunday after the Feast of the Epiphany always commemorates Jesus's baptism and the beginning of his public ministry. Subsequent weeks introduce us to the calling of Jesus's disciples, his first miracle at the wedding at Cana in Galilee, his first confrontation with religious authorities, and his early teaching and preaching.

The weeks following the Feast of the Epiphany are about appearance, visibility, recognition, and public action. Having come into the world at Christmas in the form of a vulnerable baby, God now sets out to challenge and heal the world through the ministry of the adult Christ. The Light *of* the world now shines clearly *in* the world and will become even brighter as Jesus's earthly ministry takes its course through the remainder of the church year.

As we will see in subsequent chapters, the world into which the Light of God came was—and still is—a world mostly unreceptive and hostile to that Light. The Incarnate Word fell upon both open and closed ears. Even our own hearts can be places where there is a mixture of receptivity and rebellion, all at the same time. But as we journey through Epiphany and the season that follows it, the Light of the season faithfully comes to us anew. The Light shines *upon* us and *within* us in ever-deepening ways. It illumines us, and it challenges us. It comforts and confronts us at the same time. It preserves and protects us. And it pushes us out into the darkness, where we seek to spread the Light of Christ to all nations and peoples.

Advent

Chapter One

As It Was in the Days of Noah

I cannot myself imagine a more fearful fate for our species
than that they should so habituate themselves to their earthly
circumstances as to be finally contented in them.

—MALCOLM MUGGERIDGE

Complacency is the deadly enemy of spiritual progress.

—A. W. TOZER

SUGGESTED READINGS

Isa 2:1–5; Ps 122; Rom 13:8–14; Matt 24:37–44

IN SOME WAYS IT does not seem possible that we have eclipsed the twentieth anniversary of the events of September 11, 2001. I remember vividly the sharp increase in church attendance and the dramatic rise in attention to spiritual things following that event. People lived in a heightened state of awareness, and this was especially true in spiritual matters.

That crisis in our nation also led to a revival of rampant speculation about the time of Christ's return. Even though Jesus and the New Testament writers warn repeatedly that the time is unknowable, there's nothing like a good crisis on the national or world stage to send people running for their charts and timelines. Endemic to human nature is the desire to want to know.

But interestingly, Matthew steers the conversation about Jesus's return in a completely different direction in his gospel. Rather than linking Jesus's coming to some sort of crisis, Matthew does the opposite. He gives us no hint whatsoever that Christ's return will be fraught with natural disaster, personal trauma, or mysterious signs of the impending judgment. Instead, he talks to us about Noah and the state of life just prior to the flood. He reminds us about ordinary folks engaged in the everyday things of life: eating, drinking, marrying, and enjoying life in a carefree state of mind. He speaks about the *unexpected* occurrence of an event to an *unprepared* people. The great flood was not linked to any crisis. It came in the midst of the normal routines and activities of life. Matthew also speaks of this reality in terms of a thief who strikes without warning or hindrance. There is no crisis precipitating the thief's coming. There is no warning to tip off or alert the homeowner, otherwise the homeowner would take action.

It can be easy for us to forget that Matthew writes these words not primarily to outsiders, but to a faith community, to followers of Jesus. He writes for a people who were living in between two very important events— between the resurrection of Jesus and the return of Jesus. The more time that passed as they awaited Jesus's return, the more the people in Matthew's faith community were tempted to become apathetic.

Like the readers of Matthew's Gospel, we also live in between the events of Christ's resurrection and his return. And what was true for Matthew's church is arguably more true for us because more time has elapsed between Christ's resurrection and his return. When the passage of time grows ever longer between a promise and its fulfillment, it becomes easier to live as though the promised fulfillment might never occur. We adjust in ever-increasing ways to life as we now experience it, with less attention to what is to come. It becomes possible to experience a sort of spiritual accommodation to our present cultural circumstances. Without warning, we become satisfyingly comfortable in the ordinary, everyday affairs of life. The apostle Paul describes this spiritual apathy in terms of falling asleep as he writes his first letter to the church at Thessalonica.[1] If Jesus's disciples are not careful, they may be caught spiritually "napping."

---

1. See 1 Thess 5:1–10.

Matthew writes to remind us that the more we accommodate ourselves to life's daily routines and activities, the less prepared we are for God's unexpected arrival in our lives. Life becomes business as usual. We forget our calling as followers of Christ and become mere consumers of goods. Like the folks in Noah's day, we slip into a state of ignorant bliss. Life is reduced to shopping at Trader Joe's, checking your Facebook status, or dozing off at a stoplight. In a word, we become *complacent*.

The dictionary defines complacency as "being pleased with one's situation, often without awareness of some potential danger." A related definition involves being in a state of "self-satisfaction."[2] For Matthew and the other writers of the New Testament, complacency is a serious threat to living authentically as disciples of Jesus precisely because Christ's return in judgment will not come tied to some 9/11-type of crisis. It will come when we least expect it. It will arrive while we are busy shopping at Trader Joes, checking our Facebook status, or sitting in traffic. Advent is a season which urgently reminds of this truth and calls on us to do something about it. It challenges us to understand that our preparation for Christ's return must be a way of life, not just something we think about in times of crisis.

I remember when my wife Connie and I learned the news that she was pregnant with our first child. Almost immediately we began preparing for the baby's arrival and the changes it would bring. Within a month or two, we were buying baby furniture, clothes, and other accessories. We started to do small things to get the nursery ready. Connie began to pay closer attention to her diet and her health needs. Even though the baby's coming was months away, our whole life was now lived with the arrival of that child in view. Future reality was impinging upon our present existence.[3]

Advent is a season when we feel enormous pressure to be consumers. It is a time of heightened pressure toward cultural accommodation and being squeezed into the world's mold. Learning to live wisely and numbering our days involves relying on God's grace to resist this pressure. The Advent season invites us—through biblical texts, opportunities for worship, and devotional practices—to ponder what it means to welcome Christ into our midst both in familiar and unfamiliar ways. The biblical texts of the season are a strong wakeup call to us. They shout to us and warn us not to be deceived into thinking that Christ won't return simply because a long time has passed since he promised that he would.

---

2. Dictionary.com, "Complacency," def. 1.

3. As we saw in the introduction, the theological term for this phenomenon is *prolepsis*. See also Gross, *Living the Christian Year*, 352, for a compelling example of how pregnancy is a powerful metaphor for Advent waiting and hope.

Advent also reminds us that our struggle against complacency in the spiritual life is best undertaken with others, not individually. We are strengthened in our fight against apathy when we connect ourselves with our families, our faith communities, and the experience of the saints who've gone before us. The struggle against complacency involves finding practical ways together whereby diligent preparation for Christ's return becomes a way of life. The seasons of the church year help by providing opportunities for us to reevaluate our stewardship of time, talent, and treasure. Individual congregational practices allow us further opportunities to align our priorities in such a way as to reflect life lived with Christ's return in view. With God's help, we become more attentive to the ways that we can share his love in the day-to-day affairs of life, because that is where Jesus unexpectedly comes to us—both now and at the end of time.

Chapter Two

Someday Is Not a Day of the Week

*In all affairs it's a healthy thing now and then to hang a question
mark on all the things you have long taken for granted.*

—BERTRAND RUSSELL

SUGGESTED READINGS

Isa 11:1–10; Ps 72:1–8; Rom 15:4–13; Matt 3:1–12

IN THE PREVIOUS CHAPTER we were introduced to the danger of complacency in the spiritual life. Struggling against complacency is one of our
greatest challenges as followers of Jesus precisely because it has been a long
time since Jesus promised he would return.

During Advent—and beyond—God's people are to be vigilant, ready
for Christ's coming precisely because he promised that he will come in the
midst of the ordinary, everyday rhythms of our lives. He will come when
least expected. Our task, then, is to live and embody the gospel in word and
deed so that we will be ready at any moment for Christ's return.

The Advent season helps us in this regard by introducing us to John
the Baptist, a surly and burly figure who appears in the Judean wilderness.
On two of the four Sundays of Advent, the assigned Scripture lessons focus

on John and his unique prophetic ministry. His message: Prepare the way. Make a straight road for the Lord's coming.

In John's day roads in his part of the world were not paved or surfaced because the soil in Palestine was so hard it could easily stand the traffic of mules and oxen and carts. There were, however, a few select roads in Palestine that were surfaced. These were roads that were built *by* the king, *for* the king. They usually led from Jerusalem to various parts of the country where the king might visit. They were built exclusively for the king's travel, and so they were called "The King's Highway." Before the king was due to arrive in a given area, advance notice would be sent out instructing people to repair the King's Highway and to prepare for the king's impending visit. Matthew tells us that in a day and age when it had been a long time since God had visited his people, John the Baptist appears on the scene and tells the people: "Fix up the highway. Make the path straight."

Of course, John is talking about more than a physical road. He's calling on people to do important road repair work in their hearts, to make adjustments in their interior lives. He's calling on them to change how they see the world and others. What is more, he is calling on them to change how they relate to God and others.

Folks came from near and far to hear John preach, and many responded with faith and obedience. But when the professional religious leaders come to hear John and to be baptized, he gives them a frigid reception. He calls them snakes and challenges them to prove by their changed lives that they have turned from their sins and turned to God. He assures them that their physical descent from Abraham proves nothing.

Why does John treat the Pharisees and Sadducees so harshly? Of what are they guilty? John's answer is that these religious leaders are guilty of *presumption*. The dictionary defines the word "presume" this way: "to take for granted, assume; to undertake with unwarrantable boldness."[1]

The attitude of the Pharisees and Sadducees can be summed up by the word presumption. They took for granted many things in their lives, foremost of which was God's mercy and grace. They believed that because they were physical descendants of Abraham and part of the Covenant God had established with him that their place and position was secure. They were relying more on past blessings than present fruitfulness when it came to their relationship with God. They were in a comfortable groove.

John holds them accountable. John doesn't care about their birth certificates or passports. He doesn't care where they were born, or whose pictures are in their family album. He doesn't care about their grandmother's

---

1. Dictionary.com, "Presume," defs. 1, 3.

maiden name. What he cares about is the coming judgment of God. In that coming judgment, we will stand alone before God, just us and our deeds. We will give an account of ourselves. We will take responsibility for how we have lived.

When I was a teenager, a man in my hometown went to the doctor complaining of chest pains. After running a battery of tests, the doctor sat him down in a chair and looked him straight in the eye and said: "Look, you're traveling down a dangerous lifestyle road. You need to quit smoking, quit drinking, and you need to lose fifty pounds. You need to change your diet. If you don't make some changes and you continue down this path you're on, you'll be dead in six months."

At about that time, those of us in our small town started seeing him and his wife out walking. The teenagers in our town had a standard route that we would drive that resembled the proverbial town square. A key rite of passage in our town involved getting your driver's license, then "cruising the square" where you could honk at your friends and they would honk back in return. And every day, rain or shine, you could find this man and his wife out walking the streets of our small town.

One day I asked this man why he and his wife were out walking so frequently. He told me of his health problems, his old lifestyle, and how he had made the decision to quit smoking and drinking, to change his diet, and to start walking. So I asked him another question: "How were you able to make such drastic changes in your life?"

He responded: "When you sit across from your doctor and he tells you that unless you turn your life around you will be dead in six months, changing isn't as hard as you might think."

John's message to the Pharisees and Sadducees was similar to the doctor's message to this man in my hometown. It was a wakeup call. It was gospel medicine. In John's case, though, the gospel medicine he dispenses is a bit like cod liver oil. It may be good for you, but it has a nasty taste to it. This is especially the case for the clergy and religious leaders who come out into the desert to hear John. He prescribes gospel medicine tailored specifically for them. But the religious leaders are not the only ones in John's sights. We are also in need of gospel medicine:

> John the Baptist has some nasty tasting medicine for each one of
> us because each of us has something that does not belong in one
> of God's saints. Sit down and open your mouth wide, and John
> will feed you that unpleasant medicine you have been avoiding.

John is not concerned with trivial things. He wants to know
what stands between you and God or you and your neighbor.[2]

Sometimes, though, knowing what is good for us does not automatically
help us to do what is right. This applies to many of us with respect to our
salvation. We know what we need to do, but we do not do it. We know
that we need to change our thinking and amend our lives, but we presume
that God's mercy means that God will overlook our sinful ways. If the man
in my hometown had taken the attitude about his physical health that the
Pharisees and Sadducees held with respect to John the Baptist's message, he
might have said: "I'm not worried. I have a few doctors in my family tree.
Someone will take care of me. Everything will be alright."

Presumption is a serious threat to followers of Jesus because it tempts
us to rely on past spiritual experiences or milestones while forgetting the
need for obedience in the present. It subtly deceives us into taking God's
compassion and forgiveness for granted. And perhaps the most dangerous
characteristic of presumption is the assumption that we are guaranteed
tomorrow. In subtle and sometimes unconscious ways, we find ourselves
thinking: Someday I'll repent of treating Jesus as my *Savior* but not my
Lord. Someday I'll repent that I've been a *fan* of Jesus but not a *follower* of
Jesus. Someday I'll take more seriously the apostle John's words when he
said, "Those who say they live in God should live as Jesus lived."[3] Living
for Jesus involves more than merely calling him to mind. It involves actually
living Christ's life within the sphere of my own existence. This is what the
apostle Paul meant by saying, "For to me to live is Christ, and to die is gain.[4]

Presumption clouds our vision to the brevity and fragility of life. It
tricks us into believing that there will always be time later to make things
right, to change how we relate to God and others, to straighten the interior
paths of our lives. But *someday* is not a day of the week.

John speaks of a coming baptism, a baptism with the Holy Spirit and
fire. It is easy for us to associate this baptism with judgment, which is not
entirely wrong. But the image of fire in Scripture is not merely reserved for
judgment. More often it speaks of purification, purging, and refinement.
During the season of Advent we are summoned to open our hearts and
to hear John's message with heightened awareness. We are challenged to
open ourselves to the cleansing fire of the Holy Spirit and to repent of our
presumption.

2. Wilson, *God Sense*, 167.

3. 1 John 2:6 NLT.

4. Phil 1:21 RSV.

In the midst of Advent, the voice of the Spirit calls to us and invites us to resist the attitude that says, "Someday I'll lay aside those things in my life that I know are not pleasing to Jesus." *Someday* is not a day of the week. *Someday* is a dangerous mirage, a lie from the pit of hell. The biblical texts of the season call on us to seek deliverance from presumption, challenging us to open our hearts to the Spirit's refining power and presence so that we may fervently watch and wait for Christ's coming.

Chapter Three

New Shoots from Old Roots

God does not send us despair in order to kill us;
He sends it in order to awaken us to a new life.

—HERMANN HESSE

SUGGESTED READINGS

Isa 35:1–10; Ps 146; Jas 5:7–10; Matt 11:2–11

IN THE PREVIOUS CHAPTER we heard from John the Baptist, who called on people to prepare for the Messiah's coming by preparing the King's Highway. The preparation John had in mind was primarily the interior preparation of the heart, a turning away from sin and the old life and a turning toward God and the new life God offers. The old-fashioned word for this preparation is *repentance.*

Repentance is necessary for living wisely and authentically because it is easy for us to become both complacent and presumptuous in the spiritual life. Yes, God is compassionate and graciously pours out his mercy upon us. Yes, God eagerly desires to forgive. But if we are not careful, we can be tempted to think that we are entitled to those blessings. We presume that God's offer of mercy and forgiveness will always be available even though we may show no desire in the present to amend our lives and to change course. We presume that there will always be time later to repent and to do the necessary interior work in our hearts and lives. For those infected with presumption, the motto is: "Someday I'll change."

One of the blessings of the Advent season is that it provides us a generous portion of readings from the Old Testament prophet Isaiah. Isaiah is the most quoted book in the New Testament, and with good reason. Take, for example, the beautiful images in Isa 35. They are images of radical transformation, of the desert turning green with abundant growth. They are images of the lush, verdant region of northern Palestine becoming reality for the dry, arid southern region of the country. It turns out that the people for whom Isaiah writes these words were people whose experience of life had become as dry and barren as the land Isaiah writes about. Their sense of hope was on life support, and with good reason.

After the formation of the monarchy in the Old Testament, the children of Israel split into two kingdoms—Israel (the Northern Kingdom), and Judah (the Southern Kingdom). By the time God calls Isaiah to his ministry, the Northern Kingdom has gone into full-blown rebellion against God, and the Southern Kingdom of Judah is not far behind.

Assyria, the great world power on the stage at the time, is about to sweep down and bring the Northern Kingdom to an end. Isaiah warns Judah to repent and to reclaim its trust in God, or it will suffer the same fate. Judah's King Ahaz, however, does not listen. So Isaiah brings this message. Assyria was known for importing huge cedar trees from Lebanon. And Isaiah tells the people of Israel and Judah that a massive deforestation project is coming. The Assyrian army will invade and will pillage, plunder, and destroy all cities and their inhabitants. The people will be taken captive and thrown into exile. And Judah, with its leaders descended from King David, will be "cut down," reduced to a mangled stump. This is not a message that engenders hope! But then Isaiah speaks these words:

> There shall come forth a shoot from the stump of Jesse, and a branch shall grow out of his roots. And the Spirit of the LORD shall rest upon him, the spirit of wisdom and understanding, the spirit of counsel and might, the spirit of knowledge and the fear of the LORD.[1]

Sometimes, even stumps can grow in nature. In a similar way, says Isaiah, a new David will arise who is anointed with God's Spirit. He will defend the poor and exploited and will be clothed with righteousness and truth.

---

1. Isa 11:1–2 RSV.

Have you ever seen something growing where it has no business growing? Many years ago while moving from Illinois to Idaho, a friend and I were driving our belongings cross country. Driving along Interstate 80 in Wyoming, we passed through Cheyenne and were heading west toward Laramie. At one point I noticed a huge granite boulder in the center space between the eastbound and westbound freeway. I looked again, and noticed a small, twisted tree emerging from the middle of that granite boulder.

Isaiah tells a brokenhearted and hopeless people that from the stump of destruction and despair, a new shoot can emerge. From the stump of utter discouragement, hope can be resuscitated. Out of the darkest, most painful circumstances, new life can come forth.

The people to whom Isaiah wrote were indeed taken captive. They were forcibly removed from their homes and their livelihoods. They spent decades in a foreign land, subjugated by foreign rulers. They prayed daily for God to deliver them. Days turned to weeks. Weeks turned to months. Months turned to years. And still no change. No word from God. No one to come and set them free and lead them home.

We can be relatively certain that when persons find themselves in this kind of situation, complacency is not their major obstacle. When life has become all black-and-white with no color, when hope begins to dissipate as fast as Advent candles burn from top to bottom, presumption is not the primary danger to the spiritual life. When hope is gone and life is a colorless blur, the most daunting challenge for followers of Jesus is often *despair*. And as with complacency and presumption, we must help each other and encourage each other to guard against it, because we often find ourselves in circumstances where we become spiritually discouraged. Hands and knees are not the only things in life that can become weak and tired. Hearts and spirits can also reach a breaking point.

We need not look far to see that this is true. Many in our country who have been without work for a long time are discouraged. In such situations it is understandable how discouragement gives way to despair.

There are many today who are bowed low with the pain of grief, wondering how they are ever going to go on. There are parents today who sit next to a hospital bed where a young child lies who likely will not be here to celebrate Christmas or the next birthday. There are families who will stand over grave sites this week, wondering how an apparently healthy person could suddenly be taken from them. We can empathize with persons in these circumstances who feel the increasingly heavy weight of despair.

There are many in our society who are aging and who are discovering that growing old brings with it many fears and uncertainties, far more questions than answers. We empathize with those who are tempted to lose heart and to lose hope.

As I write this, we are experiencing record levels of inflation at home and abroad. The cost of food, housing, gasoline, and other staples continues to increase with alarming consistency. Financial pressures mount on average, working-class families, creating debilitating stress. We empathize with this reality. Some of us are living it.

There are many persons today who are spiritually tired. They look at the insurmountable challenges confronting them and they are tempted to give up. Their circumstances have worn them down to the point where they believe their only remaining option is to resign themselves to the fact that things are never going to be different, that the way things are now is the way things will always be.

No one can endure endless suffering. The onset of despair often develops slowly after years of accumulated loss and pain have reduced persons to a grim version of their former selves. Protracted pain and loss wear on us until we are unable to see the proverbial light at the end of the tunnel. Author Jeannie Ewing observes:

> We want to see the light. We need to see it, even a glimpse of it beyond the darkness. But the years wear on us. Then we assume that tomorrow will involve more struggles than triumphs, and days become weeks become years.[2]

In churches that use the Advent Wreath with candles during the Advent season, the third Sunday's candle is rose-colored rather than purple that is common for the other Sundays. The rose-colored candle is customarily lit on the third Sunday of Advent because in many churches the day is known as *Gaudete* Sunday, which comes from the Latin word that means "rejoice." In many churches on this day cantors or choirs begin the service by singing "Rejoice in the Lord," and the Scripture lessons for the day focus our attention on the theme of joy.

Lighting the rose candle is not merely a decorative, liturgical act. *It is the church standing up against despair.* It is all of us standing together, arm in arm, firm in the belief that we are going to exchange exile for homecoming, just like the tired and discouraged people to whom Isaiah wrote. Do you remember what Isaiah said to those who longed to return home?

---

2. Ewing, "When You Feel," para. 8.

> The ransomed of the LORD shall return, and come to Zion with singing; everlasting joy shall be upon their heads; they shall obtain joy and gladness, and sorrow and sighing shall flee away.[3]

Indeed the day came when they did return, just like Isaiah promised. But the feelings and experiences of the lives of God's people to whom Isaiah wrote are feelings and experiences that are shared by many followers of Jesus today. People feel trapped in their circumstances, powerless to do anything constructive to change their lot. They experience a loss of control, and with that, a loss of hope that things will ever change. Discouragement is an ever-present reality that brings forth the bitter fruit of despair.

Advent is a season where Isaiah reminds us that our struggle against despair is not new. It is a perennial struggle, borne from the harsh twists and turns of life and at times the painful consequences of our own poor decisions. But it is also a season permeated with hope borne of God's enduring faithfulness to God's people in difficult times. It is a season that reveals God's faithfulness. God is the great Promise-Keeper. To be sure, God is sometimes much slower in keeping his promises than we would prefer. His wisdom and his timing are beyond our finite understanding. But the Scriptural record and the experience of God's people throughout history show us that God is faithful and can be trusted to keep his promises.

When life brings you to the place where you are sitting on the stump of utter despair, it's hard to imagine that anything new can emerge from that circumstance. At such times, and especially during Advent, God's word comes to all of us who have ever occupied the stump, or who sit there now. It says to us: *Out of the stump of David's family will grow a shoot . . . a new Branch bearing fruit from the old root.*[4] And indeed, this tender shoot did come forth. Fragile, yet tenacious, this new David grew like a plant out of the barren ground of Israel's lived experience. And in the end, he pushed back a stone from a rock-hard tomb.

So on the third Sunday of Advent, churches light the rose candle. And God's people open their hearts again to the truth in sacred Scripture. They stand together with a fresh resolve to trust their hopes and not their fears. They resolve anew to trust God even in the midst of unbearable circumstances. They trust by faith that the barren and hopeless place that confronts them is the very place where God chooses to reveal his awesome power.

One additional note. Our battle with despair is waged far more effectively in community, with brothers and sisters of faith. Through our acts of

3. Isa 35:10 RSV.
4. Isa 11:1–2 NLT.

compassion and understanding, empathetically shared with those who are hurting, we can be the antidote to their despair:

All of us face moments in life that tempt us to despair. We know all too well what it's like to see only through our tears. We feel acutely the anguish where joys give way to sighs. In those moments, we desperately need a word of hope from God. We need assurance that we are not alone.

From where does that assurance come? Sometimes the Holy Spirit comes directly to us, speaking to us from Scripture or the writings of the saints. But at other times, God uses people to speak that living word of hope to us. In the fall of 1997, my wife Connie and I stood in an ICU room at Riley Children's Hospital in Indianapolis, Indiana, where our seven-year old daughter Emily lay intubated and comatose. It was 3:30 in the morning. Darkness and a somber quiet enveloped us. I sat on a chair and my wife sat on the end of the bed. She looked at me and said, "She's not coming home, is she?" Emily was undergoing treatment for leukemia and had suffered severe complications. In that moment, I began mentally to prepare myself for the death of our firstborn child.

A few hours later, my cell phone rang. On the other end of the line was Bob Anderson, a fellow pastor and colleague from Joliet, Illinois. The conversation was brief, and I don't recall the details. What I do recall was what he said to me at the end. With a strong tone of reassurance, he said: "You are not alone." In the dark quiet of that hospital room, however, I never felt more alone. And yet, I knew that we were surrounded by people who genuinely cared.

Never underestimate what God can do for others through just a simple word or gesture. One more dayspring is what they, and so many others, need. What can we bring to those who only see through their tears, trapped in their years? The answer is simple. We can bring them ourselves, our willingness to walk with them, to assure them they are not alone. Our prayers and our presence—not platitudes—is the antidote to despair. Bearing one another's burdens, weeping with those who weep, rejoicing with those who rejoice. This is the time-honored balm in Gilead for those wounded by despair.

Chapter Four

Believing the Unbelievable

To give life to someone is the greatest of all gifts. To save a life is the next.
Who gave life to Jesus? It was Mary. Who saved his life? It was Joseph.

—WILLIAM JOSEPH CHAMINADE

SUGGESTED READINGS

Isa 7:10–17; Ps 24:1–7; Rom 1:1–7; Matt 1:18–25

THE ADVENT SEASON CALLS on us to prepare, to wait actively for Christ's
coming into our midst. We began our exploration of Advent with the warning to be on guard against *complacency*, the attitude that dispels any sense
of urgency to work on our interior lives or to amend our relationship with
God and others.

Then we were introduced to John the Baptist, who warned us of the
danger of *presumption*, of depending on past blessings or spiritual experiences to be our spiritual currency in the present, and of thinking that
there will always be time later to obey God or to plead for God's mercy and
forgiveness.

Moving deeper into the journey we saw how tempting it can be to succumb to *despair*. The circumstances of life can crush our bodies and our spirits, leaving us weak and spiritually depleted. Lighting the rose-colored candle in the Advent Wreath becomes a corporate act of standing together against despair, that subtle yet powerful condition that tempts us to lose hope, to give in, to believe that the way things are now is the way things will always be.

In this chapter, Advent introduces us to Mary and Joseph, particularly Joseph. Given the exciting role that Mary plays in the drama of our redemption, it can be easy to neglect Joseph and to underappreciate the unique role he plays in salvation history.

The story of Mary and Joseph is somewhat familiar to us. While Joseph and Mary are betrothed, she becomes pregnant through the power of the Holy Spirit. It is important to remember that a betrothal was not the first century equivalent of an engagement as we typically think of it. Couples who were betrothed were legally married.[1] It may be popular for modern preachers to describe Mary as an "unwed mother," but that moniker is inaccurate. Joseph and Mary were fully married in the eyes of the law.[2]

The Old Testament law in Deuteronomy afforded Joseph two options. He could sue Mary for divorce and go through the very public and messy legal process. Or he could annul the marriage quietly, spare Mary a very public humiliation, and try to pick up the pieces of his life.

Joseph decides to do things quietly. Then one night he has a dream where he is told by an angel that God is at work in a miraculous way. Mary's pregnancy is part of a larger plan where God is orchestrating the salvation of the world. It's not surprising, then, that in the dream the angel says to Joseph, "Don't be afraid to go through with this."

Perhaps one impediment to us hearing this story in its fullness is the assumptions we bring to it. For example, the common interpretation of this story is that Joseph believed Mary had relations with another man. This is a natural explanation and has a substantial interpretive following in the history of the church.[3] But it is not the only way to interpret Joseph's actions. There are other possibilities worthy of consideration.

---

1. See Deut 20:7; 28:30; Judg 14:15.

2. Jewish marriage had three stages. First, the parents worked together to arrange the marriage by selecting the couple. Then came a betrothal, a public ceremony with vows, like our experience of marriage vows today. The betrothal was then followed by a lengthy period before the couple actually came together as husband and wife, often as long as a year. Mary and Joseph were in the betrothal stage, which meant they were married but had not yet come together as husband and wife.

3. The ancient fathers Justin Martyr, John Chrysostom, and Augustine held this view.

For starters, if the common reading of this text is true, why does Matthew take great care to say that Mary is found with child *through the Holy Spirit*? Many scholars believe that Matt 1:18 is referring to Joseph, i.e., that Joseph discovered that Mary was with child by the Holy Spirit.[4]

Additionally, if the common interpretation is correct, why does the angel begin by telling Joseph: "Do not be afraid to take Mary as your wife"? In the common interpretation where it is assumed that Joseph believed that Mary had been unfaithful, fear would have nothing to do with Joseph's decision. If the common reading of the text is correct, Joseph would not be suspecting that Mary had committed adultery—he would be certain of it. Consider also that Nazareth was a very small village of about a dozen stone homes on a hillside. Few things happen in such a small place unobserved or unnoticed.

Third, the text tells us that Joseph is a godly and devout man. He was thoroughly acquainted with his own Scriptures, probably more so than most. With such knowledge of his own Scriptures, he would be familiar with the prophecy of Isaiah that a virgin would conceive and bear a son.[5] Joseph and Mary lived during a time when there was a heightened and widespread expectation that a Messiah was coming. Surely it is no coincidence that the angel's words to Joseph correspond exactly with Isaiah's prophecy. It is entirely possible that Joseph understands Mary to be the fulfillment of that prophecy.

These factors suggest that the popular understanding we hold of Joseph's actions is worth rethinking. If Joseph believes the angel's message that Mary is the promised virgin of Isa 7:14, then as a humble and righteous man he does not want to presume to join himself to her as her husband without God's divine approval. Joseph is hesitant to live with Mary because he believes he is unworthy to live with this miraculous child and his mother. This would explain why the angel says to Joseph: "Do not be *afraid* to take Mary as your wife (Matt 1:20). Joseph's struggle was not with Mary's perceived unfaithfulness, but rather that he did not feel worthy to be married to the young woman who would bring the Incarnate Son of God into the world. The ancient church father Origen says, "Joseph sought to put Mary away because he saw in her a great sacrament, to approach which he thought himself unworthy."[6]

Joseph's actions further highlight the mystery of the incarnation. Jesus's miraculous conception comes with no mighty fanfare but is itself

---

4. See Pakaluk, "Doing Justice to St. Joseph."

5. Cf. Isa 7:14.

6. Thomas Aquinas, *Catena Aurea*, 46. This view is also held by modern theologians like Karl Rahner and Ignace de la Potterie. See Barber, *True Meaning of Christmas*, 77.

concealed within the hidden life of a family. Joseph plays a critical role in keeping the mystery hidden. Joseph himself occupies a place of hiddenness, and he quickly recedes into the background of the narrative. Origen notes that it is because of Joseph that the virginal conception and birth of Jesus by Mary are kept hidden from the evil one. The miracle is received into the intimacy of marriage and family life. It is hidden there, and welcomed there, not only by the grace of Mary but also by the righteous Joseph, whose

> solicitous protection and providing for a Son who is not naturally his own weaves a cloak of invisibility, of paternal love, around this whole family, an exhibition of "foolishness" that the devil cannot see through because he, who does not believe in love, expects any divine power worth its salt to be exhibited in a daunting and dazzling display. But the foolishness of God is wiser than men, and the weakness of God is stronger than men.[7]

It can be easy for us to assume that Joseph's decision to divorce Mary quietly is logical because of the assumption we bring to it that Joseph believed she had been unfaithful. But as we've seen, there is more to the story than meets the eye. Imagine what it would have been like the morning after Joseph awoke from his dream. In the light of day Joseph may have thought to himself: *What happened last night? Could this really be true, or am I imagining all this?* Surely, this is what many of us might have thought.[8]

In the late nineteenth century, a French artist by the name of Tissot stepped inside a church in Paris. He had a profound religious experience in the church and devoted the rest of his life to painting spiritual themes. In the Brooklyn Museum hangs one of Tissot's paintings, a portrait of Joseph. The painting depicts Joseph leaning heavily over his carpenter's table. His shop is cramped, with tools and wood shavings everywhere. The windows look out onto the streets of Nazareth, where townspeople go about their business. But in the middle stands Joseph, his bearded chin in his hand, deep in thought. The painting's title says it all: *The Anxiety of St. Joseph.*

We may not typically think of him that way. Even the text of Matthew tells us that when Joseph woke up from his dream, he did as the angel commanded. But we should not assume that the outcome was a foregone conclusion. I'm not sure what kind of deliberations went on in Joseph's mind, but I know how I might have felt in this situation. I'm confident that

---

7. Barber, *True Meaning of Christmas*, xv. See also Cavadini, "Fatherly Heart of St, Joseph."

8. Other scholars interpret Joseph's decision to divorce Mary quietly as the fruit of great perplexity and bewilderment. The ancient father Jerome held this view.

I would have struggled. I'm certain I would have been filled with questions and riddled with anxiety.

If Joseph's experience was anything like ours, there is a fourth challenge to authentic discipleship that we must confront at numerous points in our life of faith. We battle against complacency, presumption, and despair, to be sure. But to these three we add a fourth challenge: *incredulity*.

The word "incredulity" is the noun form of the adjective *incredulous*. It means "disinclined or indisposed to believe." Another definition: "showing unbelief, especially in religious matters." Synonyms for incredulity are doubt, unbelief, and skepticism.

Joseph was undoubtedly confused and perplexed by what had transpired. But with the angel's help he worked it all through and ultimately said yes. Yet I cannot help but wonder whether Joseph at some point had to do battle with incredulity, a skepticism borne of a situation that made him think that what was being asked of him was completely irrational. In fact, on the surface of things, much of Joseph's life to this point doesn't seem to make sense. Joseph was of royal descent in the line of David, but where has that gotten him? He is of royal lineage but lives humbly as a carpenter. And now he discovers that his wife is mysteriously pregnant.

We pride ourselves on our rationality. No doubt Joseph was a rational man. But consider: If, in the midst of your everyday life, you sensed that God was leading you to do something that was irrational and contrary to human experience, would you do it?

If I were totally honest, I would have to admit that my answer would likely be no. I would not base a major decision on something that seemed irrational. But Joseph said yes. Christ's advent, Christ's coming into the world, didn't begin with a *day*. It began with a *word*. It began when a young woman—and a man—said yes.

I like to think that one of the things that helped Joseph say yes was an understanding that some truths are not so much *against* reason as they are *above* reason. Some truths transcend human reason because human reason is finite. Christianity makes such a claim. Christian faith asserts that parts of the gospel message transcend reason. Any revelation of the infinite to the finite is logically limited to what the finite can understand. Ultimately, each of us must decide what we will do when confronted by the demands of the gospel that confound our ability to understand fully with our minds. Joseph is a great model for us because once the angel speaks clarity into the confusing circumstances of his life, he says yes. He responds with faith and obedience. He is powerless and without status in the eyes of the world, but he is the very one responsible for the Messiah's identity as the Son of David.

Joseph's experience brings to mind another example from sacred Scripture where two persons had to battle incredulity. In the book of Genesis, God appears to a man named Abram and promises him that he is going to bless the world through him by establishing a covenant.[9] The covenant promise includes a son, through whom Abram's descendants will become a large and great nation. As a result of this covenant promise, God changes Abram's name to Abraham (father of many).

One of the intriguing things about God's promise in this narrative is that Abraham and his wife Sarah are well advanced in years when God makes it. And in spite of God reaffirming the promise more than once, many years elapse and Sarah is still barren and childless. Then, after God ratifies the covenant with Abraham by the sign of circumcision, three men appear to Abraham while he is in his tent at Mamre. In this unusual episode, one of the messengers promises to return within a year and that Sarah will have a son before he does. Sarah, overhearing the conversation from inside the tent, laughs.

She is incredulous, and with good reason. By this time, she is ninety years old. God made a promise many years prior, but to date nothing has happened. Having a child at her age is a physiological impossibility. Surely we can empathize with Sarah as she stands in the tent and hears the words of the mysterious guest. With her, we can feel the belly laugh bubbling up from within her barren womb and making its way to her chest and nearly exploding from her lungs. We can forgive her this moment of unbridled incredulity. When the Lord asks, "Why did Sarah laugh?" I can breathe a sigh of relief that it was Sarah and not me in this situation. But in less than a year, Isaac—the promised son whose name means "laughter"—is born. It seems that God always gets the last laugh. But it is interesting that in the case of both the son of promise of the Old Covenant and the divine Son of promise of the New Covenant, God asks earthly parents to trust him in ways that boggle the mind because what God promises is physically impossible and by all appearances completely contrary to reason.

The Advent season is very much about waiting, about our waiting on God. But there is more to Advent than our waiting on God. During the Advent season, God is also waiting on us. God is waiting on us to say *yes* to him. God is waiting on us to open our hearts and our minds to possibilities that by human standards may appear to be foolish.

The Advent season confronts us with many challenges and opportunities. One such challenge is the temptation to believe that human reason alone defines the parameters of our world and our experience. When that

9. Gen 12–18.

happens, it becomes easy for us to refashion God in our own image. God longs to come to us and to touch our lives in miraculous ways, but our incredulity shuts down the flow of supernatural grace in us, and in those whom God wishes to bless through us.

The Advent season reminds us that there are times when God asks for our obedience in ways that transcend reason. When that happens, Mary and Joseph serve to inspire us. They are powerful examples to us of what can happen when we win the battle with incredulity and step out in radical faith and obedience.

Chapter Five

When God Is Late

*Delay has to be—sometimes. Your lives are so linked up with those of others,
so bound by circumstances that to let your desire have instant fulfillment
might in many cases cause another, as earnest prayer, to go unanswered.*

—A. J. RUSSELL

SUGGESTED READINGS

Zech 9:9–10; Ps 40:1–3; Heb 10:32–39; Matt 7:7–12

SOME TIME AGO I spoke with a friend who shared with me the story of how his father left the practice of his faith. Thus began a lengthy journey where my friend prayed for his father to come back home to the faith and to the church. Part of the struggle during this process was that my friend knew that it was God's will for his father to come back to Christ, so it became discouraging at points when there was no visible evidence that his father was receptive to the advances of the Holy Spirit or to the prayers of his son.

I suspect that each of us could share our own stories of discouragement and consternation in the presence of unanswered prayer, especially in those cases where our prayers seem to be in clear alignment with the will of God as revealed in sacred Scripture. We know, for example, that it is God's will that all come to repentance and experience the joys of becoming children of God. Praying for our loved ones and friends is a primary focus of our prayer life, but at times we sense that our prayers are not being heard, and there is little discernible evidence that God is at work in the lives of those for whom we pray.

One of the prominent themes of the Advent season is that of *waiting*, of patiently trusting God and waiting on him to answer our prayers and to accomplish his purposes according to his divine providence. The Scripture lessons during this season are full of admonitions to wait patiently, to trust that God is at work in the lives of God's people. At times, this posture of waiting must take the form of tenacious trust that God hears our prayers even when our experience seems to argue to the contrary. One example of this during Advent comes from the Old Testament prophet Zechariah. Although he is not a household name, he was an important figure in the prophetic tradition of the Old Testament, and Jesus is very tuned in to Zechariah's prophecies as he appears on the scene in the first century.

Zechariah lived and wrote near the turn of the sixth and into the fifth century BC, which was the period when the children of Israel had returned from Babylonian captivity.[1] Returning to their land after more than seven decades in exile, the people very much wanted to rebuild the nation.

This desire to reconfigure their national identity involved more than mere patriotic pride, however. At the heart of Israel's identity was the deep-seated belief that they were the chosen people of God. They were chosen to learn the heart and mind of God so that through their life and worship they would become a magnet to the nations, drawing all people into relationship with God. The prophet Isaiah captures the peoples' self-understanding:

> It shall come to pass in the latter days that the mountain of the house of the LORD shall be established as the highest of the mountains, and shall be raised above the hills; and all the nations shall flow to it, and many peoples shall come, and say: "Come, let us go up to the mountain of the LORD, to the house of the God of Jacob; that he may teach us his ways and that we may walk in his paths. For out of Zion shall go forth the law, and the word of the LORD from Jerusalem."[2]

---

1. In 587 BC, Jerusalem was sacked and burned to the ground by the Babylonians. The temple, the locus of God's presence and activity, was destroyed. People were forcibly removed from their homes and taken into exile.

2. Isa 2:2–3 RSV.

Centuries before Zechariah, at the time of King David, this dream seemed far more realistic. David had gathered the tribes and was beginning to build a unified nation. But under David's descendants, the nation fell apart. Things totally unraveled as foreign powers like Assyria and Babylon completely overran the country, destroying the temple and with it the collective identity of the people. Into this collective discouragement comes Zechariah, speaking his prophetic word:

> Rejoice greatly, O daughter of Zion! Shout aloud, O daughter of Jerusalem! Lo, your king comes to you; triumphant and victorious is he, humble and riding on an ass, on a colt the foal of an ass.[3]

Who is the king in question? He is the *new* David, the One who would unite the country and make it a beacon for the nations. He's ascending Mount Zion—the place of the temple—to lead the right praise of God that will draw all nations of the world to the holy place.[4]

And how does this king arrive? He comes not on a war horse, but on a donkey. Not exactly imagery befitting a king! But Zechariah does not stop there. He goes on to describe what the reign of this coming king will look like:

> I will cut off the chariot from Ephraim, and the war horse from Jerusalem; and the battle bow shall be cut off, and he shall command peace to the nations; his dominion shall be from sea to sea, and from the River to the ends of the earth.[5]

This king, says Zechariah, comes peacefully and will rule peacefully. He will not be like the kings of the world. His kingship will be one of reconciliation and nonviolence, not just for Israel, but for the whole world. His reign will be a universal reign.

Consider how ridiculous these words of Zechariah would have sounded to those who initially heard them. As he writes them, Israel had been conquered and overrun by foreign powers. They had fallen a long way from their glory of centuries earlier. They were just now entertaining hope that they could start to rebuild from the ruins. Zechariah is not writing to a world-conquering power. Israel has no status on the world scene. Nevertheless, Zechariah says that a king is coming who will rule in peace, and his dominion will stretch from sea to sea. This is quite a bold claim, given that all the evidence points to the contrary.

3. Zech 9:9 RSV.
4. See Barron, "Zechariah and the New David."
5. Zech 9:10 RSV.

The salient point here is that Zechariah's promise did not come true in his lifetime. Israel continued its drift and decline. A century or so later, the Greeks would overrun the Holy Land. Subsequent to that, the Romans would arrive and conquer. Long after Zechariah's words, what followed was more oppression and subjugation. But in spite of centuries of continued hardship, the promises of Zechariah lingered in the collective consciousness of the people. They remembered. They clung to these promises, even when all of the evidence argued against their coming to pass.

More than five hundred years later, a young rabbi begins to preach in the hill country of Galilee. His theme: "The kingdom of God is upon you." It is so easy for us moderns to spiritualize the kingdom of God. But those listening to Jesus knew what he meant. He was announcing that Zechariah's prophecy was coming true. The tribes were being gathered. The new David had arrived. That's what the kingdom of God meant to first-century Jews listening to Jesus preach.

So as Jesus preaches, the people remember Zechariah. But the upshot of Jesus's message is that what Zechariah promised is now happening in relationship to *him*. And at the end of his life, he enters the city of Jerusalem, just as David did. But he does not enter on a war horse or in a military chariot. He enters on a donkey. Not as a conquering king, but instead just as Zechariah said he would more than half a millennium earlier. As he does, the people would have instantly called Zechariah to mind.

What a shock it must have been, then, when Jesus's followers saw him brutally crucified by the Romans. Could they have been wrong about him? Perhaps he wasn't the new David after all. So much for the coming king of peace!

But maybe, just maybe, some of them remembered another of Zechariah's promises as they witnessed Jesus die on the cross:

> I will pour out on the house of David and the inhabitants of Jerusalem a spirit of compassion and supplication, so that, when they look on him whom they have pierced, they shall mourn for him, as one mourns for an only child, and weep bitterly over him, as one weeps over a first-born.[6]

It was after Jesus's resurrection when the disciples began to piece things together, when they realized that Zechariah's words had indeed come true in Jesus. And they realized that it was precisely in his crucifixion and resurrection that Jesus was reigning as the promised king of peace. The fulfillment of Zechariah's promise continues to reverberate through the centuries today.

6. Zech 12:10 NLT.

For we recognize that, in the church, Christ's reign does indeed span from sea to sea, to the ends of the earth.

The purpose of this lengthy Old Testament excursion about Zechariah is to provide us some perspective when God seems slow or even unwilling to answer our prayers. When we pray fervently and persistently for a long period of time without an answer, it tests our faith. When we intercede for months or even years on behalf of others and we see no discernible signs of change, it is disheartening.

The reasons for this may be many, but certainly one factor may be cultural. We live in a society characterized by instant access to information. Technology has made the possibility of instant gratification such a reality in our lives that it intensifies our impatience. It shapes our lives to the point where it is difficult for us to wait for anything. Those of us who are older can remember stories of people who used to have to wait for their radios and televisions to warm up before they could see or hear anything. This is unimaginable now. I can remember when we had to dial a phone number with a rotary dial. What a stone-age concept! But now, we can't even keep last year's computer because it takes too long—perhaps three or four seconds—to perform functions that used to take hours. We have become habituated to instant gratification.

This underlying reality subtly creeps into our spiritual lives and shapes our attitudes in powerful ways, not the least of which is our experience in prayer. With a click of our computer's mouse we purchase the latest product and find it on our doorstep within two days, sometimes sooner. In this kind of world the notion that what we ask for in prayer may not instantly be granted, that we may need to wait and to trust God's timing and God's providence, upsets our equilibrium.

But even when our prayers *are* aligned with God's will, God's timing is seldom in sync with our timing. God has his own timetable and works things out according to his divine wisdom which exceeds our comprehension. Hymnwriter William Cowper observes:

> Judge not the Lord by feeble sense, but trust him for his grace;
> Behind a frowning providence he hides a smiling face.
> His purposes will ripen fast, unfolding every hour;
> The bud may have a bitter taste, but sweet will be the flower.[7]

This awareness that God's providential timing is often different from ours is why sacred Scripture is full of examples where individuals or peoples are called to wait patiently on the Lord, to persevere, to remain steadfast in

---

7. William Cowper, "God Moves in a Mysterious Way," public domain.

faith.[8] In fact, learning to be directed by God's timing and wisdom is one of the most important lessons we can learn as followers of Jesus.[9] It is also one of the most difficult lessons to learn. But time is one of God's most effective tools for teaching us to rely upon him. In fact, if you consult Scripture, you will not find a man or woman whom God used in powerful ways who did not first face a long and difficult time of waiting.[10] Charles Stanley writes:

> What we desire is often what the Lord has purposed and will provide for us. But timing is everything, and key puzzle pieces are falling into place as we wait. God is changing hearts and engineering circumstances we have no idea even exist. The delays we face are not a denial of His promises; rather, they are an integral part of His strategy to arrange all the details and get us positioned for His excellent plan.[11]

Returning to the experience of my friend from the beginning of the chapter, he told me that just before his father died, he came back home to Christ and the church. After more than thirty years, my friend's prayers were finally answered.

The season of Advent introduces us to and immerses us in the counter-cultural truth that God's purposes are not something we can manipulate. We can only trust and place our lives and the lives of those we love in his care. An old prayer says it nicely:

> Almighty God, we entrust all who are dear to us to your never-failing care and love, for this life and the life to come, knowing that you are doing for them better things than we can desire or pray for; through Jesus Christ our Lord.[12]

God is our Father, not our servant. Our prayers—even when aligned with his will—will be answered in his time and in the manner he sees fit. In fact, the answer to some of our prayers may not come in our lifetime.[13] Can we

---

8. The Psalms often reflect this call to patient trust. E.g., Pss 33:20–22; 37:1–7; 40:1–4; see also Jas 1:3–4; Luke 11:5–13.

9. See, for example, Pss 25:2–3; 27:14; 37:34; 40:1–2; 62:5–6; 147:11; Isa 30:18; 40:31; 49:23; 64:4; Lam 3:25–26; Hab 2:3; Rom 8:24–25.

10. A classic Old Testament example of this is King David. First Samuel 16–30 describes how David was anointed as a teenager to succeed King Saul, but how his life took many drastic twists and turns and many years elapsed before David actually assumed his duties as king. David suffered devastating losses, attempts on his life, demoralizing injustices, and unbearable heartaches.

11. Stanley, *Waiting on God*, 15. See also Hayford, *Pursuing the Will of God*, 122–26.

12. *Book of Common Prayer*, 831.

13. See Heb 11:13, 39–40.

accept that? Are we willing to persevere, to continue to intercede for others, and to praise our loving Heavenly Father even during the times when we cannot discern him at work? An African American preacher once said: "Until you have stood for years knocking at a locked door, your knuckles bleeding, you do not really know what prayer is."[14] This is the challenge—and opportunity—afforded to us not only during Advent, but in all the seasons of life.

14. Craddock, *Luke,* 210.

Christmas

Chapter Six

A King Whose Throne Is a Manger

*Jesus left a throne in heaven and started ruling and reigning
from an animal's feeding trough in Bethlehem.*

—MARS HILL CHURCH

SUGGESTED READINGS

Isa 9:2–7; Ps 96; Titus 2:11–14; Luke 2:1–20

FOR MANY, CHRISTMAS IS a nostalgic time. The images, stories, and music lend themselves to it. I admit that Christmas makes me feel a bit sentimental, and I suspect that many feel the same way. When you hear Johnny Mathis singing "It's the Most Wonderful Time of the Year," even the most grinch-like among us whose hearts are two sizes too small feel a little twinge of sentiment.

But if all we see in the biblical stories and images is sentiment, we are missing a huge part of what Christmas is about. Nowhere is this more obvious than in Luke's account of the birth of Jesus. We might wonder why Luke is so concerned with historical details about Caesar Augustus, and Quirinius the Governor of Syria, a census, and all the rest. But Luke knows exactly what he is doing.

During the time when Mary is about to give birth to Jesus, Caesar Augustus has climbed to the top of the mountain in terms of power and world control. The Roman Empire has ascended to full strength, and Augustus is the sharp edge of the sword. He is the warrior who enforces Rome's power and control through military might, the infamous *Pax Romana*. When he commands a census to be undertaken, he is wielding his power.

By telling the story of Jesus's birth the way he does, Luke is intentionally being subversive to Caesar Augustus. He undermines Augustus's myth of power by announcing the birth of a new king. This new king, however, is not born in a palace. He is not born in Jerusalem or in the seat of political power, but in Bethlehem, a tiny blip-on-the-map village of no reputation. Remember the prophet Micah?

> But you, O Bethlehem Ephrathah, who are little to be among the clans of Judah, from you shall come forth for me one who is to be ruler in Israel, whose origin is from of old, from ancient of days.[1]

This new king that Luke announces is not wrapped in royal garments, but in swaddling clothes. When a baby is swaddled, it is wrapped tightly. Interestingly, many church fathers saw the swaddling clothes as pointing to Jesus's shroud which was wrapped around him at his death. And as Luke tells it, this new king is visited not by royalty or the king's court from the palace, but by shepherds, which in that time were men of highly questionable reputation.

What is Luke doing here? Luke is deliberately undermining the narrative of Caesar Augustus and his political power. Thanks to Luke, Christmas becomes a battle of narratives, a "war of the worlds" if you will. There is the narrative of worldly and political power which maintains its control by force and violence. And there is the narrative which announces the coming of the True Emperor. This is illustrated in the way Luke climaxes the story. After the angel announces the birth of Jesus, Luke tells us:

> And suddenly there was with the angel a multitude of the heavenly host praising God and saying, "Glory to God in the highest, and on earth peace among men with whom he is pleased."[2]

The phrase "multitude of the heavenly host" is the Greek word *stratios*, which means "army." In a world where earthly rulers maintain power through military might, Luke tells us that it is an army of angels who

---

1. Mic 5:2 RSV.
2. Luke 2:13–14 RSV.

announces Jesus's arrival. And this army is far more powerful than the army of Augustus.

The Old Testament prophets and the Gospel writers portray the coming Messiah as a warrior king in the line of David. But this warrior king comes as an infant tightly bound in swaddling clothes. C. S. Lewis, commenting on why a warrior king would be born as a baby, theorized that Jesus came quietly into the world as a baby because he was meant to slip behind enemy lines.

There are many today who are confident that if Jesus slipped behind enemy lines, he has either become a helpless POW, is missing in action, or is dead. But Jesus's kingdom is a subversive kingdom. He does not wield power through violence and coercion. It might be easy to underestimate this King and his army, but Isaiah cautions us against that kind of thinking:

> For every boot of the tramping warrior in battle tumult and every garment rolled in blood will be burned as fuel for the fire. For to us a child is born, to us a son is given; and the government will be upon his shoulder, and his name will be called Wonderful, Counselor, Mighty God, Everlasting Father, Prince of Peace.[3]

He comes as a warrior king, to be sure. But his kingdom is not of this earth, and he conquers his enemies through sacrificial love. Even the location of his birth testifies to this reality.

Luke tells us that Joseph and Mary are in Bethlehem because of a census, because Caesar Augustus actually thinks he's in charge. But as we know from Old Testament prophecy, God is the One in charge. And God writes with events, not just words. While Mary and Joseph are in Bethlehem, Mary goes into labor. She gives birth to Jesus and wraps him in swaddling clothes and lays him in a manger, because there is no room for them in the inn. Unfortunately, the KJV and many other translations mistranslate Luke here by using the word "inn." It has led many through the years to have an image of Mary and Joseph frantically searching for a motel room and repeatedly being told there is "no vacancy."

The precise rendering of Luke's words here is that Mary places Jesus in a manger "because there was no *space* for them in the *room.*" To understand this, we must understand the layout of most first-century Jewish homes. Most homes ordinarily had a dirt floor with two rooms. There was a main room where the entire family cooked meals, ate, and slept together. And there was a second private room for guests. The very front of the main room was used to house the family's domestic animals at night. Mangers—feeding

3. Isa 9:2–6 RSV.

troughs—would be placed in this space. Luke's exact words are: "Mary wrapped the baby in swaddling clothes and laid him in a manger because there was no *space* for them in the *room.*" Luke is likely referring to the private guest room at the back of the house.[4] This makes sense, because Joseph and Mary would likely have stayed with family while in Bethlehem to take part in the census.

This may seem like haggling over words to some, but it proves to be very important. Indeed, the word that Luke uses here for "room" is the same word that he uses later in the Gospel to describe where a very significant event occurs. Luke uses the same word to describe the "room" where Jesus celebrates the Last Supper with his disciples. This is not a coincidence. Luke is very intentional. Luke is saying that the One who is born and placed in a feeding trough is the One who later gives himself to his disciples as *food*.

It is understandable, then, why early Christian writers believed that the manger points to the Eucharist. The church father Cyril of Alexandria said:

> Whereas we were brutish in soul, by now approaching the manger, yes, his table, we find no longer feed, but the bread from heaven, which is the body of life.[5]

What early Christian writers like Cyril, Jerome, Chrysostom, and others are showing us is that we enter into the mystery of what happened at Christmas through the Eucharist.[6] The One who was laid in the feeding trough is the Living Bread come down from heaven. In Hebrew, Bethlehem means "house of bread." The Living Bread from heaven—the King in the line of David who was announced by angel armies—was born and laid in a feeding trough in a village that means "house of bread." Gregory the Great observed:

> The place in which the Lord was born was called the "house of bread" because it was truly going to come to pass that he would appear there in a material body who would nourish the hearts of his chosen ones by an interior food.[7]

According to the beautiful hymn, "Lo, How a Rose E'er Blooming," he arrived "when half spent was the night." He came in humility. Rather than marking his arrival with pomp and ceremonial fanfare, he entered the world in the middle of the night when most were fast asleep. He was laid quietly among the animals. The momentus event of our Lord's coming to earth

4. See Barber, *True Meaning of Christmas*, 91–93.

5. Cyril of Alexandria, *Commentary upon Luke*, 11–12.

6. Barber, *True Meaning of Christmas*, 97.

7. Gregory the Great, *Hom.* 8 (p. 51).

passed in relative silence. The hymn "O Little Town of Bethlehem" captures it well: "How silently, how silently, the wondrous gift is given."

For many today, Jesus's humble appearance in the Eucharistic bread and wine is a scandal. How can Christ really be present in such ordinary food? The answer to this question is the *manger*. Christ is willing to be laid where the animals reside. In the same way, he is eager to come to us.

For many years now Christians have been quite vocal in pointing out that there can be no Christmas without Christ. They are all too eager to remind the world to "keep Christ in Christmas." While I quite agree with this, the admonition is incomplete. Not only should we guard against removing Christ from Christmas; we should also guard against removing the "mass" from Christmas. Christmas means "Christ's Mass." In the liturgy of the church, Christ continues to come to us. Christmas is not a past event. Our "feeding troughs" look a bit different from those in the first century. Nevertheless, Christ continues to be found there, humbly and unobtrusively. He comes silently and without fanfare. He comes, veiled under the appearance of bread and wine. He comes to us while the world just hurries on by and pays no attention. But in the manger the Bread of Life is truly present. Every time we come to the Eucharist we are coming to the manger.

Christmas is a sentimental time. I enjoy the sentiment. But what Luke describes for us cannot be reduced to sentiment. The images and stories that we enjoy so much as kids (and older kids!) are a window that opens to us and plunges us into a bloody warfare between two competing kingdoms that could not be more different. One exerts control through coercion and intimidation. The other exerts control through humble and sacrificial service, through extending mercy, and by the King giving himself as food to his subjects. At the Eucharistic table, the church celebrates and participates in Christ's reign. This has been celebrated and proclaimed as true since the earliest days of the church:

> The table of the Lord was the kingdom of God on earth, the down-payment of the Christian's heavenly inheritance. Therefore, salvation itself, as participation in Christ, was embodied in the Eucharist, and so the Church came to be defined by the table.[8]

Christ's incarnation—the miracle of Christmas—points us to and calls us to the Eucharistic table. The One who was born in Bethlehem—house of bread—and who was laid in a feeding trough continues to feed his people today with himself. This is a mystery which we apprehend by faith. Saint Thomas Aquinas helps us:

---

8. Papandrea, *Reading the Church Fathers*, 31.

Humbly I adore Thee, Verity unseen,
Who thy glory hidest, 'neath these shadows mean,
Lo, to thee surrendered, my whole heart is bowed,
Tranced as it beholds thee, shrined within the cloud.
Taste, and touch, and vision, to discern thee fail;
Faith, that comes by hearing, pierces through the veil.
I believe whate'er the Son of God hath told;
What for truth hath spoken, that for truth I hold.[9]

Christmas heralds the wonderful news of a King whose throne is a manger, and whose kingdom is peace. We participate in Christ's kingly reign by humbly taking our place at his Eucharistic table. This safeguards us from too easily identifying Christ's kingdom with earthly rule and power or political ideology.

9. Aquinas, "Adoro te Devote."

Chapter Seven

God Incognito

*The act of thanksgiving presses the sweet nectar of joy
from the husks and hulls of everyday life.*

—Wendy M. Wright

Thanksgiving is the highest form of thought.

—G. K. Chesterton

SUGGESTED READINGS

Isa 61:10—62:3; Pss 147; Gal 3:23—4:7; John 1:1–18

Growing up as a kid and for much of my adult life, Christmas was one of my favorite days. And I saw it as precisely that—a *day*. Because there was a great deal of anticipation leading up to Christmas, once Christmas Day had come and gone there was always a bit of a letdown. It was not until I was much older and discovered the liturgical year that I learned that Christmas does not end on December 25 but *begins* on December 25. Christmas is a twelve-day season where we ponder and reflect deeply about the coming of Jesus into the world.

We are speaking, of course, of the mystery of the incarnation. The word comes from the Latin word "carne," which means "meat." The incarnation involved the Creator God becoming a human being in the person of Jesus Christ.

Jesus is God in the flesh. This is the stuff of mystery. It is a mystery that the Creator God would so love the creation that he would himself become a creature. It is beyond our understanding that Eternity would invade time, that God would come among us in Jesus Christ.

Part of what contributes to the mystery of the incarnation is that it constitutes a uniquely distinctive feature of Christianity among all religions, namely, the idea that the eternal God became a human being. The eternal God became an embryo. In the first century when John wrote the prologue to his Gospel and made this claim, it was not only a strange claim, it was a *scandalous* claim. The notion that God would become human was an audacious assertion in itself, but the notion that the Incarnate God would suffer and die was even more outrageous.[1]

What would motivate the Creator to take upon himself our human nature in Jesus? Theologians have written volumes exploring that question, but it seems to me that the fundamental motive in the heart of God was *love*. The New Testament affirms this truth frequently, as the famous words from the apostle John show: "God so loved the world that he gave his only son, that whoever believes in him should not perish but have eternal life."[2]

John not only identifies love as the motive for the incarnation, he also describes more fully the nature of that love when he says: "The Word became human and lived among us. He was full of unfailing love and faithfulness."[3] The apostle Paul sounds a similar theme in his writings when he speaks of Christ as the Bridegroom and the church as Christ's bride.[4] Theologian Brant Pitre observes:

> When Paul refers to the Church being "washed" and "presented" to Christ, he is describing the ancient Jewish bridal bath and wedding ceremony. From Paul's point of view, the torture and crucifixion of Jesus on Calvary was nothing less than an expression of spousal love.[5]

---

1. See 1 Cor 1:23.
2. John 3:16 RSV.
3. John 1:14 NLT.
4. Eph 5:21–23.
5. Pitre, *Jesus the Bridegroom*, 2.

Paul was thoroughly acquainted with Jewish Scripture. He was able to see the crucifixion of Jesus as more than an unjust martyrdom or cruel Roman execution. Paul sees in Jesus's passion and death the fulfillment of God's eternal plan to wed himself to humankind in an everlasting marital covenant. This helps us to see John's description of the incarnation as God's "unfailing love and faithfulness" with deeper insight.

In 1964 a young woman by the name of Kitty Genovese was brutally murdered outside her apartment building in Queens, New York. Reports vary as to what exactly happened, but as Genovese's attacker began stabbing her, she cried out for help. As many as thirty people apparently heard her screams, and numerous lights went on in the apartment complex (the attack happened in the middle of the night). But no one came to her aid. In fact, when the lights went on in many apartments, the attacker stopped his assault. But after five minutes when no one came, he returned and began beating and stabbing his victim again.

Psychologists later coined the phrase "the bystander effect" to describe what happened on that fateful night in March of 1964. The most pressing question, of course, was: Why did no one come to the aid of this woman? One answer to that question is that anyone who would have come down from that apartment complex to help this woman would have been putting his or her life at risk. That's a serious and frightening prospect. To come down was to risk one's life.

The apostle John tells us that the Creator, the Eternal Word of God, *came down to us and for us*. Into a world marred and scarred by rebellion, violence, and pain, Jesus heard our cries and came down. But in Jesus's case, coming down involved more than just the awareness that he was putting his life at risk. In Jesus's case, coming down meant that he knew full well that it would cost him his life. He was not merely putting his life at risk. He was laying his life down.

The twelve days of Christmas is far too short a time to ponder the depth of God's love to us in the incarnation.[6] For not only is God's love steadfast and unfailing, God's love surrounds and enfolds us long before we ever know who God is, or that he exists at all. Long before we ever speak God's name, Christ came down and entered into our human existence with all of its pain and brokenness. John reminds us of this but the words are so familiar to many of us that the power behind them eludes us. God so loved the world that he *gave* his only Son. Christmas is God's consummate gift to

---

6. In some traditions, Christians informally extend the celebration of Christmas until February 2 and the Feast of Candlemas, which commemorates the presentation of Jesus in the temple forty days after his birth.

the world, motivated by love. It is the story of the divine Lover coming to wed his beloved.

When we receive a gift of any significance, the typical response it engenders in us is gratitude. How much more should this be the case with respect to God's singular act of love in sending his Son to be with us? The message of Christmas, and the reality that it brings, is that *God is with us*. The incarnation signals that God is with us not in a sterile, antiseptic, distant way, but in the ordinary, messy, everyday kind of way.

God's gift of love to the world in Jesus should engender gratitude as an immediate and obvious response. And for most of us, it does, especially at Christmas. But if we're not careful, our gratitude can become an occasional afterthought rather than a habitual practice. We dust it off at Christmas when the reason for it is obvious. But then we resume our lives in such a way that the impact of God's great gift makes very little difference in the rough-and-tumble of our daily experience.

One possible reason for this comes to us from the New Testament itself, where the biblical writers describe the incarnation as a subversive move on God's part. God comes into the world not with fanfare and pomp and power, but in a low-key, almost hidden way. God appears on the scene incognito, as it were. The apostle John describes it this way:

> He was in the world, and the world was made through him, yet the world knew him not. He came unto his own, and his own people received him not.[7]

In Luke's account of Jesus's birth, we are told that Jesus is not born in Jerusalem among the wealthy and powerful and prominent, but in the countryside among shepherds. His birth is welcomed not by flashing billboards and urban press releases and tweets, but by angels and men of low standing in the Judean countryside. God literally smuggles himself into the world through a teenage girl. Jesus's first coming was greeted only by a select few persons of nondescript and questionable reputation. In a monumental twist of irony, the One through whom the world was made enters the world he made, and the world does not recognize him. This hidden quality of God's presence with us can mitigate against developing gratitude as a habitual practice in our lives. God comes to us incognito, and it is not a natural response to give thanks and to cultivate gratitude for what we don't recognize or discern.

Many years ago on a bitterly cold January morning in Washington, DC, a man went down into a metro subway station. He found a suitable spot, removed a violin from a hard case, and began to play. It was rush hour

---

7. John 1:10–11 RSV.

as thousands of people poured through the station on their way to work. After about three minutes, a middle-aged man was the first to notice there was a musician playing. He slowed his pace briefly, then hurried on to his destination. A few minutes later a woman threw a dollar into the musician's case without even slowing down as she passed by.

Next, a man leaned against the wall to listen, but after checking his watch briskly walked away lest he be late for work. The person who paid the most attention was a three-year-old boy. His mother tugged him along, but he continued to stop to look at the violinist and to listen to the music. This action was repeated by several other children. Without exception, parents forced them quickly to move on.

The musician played for forty-five minutes and in that time only six people stopped to linger for any amount of time. About twenty people gave him money but continued to walk at their brisk pace. When he finished playing, the station became silent but no one noticed the silence. No one applauded the music, and there was no real recognition of any kind.

What the people in that train station did not know was that the musician in their midst that cold January morning was Joshua Bell, one of the world's most accomplished violinists. He had played one of the most intricate pieces of music ever written for the violin. And he had done so on an instrument worth more than three million dollars. Just two days prior, he had played a concert at a sold-out theater in Boston where tickets sold for hundreds of dollars.

Joshua Bell's performance in the Washington, DC, subway was organized by the *Washington Post* as part of a social experiment. The experiment sought to answer the question: Do we recognize talent and genius in a commonplace environment? In such an environment, do we perceive beauty? If we do not have a moment to stop and listen to one of the world's best musicians playing some of the finest music ever written, how many other things might we be missing?

Two millennia ago, God appeared incognito on the stage of human history. The location for his appearance was not a metro subway station but a small stable in a tiny nondescript village called Bethlehem. As Phillips Brooks wrote, "How silently, how silently, the wondrous gift [was] given."[8] The music of heaven filled the air that night, but only a few heard it.

The wondrous gift of Christmas—the incarnation—invites us to cultivate gratitude as a habitual disposition by training ourselves to see God personally and intimately with us in the mundane, ordinary activities of life

---

8. Phillips Brooks, "O Little Town of Bethlehem," public domain.

and by responding to God's presence with faith and obedience. Cultivating a habit, of course, requires time and focused repetition.

Because Christmas is a twelve-day season, it offers us an inherent starting place for making gratitude a habitual practice. Each day of the twelve-day season offers a new opportunity to give thanks for God's supreme gift of his Son, and to live that gratitude in concrete ways. One family that I know spreads the giving of gifts over the entire twelve days of Christmas, opening a single gift each day. The practice reinforces the nature of God's self-giving love in Jesus by experiencing it over twelve consecutive days through giving to others. The twelve days allow time for the seeds of gratitude to be planted and to find fertile soil in our hearts by meditating on God's amazing gift of love in Jesus Christ and by sharing that gift in sacrificial ways.

Gratitude as a habitual practice ultimately involves choosing to view all of life through the lens of God's love and mercy revealed to us at Christmas. It involves daily practices that connect us to the lived truth that God is *with* us. This truth becomes the lens through which we see and experience all of life. Thus, the apostle Paul could write to the Christians in Thessalonica:

> Rejoice always, pray constantly, give thanks in all circumstances; for this is the will of God in Christ Jesus for you.[9]

Pastors and theologians remind us that Paul's exhortation to give thanks is to be done *in* all circumstances, not necessarily *for* all circumstances. But it is precisely through the lens of Christmas and the coming of Emmanuel—God with us—that makes possible our ability to see our circumstances within a larger perspective, thus enabling us to respond with gratitude.

God continues to show up in our daily lives in hidden and unexpected ways, disguised to most but perceptible to those who have trained themselves to see. This seems to be God's pattern, recognized by the poet Elizabeth Barrett Browning when she wrote: "Earth's crammed with heaven, and every common bush afire with God; but only he who sees, takes off his shoes, the rest sit around and pluck blackberries."[10]

Cultivating gratitude as a way of life is best done in community, with brothers and sisters in faith and with fellow travelers along life's journey. We help each other through encouragement and mutual accountability. The celebration of Holy Communion is also a primary way in which the church offers up gratitude to God for his indescribable gift to us in Jesus. The term "Eucharist," used to describe the sacrament of Holy Communion in many traditions, means "to give thanks." As the church gathers around the Lord's

---

9. 1 Thess 5:16–18 RSV.

10. Browning, "From Aurora Leigh," 152.

Table, we are reminded that life is a gift to us. Every moment is *given*. When we are empowered by grace to be thankful for whatever is given to us, that thankfulness itself makes us happy. The saints of the church are examples of this truth. They lived lives of humble thanks for whatever life brought them.

Living from a posture of gratitude begins by being attentive to the *givenness* of life, by a heightened awareness of simple things that we often take for granted. In fact, the opposite of gratitude is taking everything for granted. A sunrise, for example, comes to us completely unbidden. We don't produce it. The light is given to us. The world is reborn each morning and a new window of opportunity is opened to us. Even if yesterday's problems are still present today, we can choose to face them in a new way with renewed grace and strength. This gives new meaning to the old saw, "Rise and shine!" When we view the morning sun as a gift, its light fills our lives with gratitude. It is the response produced in us at Christmas, where the Daystar dawns on us from on high and shines his light on those who dwell in darkness and the shadow of death.

Chapter Eight

An Unopened Gift

In the most difficult circumstances of life, there is often only one source of peace.

—DONALD HALLSTROM

But peaceful was the night wherein the Prince of Light
His reign of peace upon the earth began.

—JOHN MILTON

SUGGESTED READINGS

Isa 9:2–7; Ps 96; Titus 2:11–14; Luke 2:1–20

IN THE MARVELOUS STORY of Jesus's birth from the second chapter of Luke's Gospel, we find a profoundly simple declaration in verse 14, where the heavenly hosts say: "Glory to God in the highest, and on earth peace, good will toward men."

In one sense the entirety of Christ's mission in coming to earth could be summarized in this declaration. Christ came to bring glory to God and to bring peace to a hurting and broken world. He came to bring peace to wounded, hurting people. The apostle John reminds us of this. As Jesus prepares his disciples for his impending departure from this world, he tells them:

> Peace I leave with you; my peace I give to you; not as the world
> gives do I give to you. Let not your hearts be troubled, neither
> let them be afraid.[1]

We also call to mind the experience of Jesus's disciples subsequent to his crucifixion. They are hunkered down behind locked doors and pulled drapes, terrified that they may suffer the same fate as Jesus. In that moment, the risen Jesus appears and says to them: "Peace be with you."[2]

It is amazing to me that of the many things Jesus could have said to his disciples in that moment, he says: "Peace be with you." And he says it twice! Instead of criticizing or condemning them for their failure and weakness, Jesus reassures his frightened followers by bestowing his peace upon them. Indeed, as the prophet Isaiah foretold, Jesus was the promised Prince of Peace.

But if I were to be totally honest, the peace that Christ came to bring sometimes seems more an elusive ideal than a present reality in my life. There seems to be a great lack of peace not only in our world, but at times also in my soul.

To be clear, the fault is not with Christ, but with me. He paid the utmost cost to secure my peace, and the fact that I sometimes allow myself to be robbed of that peace is my fault, not his. I hear him say: "My peace I give to you, my peace I leave with you." And yet, the cares and worries and fears that I allow to grow in my mind often rob me of that promised peace. I allow my circumstances and my fears of the future to plunder me of one of the greatest gifts his birth into the world affords me—his promised peace.

If my own personal lack of peace were not enough, the apparent lack of peace in our nation and in our world is enough at times to ramp up my anxiety even further. When I look at the situation in our nation and in our world, I am sometimes tempted to doubt that Christ's promised peace is even remotely possible.

I suspect that many of us experience this sense of disequilibrium from time to time. And we are not alone. One of the great carols of the Christmas season was given to us by the poet Henry Wadsworth Longfellow. We are no doubt familiar with many of the words of the hymn:

> I heard the bells on Christmas Day,
> Their old familiar carols play,
> And wild and sweet,

---

1. John 14:27 RSV.
2. John 20:19 RSV.

> The words repeat,
> Of peace on earth, good will to men.
>
> And thought how, as the day had come,
> The belfries of all Christendom
> Had rolled along,
> The unbroken song
> Of peace on earth, good will to men.
>
> Till ringing, singing on its way,
> The world resolved from night to day,
> A voice, a chime,
> A chant sublime
> Of peace on earth, good will to men.

So far, so good. But then comes this verse:

> And in despair I bowed my head;
> "There is no peace on earth," I said.
> "For hate is strong,
> And mocks the song
> Of peace on earth, good will to men."[3]

Perhaps it is naïve of me, but I always heard those words and simply assumed that Longfellow was discouraged for the same reasons I am—namely, nation rising up against nation, power mongers grabbing for power and control, and people consumed by hatred and selfishness.

But Longfellow had better reasons than I do for his discouragement. Two years before he wrote this poem, his wife Fannie had died after her dress caught fire. Henry tried to save her, and in the process sustained severe burns on his face and body. Henry now found himself a widower with five children. Not long after his wife's death, his oldest son, Charles, slipped out of their Massachusetts home one day in March of 1863 and boarded the train for Washington, DC, where he enlisted in the Union Army to fight in the Civil War.

After being commissioned as a Second Lieutenant, Charles contracted typhoid fever and was sent home to recover, narrowly missing the Battle of Gettysburg. He rejoined his unit in August of 1863 and was shot and wounded in early December of that year. The bullet grazed his spine, nearly paralyzing him. Upon learning of his son's injuries, Henry traveled to Washington, DC, to be with him, where doctors said that his healing would take

---

3. Henry Wadsworth Longfellow, "I Heard the Bells on Christmas Day," public domain.

several months. On Christmas Day, 1863, the man who was now a widowed father of five, the oldest of which had nearly died as his country fought a war against itself, sat down and wrote this poem. Here are a couple of stanzas that may be less familiar to us:

> Then from each black, accursed mouth
> The cannon thundered in the South,
> And with the sound
> The carols drowned
> Of peace on earth, good will to men.
>
> It was as if an earthquake rent
> The hearth-stones of a continent,
> And made forlorn,
> The households born
> Of peace on earth, good will to men.
>
> And in despair I bowed my head,
> "There is no peace on earth," I said.
> For hate is strong,
> And mocks the song
> Of peace on earth, good will to men."

Fortunately, those words of despair were not the poem's last words. Longfellow continued:

> Then pealed the bells more loud and deep:
> "God is not dead, nor doth He sleep;
> The wrong shall fail,
> The right prevail,
> With peace on earth, good will to men."

On a cold, dark night long ago, the heavens rang out with this joyous truth: "Glory to God in the highest, and on earth *peace*, good will to men!" The peace that Christ came to bring was cosmic in scope, but it is also profoundly personal. It brings calm in the midst of chaos. It provides perspective in the midst of trying and difficult circumstances. It steadies us as we grieve the loss of friends and loved ones. It is God's gift to us at Christmas.

But this precious gift of peace is only useful to us when we unwrap it and allow it into our hearts and minds. We know and experience it best through the eyes and ears of faith, the kind of faith that Henry Wadsworth Longfellow had. His was a faith that saw through his difficult circumstances and beheld the greatness and power of God. That vision led to renewed hope. And the fruit of renewed hope is peace.

Why is it that we so often lack this peace in our lives? One reason may be that we are prone to mistake peace for the absence of suffering, conflict, and struggle that is part and parcel of daily existence. We may be confused into thinking that Christ's peace prevents our hearts from being troubled by anything at all. This simply is not the case, however. It is certain that we will experience suffering, trial, and hardship. The peace that Christ brings, though, frees us from debilitating anxiety. It empowers us to see beneath our immediate circumstances.

Author Luis Martinez posits that a possible barrier to our enjoyment of God's peace is an erosion of trust in God's love for us. We lose sight not only of the *fact* that God loves us, but also the *depths* to which that love penetrates the mundane details of our daily lives. We lose sight of how deeply personal God's love is for us. Our minds wander and forget God, but God does not forget us for one moment. His love arranges all the events of our life from the most far-reaching to the most insignificant:

> When we are disquieted, it is usually through such forgetfulness or because the event is not according to our liking and we do not accept it with resignation, or because we want to know the consequences beforehand, whether for good or for ill. We forget that God regulates all things, that we are not alone, but carried in the divine arms, which not only protect us, but also direct the world and arrange all of life's occurrences.[4]

A living, vibrant, active faith in God's love for us is the pathway to peace. This peace is the gift of God offered to us and to the world at Christmas— peace in our hearts, in our homes, and in our world. Such a precious gift, yet so little received and enjoyed. So many people in our world are unhappy, frantically searching and striving for the next thing or relationship that will fulfill them. They are not at peace.

Christmas is the annual reminder from a loving Heavenly Father that the peace we so desperately seek is available to us, but not as an isolated commodity. It is the fruit of a relationship with the promised Prince of Peace. It is *in* Christ and *through* Christ that this peace comes to us. Peace is the fruit of surrender. It results when we are able to pray sincerely: "Thy kingdom come, thy will be done." Peace is not the absence of danger or hardship, but the presence of God. It is the presence of the God who comes to us at Christmas.

The God who assumed our human nature and walked along the dusty trails of Palestine lives today among us, concealed under the appearance of bread and wine. He continues to say to us: "Peace be with you." The Author

4. Martinez, *When God Is Silent*, 93.

and source of our peace is available to us in the sacrament of the Eucharist and in the worship of the church. This has been the consistent teaching of the church through the centuries. When the church gathers around the Table of the Lord, peace is an inevitable and welcome fruit of that gathering. In the liturgy and the sacraments, Christ's gift of peace descends upon God's children, who in turn become an offering of peace to the world. Our hurting and broken world needs this peace, perhaps now more than ever.

Chapter Nine

When Life Doesn't Make Sense

Sometimes it is hard to tell whether you are being killed or
saved by the hands that turn your life upside down.

—BARBARA BROWN TAYLOR

SUGGESTED READINGS

Jer 31:15–17; Ps 124; Rev 21:1–7; Matt 2:13–18

ONE OF MY FAVORITE things about the Christmas season is the music,
especially the hymns. After experiencing the longing and anticipation that
define the Advent season,[1] the Christmas season allows us the opportunity to join with the Virgin Mary and ponder the mystery of God coming

1. One of the challenges of marking time through the liturgical year involves letting Advent have its full integrity by not allowing Christmas to bleed into the Advent
season, especially in public worship. Nowhere is this challenge more pronounced than
in the music we sing. During Advent the hymns and carols put us in touch with the holy
longing for God's coming and help us to anticipate and to pray for his arrival among
us. The Christmas hymns and carols are most appropriate, however, only when the
Christmas season has begun. Preserving the integrity of Advent is very difficult when
the prevailing culture (and even much of the church) begins singing Christmas carols
almost immediately after the Thanksgiving holiday.

to us in Jesus. With Charles Wesley, we find ourselves awestruck in the face of the incarnation:

> Let earth and heaven combine, angels and men agree,
> To praise in songs divine th'incarnate Deity,
> Our God contracted to a span, incomprehensibly made man.[2]

In a more practical vein, the well-known carol "What Child Is This?" invites us simply to worship Jesus. The invitation is marked by urgency: "Haste, haste, to bring him laud, the babe, the son of Mary."[3] This beautiful hymn, set to the tune of Greensleeves, is a favorite of many. But we might wonder: Why all the fuss about making haste and coming quickly to greet him? What's the rush? Can't we simply revel in the joy of this occasion for a while? Can't we just enjoy Christmas?

The answer to that question is both yes and no. Of course we should take a deep breath and enjoy the beauty and mystery of Christmas. We should allow ourselves time to ponder in our hearts what it all means. We should allow ourselves to be overcome with joy that Jesus the Bridegroom has come to unite himself to us as his bride. But in the liturgical year we're not given the luxury of too much time, because Jesus's parents are packing him up and fleeing quickly to Egypt. They are on the run because King Herod is searching for Jesus in order to kill him. For Herod, Jesus's arrival signals not hope and promise, but a threat. Herod is an evil, insecure man who will stop at nothing to secure his own power, including murdering his own wife and children. Caesar Augustus, himself a violent man, was said to have remarked that he would rather be Herod's dog than his son.

Afraid that he might be bumped from his throne, Herod orders the slaughter of all boys two years old and younger in Bethlehem and the surrounding region. Herod had interrogated the Magi, wise men from the East who had traveled a great distance in search of the newborn child. He had learned their astrological calculations and determined that the new king of the Jews—if such a child had been born—could be no more than two years old. So he sent his henchmen to do the dirty deed.

Matthew is the only Gospel writer to mention this horrific incident, and it is gruesome to contemplate it. In Pier Paolo Pasolini's film, *The Gospel According to St. Matthew*, it is portrayed by horsemen galloping through Nazareth wrestling the babies from the arms of their mothers. The terrorized mothers fight valiantly, but eventually lose the struggle.

---

2. Charles Wesley, "Let Earth and Heaven Combine," public domain.

3. William Chatterton Dix, "What Child Is This?," public domain.

Scholars are divided about the number of children who died that day. But when Herod's horsemen departed, Matthew tells us that the moaning and the mourning that rose from the village could be heard five miles away in the village of Ramah.[4] From the earliest history of the church, these children were considered martyrs because they died not only *for* Christ but also *instead* of Christ. Remembrance of their sacrifice has been observed in the West from the fourth century of the Christian era, where they have been known as the Holy Innocents. In the fifth century, Saint Augustine described them as *flores martyrum*, as buds killed by the frost of persecution the moment they showed themselves. For centuries in England, this day was called *Childermas*.

This horrific act of violence by Herod reveals a common struggle for those who follow Jesus, namely, how to reconcile the presence of injustice and random evil with a loving and benevolent God. From a human perspective, the fact that God would allow random evil when he is capable of preventing it seems to call into question both his omnipotence and his benevolence. Either God is incapable of preventing such acts, or if he is capable, the fact that he does not always do so seems to impugn his character as loving.[5]

Part of what makes the struggle so difficult for many is that we often live our lives out of an underlying or unconscious cause-and-effect paradigm. This is partly understandable, given that the raw material for such cause-and-effect religion is found in Scripture. The book of Deuteronomy seems to do so when it frames the relationship of the children of Israel to God in terms of blessings for obeying the covenant, and curses and calamity for disobeying it.[6] Parts of Deuteronomy even imply that wealth and material blessing are a sign of divine favor due to obedience, while hardship and calamity are a sign of disobedience.

In the New Testament epistle to the Galatians, the apostle Paul frames the notion of cause-and-effect religion using the metaphor of sowing and reaping: "Do not be deceived; God is not mocked, for whatever a man sows, that he will also reap."[7] The difficulty lies precisely in the fact that most

---

4. Matthew is quoting the prophet Jeremiah's anguished prophecy: "A voice was heard in Ramah, wailing and loud lamentation, Rachel weeping for her children; she refused to be consoled, because they were no more." See Matt 2:16–18 RSV.

5. See Boone, *Dark Side of God*. See also Fringer and Lane, *Theology of Luck*. Tom Oord has written extensively on this issue from the perspective of open and relational theology. See Oord, *Uncontrolling Love of God* and *God Can't*. See also LeClerc and Peterson, *Back Side of the Cross*.

6. Deut 4:39–40; 5:33; 7:12–15; 11:13–17, 26–29.

7. Gal 6:7 RSV.

of the time, cause-and-effect *is* an apt and accurate description of how life works. There are consequences to our behavior. There are rewards and blessing for obedience, and discipline and punishment for sin. This seems to be the way of God—*most of the time.*

The problem with cause-and-effect religion is that it doesn't explain or account for *every* situation. Sometimes people do good and get bad, while others do bad and get good. The story of Job in the Old Testament is perhaps the most compelling example of this seemingly inexplicable phenomenon.[8] God, in the mystery of his providence, permits Job to suffer incomprehensible pain and loss, even though there is nothing in Job's life to warrant such tragedy. In fact, the opposite is true. Under the cause-and-effect model, Job should receive blessing and honor because of his upright life.

Job's friends, however, are convinced that Job has violated the inviolable law of cause-and-effect, so they try to convince him that he has sinned and needs to repent before God. Job, however, steadfastly asserts his integrity. He cries out to God and demands to be heard.[9] He accuses God of stalking him like a hunter stalks a wild animal. He challenges God to a debate, accusing God of wildly and freely doing what he pleases with complete immunity from any law. He summons God to court and demands that God defend himself. As one writer notes, had Job talked like this in church we would have had the ushers escort him to the atheists club![10]

As it turns out, Job is ultimately vindicated and God indicates that he is pleased with Job's brutal honesty that is the fruit of wrestling with the side of God that he does not understand. Job's faith seeks understanding. He asks the God he understands to help him get justice from the God he doesn't understand. He discovers that justice is not a cause-and-effect outcome, but a world being made right by the love of God.[11]

Job is not the first person to ask the question: Where is God? Elie Wiesel tells the harrowing story from his experience in a Nazi concentration camp about a young boy who was executed with two adults whom the Gestapo suspected had collaborated to blow up a German power station. On the day of the executions, prisoners in the camp were forced to march past the gallows in procession, fixing their gaze upon the three victims who had been mounted onto chairs, nooses around their necks.

---

8. See also Luke 13:1–5, which tells the story of the Tower of Siloam which fell and killed innocent bystanders. See also Eccl 8:9, 14.

9. Job 29–31.

10. Boone, *Dark Side of God*, 416.

11. Boone, *Dark Side of God*, 607.

"Long live liberty," cried the two adults. But the child remained silent. As the camp commander read the verdict, all eyes were on the child. To hang a child in front of thousands of prisoners was extreme, even for a concentration camp. At that moment a prisoner softly asked: "Where is God? Where is he?"

Then the head of the camp gave a signal, and the three chairs toppled over. As the prisoners marched by, they could see that the two adults were dead. But the third rope was still moving because the young boy was so light. The prisoners had to stare at him for more than thirty minutes as he hung suspended between life and death. He was still alive as Weisel passed in front of him, where he heard the voice again: "Where is God now?" In that moment Weisel heard a voice inside himself that replied: "Where is he? He is here—hanging on this gallows."[12]

Noted author C. S. Lewis also asked the question after the death of his wife:

> Meanwhile, where is God? This is one of the most disquieting symptoms. When you are happy, so happy that you have no sense of needing Him, so happy that you are tempted to feel His claims upon you as an interruption, if you remember yourself and turn to Him with gratitude and praise you will be—or so it feels—welcomed with open arms. But go to Him when your need is desperate, when all other help is vain, and what do you find? A door slammed in your face, and a sound of bolting and double bolting on the inside. After that, silence. You may as well turn away. The longer you wait, the more empathic the silence will become. There are no lights in the windows. It might be an empty house. Was it ever inhabited? It seemed so at once. And that seeming was as strong as this. What can this mean? Why is He so present as a commander in our time of prosperity and so very absent a help in time of trouble?[13]

And, of course, Jesus himself asked it as he hung on the Cross. Quoting from Ps 22, he cried: "My God, my God, why have you forsaken me?" Inevitably, we take our places alongside them, asking: "Where are you, God? What did I do to deserve this? Why did I do good and get bad?"

The law of cause-and-effect, the principle of sowing and reaping, is true *most of the time*. But G. K. Chesterton cautions us:

> The real trouble with this world of ours is not that it is an unreasonable world, nor even that it is a reasonable one. The

12. Wiesel, *Night*, 60–61.
13. Lewis, *Grief Observed*, 443–44.

commonest kind of trouble is that it is nearly reasonable, but not quite. Life is not an illogicality; yet it is a trap for logicians. It looks just a little more mathematical and regular than it is; its exactitude is obvious, but its inexactitude is hidden; its wildness lies in wait.[14]

Ultimately, the answer as to how and why God allows evil into our lives and into the world—and its apparent randomness—is elusive. Perhaps the philosopher Peter Kreeft was right when he observed that Christianity has the burden of explaining the presence of evil in the world while atheism faces the challenge of explaining everything else. Dan Boone may be helpful when he observes:

> The God who is free to do as he chooses, chooses to receive into himself the injustice of evil, because he wishes to be with us in the place where we are abandoned.[15]

Picture Jesus, hanging on the cross. Bound by nails, immobile, without hope of tomorrow, a victim of pure evil and injustice, abandoned on the ash heap of human rejection. Then consider: When we cry out to him and sense that he is absent, maybe he is the cry inside us, so near to us that we do not even know it.

It is also important to observe in this discussion the distinction between physical evil and moral evil. Physical evil involves negative occurrences such as sickness, pain, natural disaster, and death. Moral evil is something that is done by a culpable actor. In both cases, evil does not exist *in* itself, but is a privation, e.g., the absence of good. Evil is not a *thing* and is alien to God's creation. It does not originate in God. Nevertheless, the pesky question still remains: Why, if God is both good and all-powerful, does evil exist? C. S. Lewis may have been right in observing that the answer to this question is elusive because of the juxtaposition of human freedom with divine omnipotence. Scott Hahn concurs:

> When God made both human beings and angels, he made us rational, free, and capable of loving. This means, however, that we have the possibility of choosing something other than God. It was necessary for us to have this choice, because true love cannot be coerced. If we did not have the freedom to say no to God, we could not truly love Him. Thus, God could not create a species with free choice without also permitting the possibility of evil.[16]

14. Chesterton, *Orthodoxy*, 74.
15. Boone, *Dark Side of God*, 629.
16. Hahn, *Reasons to Believe*, 51.

In a similar vein, author Madeleine L'Engle reasons that when life is particularly difficult or we encounter some grievous tragedy that makes us ask why God doesn't intervene in order to manipulate those tragic circumstances, all we need to do is read a novel by a writer who is a manipulator, who controls characters and denies them their freedom. Doing so helps us to realize that no matter how terrible life can sometimes be, we do not want a dictator God.[17]

It is beyond the scope of this book to explore issues of theodicy, the branch of theology that is concerned with the vindication of God's goodness and providence in relation to the existence of evil. Nevertheless, there is a long history of interpretation in Christianity that views God allowing evil and injustice as a consequence of human beings being free moral agents, as stated above. In this line of thinking, God foresaw that human beings would misuse our freedom without causing us to do so. In spite of our rejection of his love and the misuse of our freedom, God is able to use evil to show forth his infinite goodness and power by bringing forth from it a greater good. Native American poet Alexander Posey reflects this understanding in his poem entitled "Assured":

> Be it dark; be it bright;
> Be it pain; be it rest;
> Be it wrong; be it right—
> It must be for the best.
> Some good must somewhere wait,
> And sometime joy and pain
> Must cease to alternate,
> Or else we live in vain.[18]

Often, the harm or evil that we experience at the hands of others is difficult to comprehend precisely because of its senselessness. It defies logic and runs contrary to the natural order of things. Christian faith insists, however, that where events may appear random and senseless to us, God has the power to bring good from those circumstances so that the evil intent of those who abuse their freedom will not be the final word. This requires strong and determined faith that God sees what we cannot see, that God's purposes are loving and benevolent. Saint John Henry Newman captures this truth based on his own life experience:

> God has created me to do Him some definite service; He has committed some work to me which He has not committed to another. I have my mission—I may never know it in this life, but

---

17. Quoted in Sayers, *Mind of the Maker*, xix–xx.

18. See "Assured" in Posey, *Poems of Alexander Lawrence Posey*, 92.

> I shall be told it in the next. . . . I am necessary for His purpos-
> es. . . . He has not created me for naught. . . . Therefore I will trust
> Him. Whatever, wherever I am, I can never be thrown away. If
> I am in sickness, my sickness may serve Him; in perplexity, my
> perplexity may serve Him; if I am in sorrow, my sorrow may
> serve Him. My sickness, or perplexity, or sorrow may be neces-
> sary causes of some great end, which is quite beyond us. He does
> nothing in vain. . . . He knows what He is about.[19]

What is striking about this observation is Newman's realization that
his life's mission—the purpose for which he was created—may not be fully
revealed to him in this life. This amazes me, as I've never thought about my
life's purpose in this way. To think that I may never know fully on this side
of the grave why my life has unfolded as it has seems daunting at first glance.
Surely this must include those things that happen to us that are inexplicable,
things that seem to have no purpose other than to bring us pain and heartache. But as the apostle Paul reminds us, all of our knowledge on this side
of the grave is partial:

> For now we see in a mirror dimly, but then face to face. Now I
> know in part; then I shall understand fully, even as I have been
> fully understood.[20]

Newman intuitively grasps the thrust of Saint Paul's words to the Corinthians. When we are confronted with painful and inexplicable circumstances,
some greater end that is beyond us is at work. We may not be privileged to
know that end just yet, but God does. And, as Newman says, God knows
what he is about. In prayer he states:

> I am born to serve Thee, to be Thine, to be Thy instrument.
> Let me be Thy blind instrument. I ask not to see—I ask not to
> know—I ask simply to be used.[21]

Newman reaches a place where he gives up his demand to know from God
why things unfold in his life as they do. He accepts his finite understanding
in the face of God's infinite wisdom and prays simply to be used by God for
the accomplishment of God's purposes. When confronted with the apparent
inexplicability of tragic events and injurious circumstances, we are invited
to trust that God sees what we cannot see and that what confronts us in the
present is being shaped by God to conform to his ultimately loving purpose.

19. Marr, *John Henry Newman*, 121–22.

20. 1 Cor 13:12–13 RSV.

21. Marr, *John Henry Newman*, 122.

There is an additional consideration for us as we ponder issues of injustice and random evil. We must be concerned not just with understanding the mystery of how God can allow evil, but we must also come to grips with the capacity in our hearts to commit such evil. In the midst of the Christmas celebration, we are forced to confront the Herod in all of us, to acknowledge the darkness in our hearts that renders us capable of doing what Herod did, and more.

Jesus's coming can be threatening not merely to the Herods of this world, but also to us. For he comes to shine the light into our hearts, to put to death in us all that is not God's best for us, to shake us out of the status quo and take us on a journey of adventure and discovery. But something in us, something in our human nature, resists that sacrificial love. Herod may grab the storyline, but the darkness in all of our hearts forces Joseph and Mary to grab Jesus quickly and to flee to Egypt. The love that can heal us and save us comes to us, but we struggle to embrace it.

When my wife Connie and I were teenagers, our church presented a live nativity scene every year in the days just before Christmas. The church parsonage was on a large corner lot, which made a perfect setting to stage the scene. It was a big production, complete with strategically arranged hay bales and sometimes a few live animals. There were costumes, lights, shepherds, angels, wise men, the complete package. But in the years that Connie and I participated in that event, I do not recall one single time when Joseph and Mary ever grabbed Jesus out of the cradle, bundled him up, and ran off into the night in order to flee the wrath of Herod. The closest thing we got to that was Mary and Joseph scurrying off to the fellowship hall for hot chocolate, while a new Mary and Joseph quickly ran out to take their place before a set of headlights appeared in the distance.

But what Herod did was real and is an integral part of the Christmas story. It reminds us that the precious gift that arrived for us in the manger was a gift procured at the greatest possible cost. It shows us that although God's love for us is deep and profound, our brokenness and our self-sufficiency also run deep and push hard to reject that love. And in some cases, we even try to destroy it. In an act unimaginable to us, Herod orders the murder of innocent children. Their lives become little more than collateral damage to him as he flees from the love that has come to heal him and to save him. The good news of Christmas, however, is that God's love to us in Christ cannot be thwarted or defeated. The light shines in the darkness, and the darkness cannot overcome it.

Epiphany

Chapter Ten

The Long and Winding Road

Adversity is the first path to truth.

—Lord Byron

Were we led all that way for Birth or Death?

—T. S. Eliot

SUGGESTED READINGS

Isa 60:1–9; Ps 72; Eph 3:1–12; Matt 2:1–12

Growing up in a rural Nebraska farming community, one of the staple enjoyments of childhood involved spending weeks at a time camping with my family. The presence of a beautiful lake only seven miles from our home made camping an attractive option. I would often accompany my mom to the store to buy groceries, and once we were home we would load everything into the camper in preparation for several days at the lake. My stepfather purchased a nice boat when my siblings and I were young, adding fishing and skiing to the pleasures of being at the lake and escaping the routines of life and work. On many occasions, our camping excursions were spent with cousins and extended family or other friends from the community.

Some of my fondest memories of those times spent camping involved watching the sun set over the lake and looking up at the stars. In the pitch-black darkness of the night, the stars were like enormous diamonds, glowing and sparkling against the velvety black sky. There is something about stars that captures our attention and imagination.

The Feast of Epiphany tells the fascinating story of a star and a group of foreigners from the East who follow it more than a thousand miles to the Judean countryside. Matthew tells it like this:

> Now when Jesus was born in Bethlehem of Judea in the days of Herod the king, behold, wise men from the East came to Jerusalem, saying, "Where is he who has been born king of the Jews? For we have seen his star in the East, and have come to worship him."[1]

Who were these men, and why did they ask this question about the star?

Although our knowledge is limited, the Magi were likely astrologers, considered at the time to be wise because of their lifelong commitment to studying the skies and finding meaning in the cosmos. They probably came from Persia, and some scholars believe that they may have been part of a school of wise men over which Daniel, the Jewish prophet, had been given authority hundreds of years earlier.[2]

Why, though, do these scholars make the long journey and follow this star? To answer that, we need Matthew's help. Matthew, more than any Gospel writer, makes numerous connections to the Old Testament. Sometimes Matthew connects his writing to the Old Testament Scriptures by directly quoting them. At other times, Matthew just assumes a worldview and context that his first-century readers possessed but that is foreign to us. We must remember that those to whom Matthew wrote did not have Netflix and smartphones. Their culture was shaped by their Scriptures. Life revolved around what they heard in the Synagogue, what they pondered in prayer, and what they celebrated in their feasts. And they were acutely aware of the prophecies that were part of their Scriptures.

---

1. Matt 2:1–2 RSV.

2. Daniel was part of the group of Israelites who were taken captive by the Babylonians in 586 BC. The book of Daniel describes how Daniel remained faithful to God in the midst of a pagan land. God gave him wisdom, and he was able to interpret a dream of King Nebuchadnezzar that no one else could discern. In gratitude, the king made Daniel the "chief prefect over all the wise men of Babylon." See Dan 2:48.

This story of the Magi from Matthew, while strange and perplexing to us, would have resonated deeply with Matthew's audience. For as Matthew tells the story in all of its detail, he is alluding to a story right out of their Scriptures. The story is found in the book of Numbers.

As the children of Israel made their way toward the promised land after leaving Egypt, they encountered Balak, the wicked king of Moab. Balak felt threatened by the Israelites, so he summoned a man named Balaam, a wise man from the East, to put a curse on the people of Israel. But every time Balaam tried to curse the Israelites, God intervened, and words of blessing came out of his mouth instead of curses. Even a donkey was involved in this strange story!

The story of king Balak and the wise man Balaam foreshadows the events surrounding Christ's birth. Just as the wicked king Balak tried to use a seer from the East to harm Israel, so the wicked king Herod tries to use the Magi from the East in his plot to discover where the Christ child is residing. And just as Balaam didn't cooperate with Balak's plan, blessing the people instead of cursing them, so the Magi don't assist Herod in his plan. Instead, they worship the baby and do not reveal his location to Herod.

But perhaps the most telling thing about the story of Balak and Balaam is how it ends. After attempting to curse Israel three times, Balaam experiences God taking control of his speech once again. This time, Balaam utters a prophecy about a great king who will come to Israel in the distant future:

> I see him, but not now; I behold him, but not nigh; a star shall
> come forth out of Jacob, and a scepter shall rise out of Israel.[3]

If we unpack the symbolism, we notice that the scepter is a royal staff, symbolizing a king who will one day come to Israel. And according to the prophecy, a star will be the sign of the king's arrival. So when the Magi see the star in the direction of Israel, their traveling to Jerusalem in search of a king would make perfect sense to those reading Matthew's words. It rings perfectly true to what Balaam had prophesied centuries earlier.

Balaam's prophecy also makes sense of Herod's anger as recorded by Matthew. For right after Balaam speaks of the star coming forth out of Jacob, he mentions that because of the rising star, "Edom will be dispossessed."[4] And who was Herod? Herod was an Edomite, a usurper to the throne in Jerusalem. Matthew's intriguing story of the Magi following the star is simply the full flowering of Old Testament prophecy. The star that the Magi

3. Num 24:17 RSV.
4. Num 24:18 RSV.

followed was the Star that was promised to rise from Jacob, the Scepter who was to emerge from Israel.

This is confirmed in Luke's Gospel. Luke tells us that after John the Baptist is born, his father Zechariah breaks forth in a song of prophetic praise. In the prophecy, Zechariah announces that John will go before the Lord to prepare people for his coming. Then Zechariah speaks these words:

> By the tender mercy of our God, the dawn from on high will break upon us, to give light to those who sit in darkness and in the shadow of death, to guide our feet into the way of peace.[5]

Matthew and Luke take great care to place this story of the Magi following the star into its Old Testament prophetic context. But the story doesn't end with Matthew and Luke. In the apostle John's vision which we know as the Revelation, Jesus reveals to John how God is going to bring his plan for saving his people to its grand conclusion. Near the end of the vision, Jesus says to John:

> I, Jesus, have sent my angel to you with this testimony for the churches. I am the root and the offspring of David, the bright morning star.[6]

Indeed he is. Matthew, Luke, and John all see Jesus as the fulfillment of Balaam's prophecy. Jesus is the true Daystar, the Light of God who comes not just for the children of Israel, but for all people.[7]

We are fascinated by stars. But have you ever hitched your life to one? Have you ever pinned all of your hopes and dreams on one? Have you laid aside everything you hold dear in order to follow one? The Magi did. And through the centuries, so have a host of others. One such person was the poet T. S. Eliot.

Eliot was born in America and educated at Harvard, but subsequently moved to London and became a British citizen. He became famous for his poem "The Love Song of J. Alfred Prufrock" in 1911. Eliot was masterful in his use of images to suggest meaning. In 1922, he published *The Wasteland*, a collection which earned him great notoriety. Regarded by many as the greatest poet of the twentieth century, Eliot's poem *The Journey of the Magi* reveals the doubts and struggles he faced in embracing Christianity.

---

5. Luke 1:78–79 NRSV. The canticle of Zechariah is an integral part of Morning Prayer in those traditions that pray the Divine Office, also known as the Liturgy of the Hours.

6. Rev 22:16 RSV.

7. See Eph 3, where the apostle Paul explains God's love for the gentiles as part of his redemptive plan.

He does so by writing the poem from the perspective of one of the wise men who make the journey to worship Jesus.

Part of the poem's power, in my view, lies in its stark realism. While it is easy for us to romanticize the story of the Magi, Eliot focuses on the harsh realities of what the journey must have involved, a path fraught with hardship.[8] The journey to follow the star is characterized by severe cold, distance, dirt, sleepless nights, memories of the comforts left behind, and the hostility of those encountered along the way coupled with their lack of understanding and encouragement. All of this leaves this particular Magi with a voice ringing in his ears that what he is doing is foolish. He experiences doubt as he pushes toward his goal, and his confidence diminishes that he will find what he seeks at the end of his travels. Still, the wise man forges ahead, eventually arriving at the place where Jesus resides with his parents. The scene is anticlimactic. There is no warm fuzzy, no special feeling of fulfillment. There is no drama, no excitement, no ecstasy. There is only perplexity and paradox.

After reflecting on the experience, the Magi traveler concludes that he would do it all again. But in his heart he wonders about the real purpose of his lengthy journey. Was it to celebrate Jesus's birth, or was it to be confronted with the *meaning* of Jesus's birth, which involved dying to himself and coming under Jesus's lordship?[9]

This becomes a pertinent question for us. The birth of Jesus, heralded by the bright star shining in the Judean countryside, changed the world. That birth changes everything. Jesus's birth makes possible our new birth whereby we become God's sons and daughters and share in the very life of the Trinity.

But there is a paradox at work here. Eliot does not regret his decision to become a Christian and to follow Jesus. But he had no idea how much it would cost him to complete his journey when he initially began it. And so it is with us. If you desire to follow Jesus, you will discover that following him is sometimes more a death struggle than a growth process. The grace that Jesus offers us is profoundly costly, inviting us on a journey where we die to sin and self-rule. The adversity we encounter in following Jesus can at times lead us to question our faith. When we discover that following Jesus involves the way of the cross and sharing in Jesus's sufferings, it forces us to reevaluate our priorities. When sharing in Jesus's suffering moves from an

8. Christianity came very hard for Eliot, who once remarked that he was "dragged into the kingdom kicking and screaming." His path to Christianity involved overcoming bitter cynicism, a journey characterized by a great deal of doubt and uncertainty, a "wavering between profit and loss," as he put it.

9. See Eliot, *Collected Poems*, 99–100.

abstract idea and manifests itself in our personal experience, we may find ourselves asking: *Is is worth it?*[10]

The birth of Jesus changes everything. Yet T. S. Eliot's experience challenges us, especially in moments where we come face to face with the possibility that Jesus's birth signals our death in the sense that Jesus's claim on our life is total and complete. Jesus's birth involves death for those who would follow him and call him Lord, because following him involves nothing less than total surrender of our lives to him. Jesus was clear about this:

> If any man would come after me, let him deny himself and take up his cross and follow me. For whoever would save his life will lose it; and whoever loses his life for my sake and the gospel's will save it.[11]

Sooner or later, we discover that Jesus is not a guru whose purpose is to give us a happy life. Christianity is not a utilitarian religion, a religion that involves serving God solely for some kind of reward. To serve God for reward, insurance, blessing, or a protective hedge is to fall short of knowing God as he is revealed to us in Jesus. To do so makes God into an idol to be appeased for the good things he can give us. Jesus is not a magic talisman on the road to a happy and prosperous life. Jesus is the Son of God, who invites us to share in his suffering and death so that we may also share in his resurrection. Ironically, this *is* the way to a happy life, but there will be times where we experience tragedy, pain, and suffering in full measure, just as Jesus did. The servant is not above the Master.

Consider these representative examples from Scripture. Abraham, nearing the century mark in age, clings to a vision that he will father a great nation. For twenty-five years that vision seems more like an impossible dream until a single son is born. And then God presents Abraham with a monumental test of faith, asking him to sacrifice Isaac as a burnt offering.

Consider Joseph, who heard from God in his dreams but landed at the bottom of a well, and later was thrown into an Egyptian prison for trying faithfully to follow God's divine guidance. Or recall Moses, the handpicked liberator of the Hebrew people. Moses hid in the desert for forty years while being hunted by Pharoah's hit squad.

Then there was David, anointed as a teenager to be Israel's king at God's demand. But David spent the next decade and more on the run,

---

10. Our personal experience can parallel that of the children of Israel who, after leaving slavery in Egypt to begin their journey toward the promised land, decided that the cost of obedience to God in the wilderness was too high, and that it would be better to return to slavery in Egypt.

11. Mark 8:34–35 RSV.

dodging spears and sleeping in caves. Or consider King Hezekiah, who is miraculously granted a fifteen-year extension to his life. But upon being granted that favor, God departs from Hezekiah for a significant time in order to test him.

These examples led author Phillip Yancey to conclude that God's guidance in his children's lives often follows a "morse code" type of pattern. There is a clear message of guidance, followed by a long gap of silence.[12] I'm also reminded of C. S. Lewis's observation that persons new to the life of faith often experience answers to prayer—even miraculous ones—but the passing of time and the maturing of their faith brings a decrease in those breakthrough spiritual moments. God does not abandon us in these times. But paradoxically, perplexing times of adversity sometimes help fertilize our faith. Deep faith in God often grows through times of testing.

When I was a young and inexperienced pastor, I was captivated by the writings of Eugene Peterson. While many may know him as the author of *The Message*, Peterson was a gifted pastor in addition to being a prolific author. His writings about pastoral ministry deeply influenced my own practice as I sought to be a faithful shepherd. I was especially impressed that this man served one congregation for more than thirty years, bearing much fruit from that long-term tenure.

But none who follow the Star of Bethlehem are immune from the high cost of that arduous journey. None of us are exempt from the harsh reality of adversity that can discourage and confuse us. Peterson acknowledges numerous times of gut-wrenching struggle during his long ministry, and the resulting confusion that often accompanied it. Times of losing his way and then finding it again. Reflecting on his experience, Peterson marveled at how anything fruitful came of those years of service, and how God was able to use his dark times of adversity to minister to people.[13]

In those moments of adversity when doubt assails us and tempts us to wonder whether following Jesus is a foolish venture not worth the cost, the Holy Spirit becomes our Advocate. He comes to us and walks beside us on the journey to strengthen and inspire us. He reminds us of God's past faithfulness. And he gently nudges us to resume our journey by drawing closer to our brothers and sisters in the faith and to the saints who have gone before us.

When all is said and done, we must remember that it is only by his grace that we can follow that Star and see our journey through to the end. The poet Christina Rosetti captures this well in her poem "Epiphanytide."

---

12. Yancey, *Disappointment with God*, 228.

13. Peterson, *Pastor.*

As we know from ancient times, no person could approach a king unless the king extended his sceptre to the person. Approaching a king without his sceptre extended meant certain death.

Rosetti, using images reminiscent of Balaam's prophecy in Num 24, offers us a King who extends his scepter to us, both in his lowly birth and in his death. And she reminds us that the King born in the manger has not come to conquer or subdue us, but to restore us, to renew us, to set us free. The poem's humble prayer can also be ours:

> Full of pity view us, stretch Thy sceptre to us,
>   Bid us live that we may give ourselves to Thee:
> O faithful Lord and True! Stand up for us and do,
>   Make us lovely, make us new, set us free –
>   Heart and soul and spirit—to bring all and
>   Worship Thee.[14]

14. Rosetti, "Epiphanytide," 161.

Chapter Eleven

Stepping into the Water

*Jesus rises from the waters; the world rises with him. He who is spirit and
flesh comes to begin a new creation through the Spirit and water.*

—Saint Gregory of Nazianzus

SUGGESTED READINGS

Isa 42:1–9; Ps 89:20–29; Acts 10:34–38; Matt 3:13–17; Mark 1:7–11; Luke
3:15–22

After waiting during Advent and preparing for Jesus's arrival; after celebrating his birth through the Christmas season and into Epiphany and the
visit of the Magi, our journey through the liturgical year does a sort of fast
forward to the place where we see the adult Jesus going out into the wilderness to be baptized by John in the Jordan River.

This episode has puzzled Christians for centuries. John sees Jesus standing in line with the rest of the riffraff and asks: "I need to be baptized by you,
and you are coming to me?" This is also our question. And finding an answer
is difficult. John, after all, was dealing with people who needed a complete re-
configuration of their lives and their worldview. His was a baptism of *sinners*.

Jesus does not fit that category. So John's question still lingers with us. Why does Jesus come out to John at the River Jordan for baptism?

The answer to this question is that Jesus's baptism is an *epiphany*, an occasion for God's divine presence and power to be revealed. Specifically, it is an occasion for God to reveal exactly *who Jesus is*. The events here take us back to the Old Testament. The voice from heaven that says, "You are my beloved son," hearkens back to Ps 2 and language there that describes the coronation of the king.

In addition, the voice says, "With you I am fully pleased." These words point back to Isa 42 and Isa 64. These are known as "servant songs" that describe the ministry of the coming Messiah as one who is a suffering servant. In using these allusions, the Gospel writers are saying that Jesus is the One anointed with the Spirit to bring justice and righteousness to earth. Jesus's baptism, then, is an epiphany which proclaims him to be the Son of God. He is both the sovereign King and the Suffering Servant. He is the Liberator of captives, the Light to the nations.

But there is more to this epiphany than just the words that are spoken. The very location of Jesus's baptism is laden with meaning. This is because in Scripture, geography is never merely about *place*. In Scripture, geography is often *theology*. Geography in Scripture is frequently infused with theological significance. This is especially true in the case of Jesus's baptism.

Jesus comes to John at the Jordan River. If we recall our exposure to John during Advent, we remember that the Jordan River was the place where the original exodus of the children of Israel from slavery in Egypt came to its end. At the very place where the original exodus ended, John now stands and announces that a new exodus is about to begin. To prepare for that, John calls on the people to undergo a baptism of repentance and to turn their lives in a new direction.

When John balks at Jesus's presence, wondering why Jesus is there for baptism, Jesus says: "Let it be so now; for thus it is fitting for us to fulfill all righteousness."[1] Quite often, when we hear the word "fulfill," our thoughts turn to Scripture, especially prophecy. And we are in good company. In Matthew's Gospel, the word "fulfill" is used sixteen times, and in almost every case it refers to the fulfillment of something in the Old Testament Scriptures. So when Jesus says to John, "Permit my baptism in order to fulfill all righteousness," he means that his baptism in some way fulfills part of God's plan for the salvation of the world.

Matthew then takes us on a tour of the Old Testament to show us what that plan involves. He begins by saying that after Jesus is baptized, there is a

---

1. Matt 3:15 RSV.

heavenly vision and a voice. Several things occur. First, the Spirit descends upon Jesus. This is not Jesus's first contact with the Spirit, for the Gospel writers tell us that Jesus was conceived of the Holy Spirit. But still, the descent of the Spirit on Jesus is a pivotal moment for Jesus. Matthew's readers, with the Old Testament firmly in their minds, would be aware of occasions in their history when the Spirit came powerfully upon the kings of Israel at the time of their anointing.

For example, when Samuel was preparing to anoint Saul as king, Samuel said to him: "Then the Spirit of the LORD will come mightily upon you, you shall prophesy with them and be turned into another man."[2] Similarly, when David was anointed king, we read: "Then Samuel took the horn of oil, and anointed him in the midst of his brothers, and the Spirit of the LORD came mightily upon David from that day forward."[3]

For Matthew's readers, it was expected that Israel's future royal son of David would also have the Spirit of the LORD resting mightily upon him. We see this clearly in the prophet Isaiah, who, speaking of the LORD's servant who is to come, says: "I have put my Spirit upon him."[4] What Matthew is showing his readers is that the Spirit's descent upon Jesus here in his baptism is his anointing as Israel's promised Messiah. The word "Messiah" means "Anointed One."

But our tour has only begun. Matthew also explains that the Spirit descends upon Jesus like a dove. Here Matthew is taking us back to Genesis, to the creation story and the story of Noah and the Flood. At creation, the Spirit of God hovers over the waters of creation like a bird. And after the great flood, Noah released a dove to see if the flood waters had receded enough for the dove to find dry ground. Eventually, the dove returned to Noah carrying an olive branch in its mouth, signaling the end of the flood and the beginning of the new world.[5] The ancient church father Tertullian commented on this story: "After the flood, by which the iniquity of the old world was cleansed away, e.g., after the baptism of the world, the dove proclaimed to the earth the tempering of the wrath of heaven."[6]

Tertullian helps us to see something happening here more significant than meets the eye. For Tertullian and other church fathers, the image of the dove not only calls to mind Noah and the flood, it reveals Jesus as a *new* Noah who comes to build a *new* Ark (the church) and to bring people safely

---

2. 1 Sam 10:6 RSV.

3. 1 Sam 16:13 RSV.

4. Isa 42:1 RSV.

5. See Gen 8:8–12.

6. Oden and Hall, *Ancient Christian Commentary on Scripture*, 11.

into the Ark through the cleansing of their sins and their reconciliation to the Father. What is happening as Jesus steps down into the Jordan River is not merely that Jesus is being baptized, but that in his baptism Jesus is making *new* the old creation! Jesus is the *new* Noah.

But Matthew's tour of the Old Testament is still not complete. The people of that day were looking for the Messiah to usher in the new age, the dramatic arrival of God's kingdom with power. Many of the Old Testament prophets had announced that certain signs would accompany this arrival. Isaiah and Ezekiel both speak of it in terms of the splitting of the heavens.[7]

By employing these Old Testament images Matthew and the other Gospel writers are saying that Jesus's baptism is ushering in the new age, that special time anticipated in the Old Testament. Jesus's baptism is literally an earth-shattering event, but your heart has to be tuned to the vibrations and the shaking.

If we ask, then, why Jesus came for baptism, the answer to that question is that Jesus's baptism was an *epiphany*, a showing forth of his identity as the Messiah, the One anointed by God to usher in the new age of God's kingdom. He is the new Noah, making the old creation new. But there is yet another reason why Jesus came to John at the Jordan River.

In Deut 18, Moses tells the children of Israel: "The LORD your God will raise up for you a prophet like me from among you, from your brethren. Him you shall heed."[8] Throughout the Gospels, Jesus is frequently portrayed as the fulfillment of Moses's words. This is especially the case for Matthew, who structures his entire Gospel in such a way as to portray Jesus as a new Moses.

We see this clearly in Jesus's *Sermon on the Mount* (Matt 5–7), which describes Jesus ascending a mountain (just as Moses did) to teach the people (even as Moses received the stone tablets from God). Jesus's sermon is based on a series of contrasts between the law given to Moses and Jesus's fulfillment of that law as the new Moses. For example, Jesus says:

> You have heard that it was said, "you shall love your neighbor and hate your enemy." But I say to you, love your enemies and pray for those who persecute you, so that you may be sons of your Father who is in heaven.[9]

Now if Jesus is a new Moses, the question becomes: What did Moses do? Moses led the children of Israel from slavery in Egypt to the promised land. On the way, their deliverance from Pharoah and his army occurred as

7. See Isa 64:1–4; 11:2; 42:1; 61:1–4. See also Ezek 1.

8. Deut 18:15 RSV.

9. Matt 5:43–45 RSV.

they passed through the waters of the Red Sea. Scholars almost unanimously agree that the waters of the Red Sea were a *type* or prefiguring of baptism.

As the new Moses, Jesus came to lead God's people on a new exodus. The ultimate destination of this exodus, however, is not a piece of geographical land in Palestine. The ultimate destination of this exodus is the promised land of heaven. The deliverance that Jesus brings as the leader of this new exodus is not deliverance from Pharoah and his armies, but deliverance from the slavery of sin. And the water through which the new Moses leads the people—water that is instrumental in their deliverance—is not the water of the Red Sea but the water of baptism.

This is what Jesus is doing when he steps down into the Jordan River. He is humbling himself to pass through Jordan's waters in order to lead a new exodus and to open up the promised land of heaven. Jesus does not step down into the water of the Jordan to be sanctified. He steps down into the water *to sanctify*. Saint Maximus of Turin explains:

> Christ is baptized, not to be made holy by the water, but to make the water holy, and by his cleansing to purify the waters which he touched. For the consecration of Christ involves a more significant consecration of the water. For when the Savior is washed all water for our baptism is made clean, purified at its source for the dispensing of baptismal grace to the people of future ages.[10]

Jesus did not merely come to be human like us. That was demonstrated in the incarnation, which we celebrate at Christmas. Jesus became flesh and blood so that he could step into the place of sinners and accomplish what John's baptism only symbolized. He submits to baptism as his first public act of *identifying* with our sin, and his baptism is his first step in *defeating* our sin.

Defeating our sin would require him to be submerged into death, into the grave. But his victory over death would be accomplished by his resurrection, symbolized here by Matthew in the opening of heaven and the descent of the Holy Spirit. In the old order, death was the end. But in the new order led by Jesus, death in the water of baptism means new life, a rebirth, a truly new start. Jesus makes this ordinary act of stepping down into the water extraordinary by sanctifying the water, enabling it to become a channel of the Holy Spirit bringing inner cleansing, rebirth, and transformation to those who will be bathed in it. He makes it possible for all of us to be born again into the relationship God originally intended for us, to restore spiritual life

---

10. Maximus of Turin, "Sermon 100," *De sancta Epiphania* 1.3 (in *Liturgy of the Hours*, 612–13).

in us that has been lost because of sin. His baptism is not only with water, but with "fire and the Holy Spirit."

And here is perhaps the most astounding part of this epiphany. Under the first exodus led by Moses, the right to be called a child of God belonged only to the children of Israel. But under the new exodus led by the new Moses, Jesus makes it possible for all people to hear in baptism the words that are pronounced over him at his baptism, namely, that they are beloved sons and daughters of God.

In concluding Matthew's tour of the Old Testament with respect to Jesus's baptism, there is one more stop. The voice from heaven at Jesus's baptism proclaims him as the "beloved son." This term "beloved son" is used of only one other person in the Old Testament. In Gen 22, God tells Abraham, "Take your son, your only son Isaac, whom you love, and go to the land of Moriah, and offer him there as a burnt offering upon one of the mountains of which I shall tell you."[11] In this episode, Isaac was a *type* or foreshadowing of Christ, the "beloved son" who would one day be offered up as a sacrifice for sin outside of Jerusalem, ironically, on Mount Moriah.

What, then, is the significance of Jesus's baptism? Why does he need to be baptized? And why does Matthew describe it in terms laden with Old Testament images and expectations?

Matthew takes us on this tour of the Old Testament to show us that Jesus's baptism was not some incidental event at the start of his public ministry. He does it to show his readers, and us, that Jesus is the fulfillment of all of the Old Testament hopes for the coming Messiah. Jesus's baptism was necessary, then, to "fulfill all righteousness." It happened as a vital part of God's plan for the salvation of the world. When Jesus is baptized and hears the heavenly voice, he finds himself called to particular obedience toward a sacrificial death, like Isaac centuries before him.

But in fulfilling the Father's call on his life, Jesus does more. By going down into the water of the Jordan, Jesus shows his complete solidarity with sinners. By being immersed in the same waters that the repentant crowds have been in, Jesus piles all of our guilt upon his shoulders and bears it down into the water. His baptism anticipates his cross.

Jesus's baptism was not an ancillary act or a merely symbolic gesture. It was an act of obedience in order to do the will of God. He is the new Noah who comes to make all things new. He is the new Moses who has come to lead the people of God on a new exodus to the heavenly promised land through the creation of a New Covenant. And the New Covenant people of God become such not through natural birth, but by spiritual rebirth

11. Gen 22:2 RSV.

through water and the Spirit.[12] Jesus's baptism anticipates and makes possible our being made sons and daughters of God through the sacramental water of baptism.

12. See John 3:1–24; Col 2:11–15; 1 Pet 3:18–22.

Lent-Easter-Pentecost
The Cycle of Life

As is the case with Advent-Christmas-Epiphany and the Cycle of Light, the celebration of Lent-Easter-Pentecost is best seen as a unity, known as the Cycle of Life. In recent years scholars have reminded us that not only is the Lent-Easter-Pentecost cycle a unity, it is foremost the celebration of the Paschal mystery, of the death and resurrection of Jesus. There is an unfortunate tendency to isolate the different dimensions of the Paschal mystery and to assign each dimension to a different time on the cycle's continuum. When this happens, Lent becomes a time to focus on Christ's suffering and death, Easter becomes a time to focus on the resurrection of Jesus, and so forth. Scholars remind us, however, that when the various dimensions of the Easter mystery are torn asunder, the essential unity of the cycle is lost:

> The liturgical year is not some sort of family album which the Christian community takes out each year to admire old photographs. We do not celebrate Lent in the pretense that the resurrection has not yet happened. Likewise we do not celebrate the resurrection forgetful of the suffering and death of Christ in the past and in the present. The suffering, death and resurrection of Christ is an ever-present reality. The cross is neither a fashion accent which one wears around the neck or on a lapel, nor is it a product that the [Church] is trying to sell with all the aggressive gimmickry of Madison Avenue.[1]

At present, the Lent-Easter-Pentecost cycle consists of the forty days of Lent, Holy Week, particularly the *Triduum*, and the fifty days of Easter.

---

1. Whalen, *Seasons and Feasts*, 76–77.

LENT

The Christian year—like all of life—is comprised of rhythms. It is filled with ebb and flow, fasts and feasts, preparation and fulfillment. Key events in life are most fully and richly experienced when thoughtful and adequate preparation has been made for those events. Consider weddings, anniversaries, retirements, or the birth of children, to name just a few examples. This is equally true in the spiritual life. The Christian year is not an artificial construct, but a living journey of transformation.

Just as the season of Advent involves preparation for the birth and return of Jesus, the season of Lent involves a forty-day period of preparation to celebrate the central and great mystery of Christian faith—the resurrection of Jesus. In the early centuries of the church, the season of Lent was a period of instruction and training for new converts (catechumens), culminating in their baptisms at Easter. Because baptism was the means by which persons were initiated into the church, it required a serious commitment borne from a radical change in lifestyle and could not be undertaken without preparation. It was important, especially in the early days of the church, to distinguish between the morals of the church and the morals of Greco-Roman culture and society. Baptism also required sponsorship, i.e., the endorsement of someone already within the church to vouch for the new convert's sincerity and readiness to accept the moral demands of a baptized Christian.[2]

Baptism thus lies at the heart of the Lent-Easter-Pentecost cycle. Historically, the initiation of catechumens was public and communal. The entire faith community participated with the catechumens in their spiritual journey.

Today, Lent serves as a yearly reentry into the faith that provides opportunities for followers of Jesus to reflect on their own baptisms. It is a period for exploring more deeply what it means to live our baptismal covenant in daily life. We all approach the waters of baptism during the Lent-Easter-Pentecost cycle for the first time either as a catechumen or in memory of our own entrance into the Christian faith. The beginning of the Lenten journey thrusts us into what one writer describes as the "rhythm of disequilibrium," into the process of dying which is essential to the formation of new life.[3] The season is designed to empty us so that new life and resurrection might come to birth in us. Lent is about changing our hearts, our perspective, our focus.

2. Papandrea, *Reading the Church Fathers*, 30. Because baptism required extensive preparation, local communities quickly developed methods for training catechumens and preparing them for baptism.

3. Wright, *Rising*, 16.

One means of changing our hearts during the Lenten season is learning to conquer our slavery to worldly things, even when those things are good. We can forget that even good things have a way of mastering us when we indulge them without discipline. God means for us to enjoy the good things of life, but those things are never to become a substitute for God. Lent is a time for demonstrating to God that we can be trusted, even with God's good gifts. We voluntarily fast some of those things and master them for a few weeks so that they do not master us for life. The Lenten journey thus becomes a time of spiritual training for eternal life. We imitate Christ and unite ourselves to him because he gave his life for our salvation.

Part of that training involves the painful recognition that most of us resist what is good for us. We resist going to the dentist for a checkup, we resist eating right and exercising, we procrastinate over a laundry list of things that are necessary. During Lent we embrace practices and disciplines that are good for both our bodies and our souls. We offer those practices to God out of gratitude for his grace and mercy.

An additional theme of Lent is forgiveness. The Scripture lessons and themes of the season patiently remind us of our need for God's forgiveness, our need to be forgiven by others, our need to forgive ourselves, and our need to forgive others, both those who seek our forgiveness and those who do not. Forgiveness in all of its facets is a characteristic feature of the season. We discover in various ways during Lent how difficult it is for us to love others as we have been loved.

We further discover that forgiving others (and ourselves) is often a long and difficult journey, especially when we have been gravely wounded. Forgiveness is not merely about politeness or the acceptance of the quirks and foibles of others. It is a courageous act of defiance that refuses to remain trapped in a cycle of hatred and recrimination.[4] The word "forgive" has at its root the meaning of loosing others from what binds them. When we are empowered by God's grace to forgive, to release someone who has hurt us from being bound and identified with pain, we release ourselves as well. Forgiving ourselves, others, and our enemies lies at the heart of the Lenten journey.

In most languages, the same word applies to the Jewish Passover as it does to the Christian feast of Easter. The word is *Pascha*. When the church speaks of preparing to celebrate the Paschal Mystery, it may be confusing to those who are used to the English name that derives from the German spring festival that we know as Easter.

---

4. Wright, *Rising*, 49.

But for Christians, the Paschal Mystery *should* invoke the ancient Passover when all firstborn children of Israel were spared, when the chosen people were liberated from slavery, and when they embarked upon their journey to the promised land. Their deliverance began, in each household, with the sacrifice of a lamb and the smearing of the lamb's blood on the doorposts of the home. In subsequent generations, the Jewish people would recall those saving events through the perpetual observance of the Passover celebration.

Christianity teaches that in the fullness of time, Jesus came as the promised Messiah who was the true Passover Lamb of God.[5] The apostle Paul speaks of Jesus as the Paschal Lamb who has been sacrificed and admonishes the Corinthians (and by extension, us) to "keep the feast," i.e., to celebrate the New Covenant fulfillment of the Passover which is the Eucharist.[6]

The Old Covenant Passover began with Israel's redemption of the firstborn and liberation from slavery, but it culminated much later with the people's entrance into the promised land. Between those two events, the people wandered in the desert for forty years. Those years were a time of *preparation*. The people experienced preparation for entering the promised land by being purged of the residual effects of decades of exposure to Egyptian idolatry.

This pattern of preparation characterized Jesus's ministry as well. Before he launched his public ministry and inaugurated God's kingdom, he fasted and prayed for forty days in the wilderness. In Jesus's case, his preparation was not because he needed to be purified, for he was the spotless Lamb of God. Jesus's preparation paralleled that of Moses, who fasted for forty days on the mountain in preparation for receiving the law of God at Sinai. As the new Moses who came to lead the people on a new Exodus, Jesus also prepared for his divine mission through a forty-day period of preparation.

The earliest historical reference we have to the church's forty-day preparation for Easter comes from the Council of Nicaea, held in AD 325. In the fifth century, Saint John Cassian described Lent as a tithe of the year, because the forty-day period is roughly one tenth of the days of the entire year. He encouraged Christians to give the forty days of Lent to the Lord as a tithe, as a special offering of themselves. In Scripture, the tithe represents the giving of both the *first* of peoples' lives as well as the *best* of their lives to God.

---

5. John 1:29 RSV. In Revelation, John refers to Jesus as the Lamb of God twenty-six times.

6. 1 Cor 5:7; 11:23–26 RSV. See also Hahn, *Fourth Cup.*

During Lent, we are called to examine our lives closely in preparation for the Easter celebration. We are invited to walk with Jesus toward Jerusalem, knowing that the journey ends with him carrying a cross. During that journey, we hear him call us to pick up our own cross and carry it. It is difficult for us to discern the depth of Jesus's call, given that the cross was an instrument of brutal torture. But as we walk with Jesus, we discover the profound truth that the love he demonstrates for all humankind as he hangs on the cross demands our life, our soul, our all, in response. During Lent, we ask the Holy Spirit to search our hearts in order that we may truly give Christ the *best* of our lives. We ask for the grace to prepare to experience the resurrection through a willingness to share in his suffering and death. There is no Easter without Lent, Holy Week, and Good Friday, either in history or in our own lives.

HOLY WEEK

The celebration of Easter in the early church was initially linked to Passover which was celebrated on the Sabbath and where the primary focus was on Jesus's sacrificial death as the Lamb of God. But as Christians began to celebrate Easter on Sunday or the Lord's Day, the emphasis gradually moved from Jesus's death to his resurrection and the separation of Easter from Passover. This shift had become so widespread by the end of the fourth century that the resurrection of Jesus became the sole focus of Easter. As a result, the *Triduum* emerged (followed by the other days of Holy Week) to commemorate the various events connected with the last days of Jesus's life.[7]

Holy Week begins with Palm Sunday, complete with processions of palms in honor of Jesus's entry into Jerusalem. The climax of the week is the *Triduum* (Latin for "three days"). The *Triduum* consists of Maundy Thursday, Good Friday, and Holy Saturday. The beginnings of the *Triduum* observance are found in the late fourth century in Jerusalem sometime around AD 380, though there appear to be numerous variations in how it was observed depending upon location.[8] Maundy Thursday recalls Jesus's institution of the Eucharist as he celebrated the Passover with his disciples in the upper room. It also calls to mind his washing of the disciples' feet and his admonition to them: "A new commandment I give unto you, that you love one another as I have loved you" ("Maundy" is from the Latin for "command"). The service of Tenebrae (Latin for "darkness") is also sometimes observed. Originally, Tenebrae was a combination of the first two nocturnal

7. Bradshaw and Johnson, *Origins of Feasts*, 68.
8. Bradshaw and Johnson, *Origins of Feasts*, 64–67.

liturgies of the Divine Office, or Liturgy of the Hours.[9] The service occurs in the late evening or early morning hours and is characterized by the gradual extinguishing of candles which symbolizes the somber and mournful quality of Jesus's impending arrest and execution.

Good Friday entails the observance of Jesus's crucifixion, and in many traditions the principal emphasis of the liturgy is the solemn collects, i.e., prayers of intercession for the world. The passion narrative from the Gospel of John is customarily read in this service, as is the Suffering Servant passage from the fifty-third chapter of Isaiah. In some traditions, the liturgy of the Stations of the Cross is held, often at noon, and worshippers are allowed the opportunity to venerate the cross. Many Good Friday services are held at 3:00 p.m., the precise hour of Jesus's death.

Holy Saturday is a day marked by somber, quiet reflection. It is the day Jesus lays in the tomb, the day he suffers the absence of his Father, which is perhaps his greatest suffering. It is Jesus's pathway into the abyss of human misery.

It is also the day when Jesus descended to the realm of the dead, or as the Apostles' Creed says, "descended into hell."[10] Holy Saturday is a time of rest and silence, as all of creation awaits a salvation it does not yet understand. A beautiful and ancient text from the early church pictures Jesus roaming the abode of the dead on this day, liberating Adam and Eve and all of the other souls who had been waiting for redemption since the foundation of the world:

> What is happening? Today there is a great silence over the earth, a great silence, and stillness, a great silence because the King sleeps; the earth was in terror and was still, because God slept in the flesh and raised up those who were sleeping from the ages. God has died in the flesh, and the underworld has trembled. Truly he goes to seek out our first parent like a lost sheep; he wishes to visit those who sit in darkness and in the shadow of

---

9. The Divine Office, or Liturgy of the Hours, is the church's historic way of praying throughout the various times of the day. The offices include: Matins, Lauds, Prime, Terce, Sext, None, Vespers, and Compline. In this way, the whole day is sanctified through prayer. For every part of the day there is a special prayer-form—an hour, as it is called—that corresponds to the particular need of that time of the day. The theme of a canonical hour is that special thought or motivation to prayer that arises from the needs of that time of day. It is that hour's prayer intention.

10. See 1 Pet 3:18–22. The early church believed that between Jesus's death and resurrection, he descended to hades, or the realm of the dead, in order to preach to souls who were there and to make the gospel available to those who preceded his incarnation. In the sixteenth century, this became known as the "harrowing" of hell.

death. He goes to free the prisoner Adam and his fellow-prisoner Eve from their pains, he who is God, and Adam's son.[11]

Martin Luther—perhaps borrowing from this ancient text—observed that "our Lord Jesus Christ did descend into hell, battered hell open, overcame the devil, and delivered those who were held captive by the devil."[12]

One writer has also observed a connection between Advent and Holy Saturday, in that in both cases the King of the Cosmos is hidden in darkness. In the incarnation, Christ descends from heaven to earth. In his Passion, Christ descends to Hades. One is the darkness of the womb, the other is the darkness of the tomb. Each sleep leads to new life. Out of the womb of Mary came God made flesh. Out of the tomb came the life and the resurrection.[13]

Holy Saturday is a time-beyond-time when Jesus entered that place where not one ray of love is found, where total abandonment reigns without any word of comfort—namely, hell. We have all, at some point, felt the frightening sensation of abandonment. We have known the terror that strikes so deeply within us that we could only be reassured by the presence of a person who loved us. This is what happened on Holy Saturday. The voice of God resounded in the realm of death. The unimaginable occurred. Love penetrated to the depths of hell.

As we contemplate this reality we become aware that in the midst of the most extreme loneliness and isolation, we may hear a voice that calls to us and a hand that takes hold of ours and leads us out of despair. We discover that in our hour of supreme abandonment we are never alone. The Word made flesh descended into our miseries and afflictions—no matter what they are—and he awaits us in these painful places. Our hidden affections, failures, frustrations, and disappointments are not places that God avoids or pretends does not exist. If we can seek him there, he will raise us up to new life. This is the mystery of Holy Saturday.

Holy Saturday culminates with the Great Vigil of Easter, which begins with worshippers gathered outside in the darkness, or in some cases a dark narthex of the church which resembles the tomb. A new fire is kindled, and from it the Paschal candle is lit. The Paschal fire symbolizes Christ, the Light of the world, who dispels the darkness of sin and death as he passes over from death to life. Gathered around the fire of the Vigil, we call to mind how we began the Lenten journey marked with the ashes of sin, failure, and defeat. But now we are filled with fire, the mighty power of the risen Christ.

11. "Lord's Descent into Hell," paras. 1–2.

12. Luther, "Easter Eve," 476–89. See also Levertov's captivating poem, "Ikon: The Harrowing of Hell," in Levertov, *Stream and the Sapphire*, 77–78.

13. Beale, "Advent and Holy Saturday."

We proclaim the resurrection of Christ as the focal point that transforms all of human history.

The people follow the Paschal candle in procession into the church, where the Minister or Celebrant chants, "the Light of Christ," and the people respond: "Thanks be to God." Then begins the lengthy rehearsal of salvation history from sacred Scripture in the Service of the Word, beginning with the chanting of the Exultet by a cantor. The Exultet proclaims God's powerful deliverance of his people from sin and death through the miraculous raising of Christ. The Service of the Word ends with the acclamation, "The Lord is risen!" Darkened sanctuaries are then flooded with light and the pealing of bells. Then comes the Service of the Table and the celebration of the Eucharist. Baptisms are also a prominent feature of the Vigil, as new Christians are received into the church on this night. Coincidentally, many in the early church believed that the Lord would return during the Easter Vigil.

The services of the *Triduum* are symbolically rich and flow together in a seamless way. While it may appear that the liturgies are separate and distinct, they are actually one continuous celebration that commemorates the passion, death, and resurrection of Jesus. The Easter Vigil on Holy Saturday is the high point of the *Triduum*, but not in a way which isolates it from the liturgies on Maundy Thursday and Good Friday. The *Triduum* is the culmination of the entire liturgical year. It looks to the whole of Christ's life, passion, death, and resurrection. During this time the church keeps watch, awaiting the resurrection of Christ and celebrating it in the sacraments. To reduce the *Triduum* or any one of its services simply to one dimension of this whole mystery is to impoverish it in a significant way.[14]

The events of Holy Week are bathed in irony. In a culture that idolizes power and strength, millions of Christians gather to honor the humiliation, torture, and crucifixion of Jesus. The weakness of the cross, the simplicity of the Eucharist, the tenderness of the foot washing, the love that seeks to embrace a traitor, a thief, and a coward, is so beyond the grasp of power politics and social hubris that it takes our breath away. If God could become that poor, humble, and vulnerable to love us, how can we ever again seek to live life out of our own self-importance?

God desires to pour out his love upon us as we experience the mysterious irony of Holy Week. Weakness becomes strength, love conquers fear, hope transforms despair, and death gives way to eternal life—all because a naked criminal was thrown down on a cross and embraced it for the joy set before him. One writer observes:

14. See Whalen, *Seasons and Feasts*, 91

The shocking, strange, and powerful events of Holy Week should lead us to tears and laughter, gratitude and praise, humble awareness of our weakness and joyful acclamation of God's victory. The Triduum is a time for God to break open our hearts, so that the gracious torrent of Divine Mercy that flows from the side of the crucified Christ will wash us clean, forgive our sins and fashion us ever more deeply in the new creation of the Lord's saving death and resurrection.[15]

EASTER-PENTECOST

The Easter and Pentecost components of the Cycle of Life consist of the fifty days from Easter Sunday to Pentecost Sunday. This fifty-day period is meant to be celebrated as one great feast, sometimes called the "Great Sunday." In the early church, Pentecost was a fifty-day period subsequent to Easter that celebrated the whole mystery of Christ's death and resurrection, culminating with the feast of Pentecost on the fiftieth day. During this period both kneeling and fasting were prohibited, as they were seen as signs of penitence. Pentecost was initially a Jewish feast that commemorated the giving of the law to Moses on Sinai. As early Christian worship developed, it became primarily the celebration of the outpouring of the Spirit on the church.

The Ascension of Jesus is observed forty days after Easter, but in many traditions it is celebrated on a Sunday. The observance of the Ascension as a separate feast appears to have originated near Antioch in AD 380, and was influenced by the text from Acts 1 which describes the event. Ironically, the emergence of the Ascension as a separate feast was a catalyst for the eventual fragmentation of the entire Lent-Easter-Pentecost cycle. But the observance of the Ascension and Pentecost within the context of Easter is intentional and should not be overlooked, for both are part of the Paschal mystery.

From a pastoral perspective, celebrating the fifty days of Easter is sometimes difficult because it is hard to sustain a celebration for such a long period. This is especially true when the Easter celebration is interrupted by a host of secular as well as religious observances, such as weddings, graduations and other events. With pastoral sensitivity and congregational cooperation, however, the "Great Sunday" can remain a joyous and festive time of celebration.

---

15. Hying, "Fully Entering Into the Triduum," para. 9.

Lent

Chapter Twelve

Rending Our Hearts

God cannot forgive our sins by taking away our part in them.

—James V. Schall

*But hope could rise from ashes even now, beginning
with this sign upon your brow.*

—Malcolm Guite

SUGGESTED READINGS

Joel 2:1–17; Pss 51; 103:8–14; 2 Cor 5:20—6:10; Matt 6:1–21

A FEW YEARS AGO I was asked by a parishioner which day of the year finds the most people in church. My immediate reaction to the question was to choose Easter, with Christmas following a close second. I was surprised to discover that I was wrong on both counts. It turns out that the day of the year on which the most people are in church is Ash Wednesday.

The reasons for this may be difficult to discern. But after many years of ministering to people, I have my own theory. In a culture that views religion as medieval superstition which rational people have outgrown, there remains a faint awareness within us that something is fundamentally wrong with the world and with ourselves. A fog of disequilibrium envelops us. In spite of scientific and technological advances, we find ourselves immersed in a severely disoriented world. The human family is a dysfunctional family, and we lack the resources to cure our dysfunction. The explosion of social media and increasing access to information creates a chasm that exists between accumulating facts and acquiring wisdom.[1] But this infectious human malaise pre-dates the advent of social media. The poet Edna St. Vincent Millay lamented this truth as early as 1939 as World War II was in its infancy. She was frustrated that American leaders were not more outspoken about the atrocities of Naziism, and she was concerned about the implications of the burgeoning computer tech industry for society.

Millay acknowledged the vast creativity and ingenuity of humanity, especially in the field of scientific research. Yet she also recognized the painful truth that there remains within humanity a fundamental *dis*-ease, a disconnect so profound that science in all its regnant glory cannot cure it.[2] Millay anticipated author Wendy Wright's poignant admission which came several decades later:

> We live in a world of both great beauty and great sorrow. We stumble along burdened by our personal limitations—our brokenness, our narrow perspectives, our fears and addictions, hatreds and suspicions. We stumble along together in a magnificent universe blighted by war, hunger, oppression, and injustice. For all our good intent and efforts, the stark reality of it is that we are not enough. And the human spirit cries out, as does the anguished voice of creation itself, Have Mercy![3]

It would seem that us moderns have the necessary acumen to cure our dysfunction, but no underlying framework by which to correlate the data into a coherent and workable solution. We have the superstructure, but no foundation upon which to build it. We have a monumental accumulation of facts, but we lack wisdom. We continue to find new ways to exploit and kill each other. This illness within human nature prompted Harry Emerson Fosdick to pray:

---

1. For a thorough analysis of the harmful impact of social media on our society, see Haidt, "Why the Past 10 Years."

2. See "Upon This Age That Never Speaks Its Mind" in Millay, *Collected Sonnets*, 140.

3. Wright, *Rising*, 22.

> Cure the people's warring madness, bend our pride to thy control. Shame our wanton, selfish gladness, rich in things but poor in soul.[4]

Fosdick reveals a clue to resolving our dilemma by suggesting that our *dis-ease* is the result of pride. Pride manifests itself in manifold ways and is a symptom that we are estranged from our Creator. Our alienation from God leads to our alienation from one another and a desire to wield power over others. Our arrogance fosters a lack of humility.[5] Our understanding of who we are in relation to God and to one another becomes distorted.

One plausible reason that more people are in church on Ash Wednesday than on any other day is because of this intuitive realization that we are broken and we cannot fix ourselves. This is precisely what Ash Wednesday reveals to us. People stand before a Priest or Minister and have ashes smudged on their foreheads in the shape of a cross. *Memento mori.* You are dust, and to dust you shall return. In that ritual moment, pride is cut off at the knees. In that moment, we come face to face with *who* and *what* we are—finite creatures who are mortal. In a culture intent on denying death, Ash Wednesday begins the Lenten season by pulling back the curtain on our denial and placing us before our Creator with nothing to offer God but our brokenness.

However, the imposition of ashes is not to be construed in a punitive or morbid way, but in a serious and reflective way. When we receive the ashes on our foreheads in the shape of a cross, we are invited to acknowledge the greater reality beneath our attempt to be the architects of our own lives and destinies. That reality involves the truth that we must turn and let go of our old prideful ways of living that lead to pain and heartache. We must start over. We must return to God. We must fast. We must empty ourselves in order to be filled with something new.

The specific shape of Ash Wednesday—especially the imposition of ashes—becomes clear when we examine the function of ashes in the Old Testament and what the ashes symbolized to people in the first century to whom Jesus preached.

For example, in Gen 3, God speaks to Adam about the consequences of his sin, and in part says to him: "In the sweat of your face you shall eat

4. Harry Emerson Fosdick, "God of Grace and God of Glory," public domain.

5. The word "humility" comes from the root *hummis*, i.e., "earth." In Christian terms, humility involves true and adequate self-knowledge based on divine revelation. It involves the recognition that we are at one and the same time both blessed and broken creatures. We are endowed with enormous potential, yet we are profoundly limited. Humility, then, involves the clear understanding that we are simultaneously blessed and broken. See also Wright, *Rising*, 31.

bread until you return to the ground, for out of it you were taken; you are dust, and to dust you shall return."[6] In this instance, ashes point to the reality of our mortality. Each of us must understand without equivocation that our life will not go on forever. We are mortal. We will return to the dust from which we came.

In another Old Testament passage Job says: "I despise myself, and I repent in dust and ashes."[7] In the context of this passage, ashes symbolize not just mortality, but also repentance from sin.

In another passage from the book of Daniel, we find Daniel saying: "I turned my face to the Lord God, seeking him by prayer and supplications with fasting and sackcloth and ashes."[8] In this context, Daniel is penitent and prayerful on behalf of all the people, not just himself. This explains why in times of national crisis or mourning, people often covered themselves with sackcloth and ashes.

Finally, in another passage from the book of Esther, the story is told of how the children of Israel are almost exterminated *en masse* by a pagan king. Queen Esther responds to the plot to destroy her people by taking drastic measures:

> Esther, seized with deathly anxiety, fled to the Lord. She took off her splendid apparel and put on the garments of distress and mourning, and instead of costly perfumes she covered her head with ashes and dung, and she utterly humbled her body, and . . . prayed to the Lord her God.[9]

In this instance, as with Daniel, Esther covers herself with ashes and prays to God on behalf of all her people who were under threat of extinction.

These Old Testament passages give us a representative idea of what first century Jews were thinking and doing when ashes were put on one's head. Ashes involved the recognition of one's mortality (like Adam), the act of repentance (like Job), and the act of interceding for others (as in the case of Daniel and Esther).[10]

6. Gen 3:19 RSV.

7. Job 42:6 RSV.

8. Dan 9:3 RSV.

9. Esth 14:1–3 RSV. This portion of the book of Esther is taken from the Septuagint, the translation of the Old Testament into Greek which was undertaken approximately 150 BC; the Septuagint is the translation of the Old Testament most often quoted by the New Testament writers.

10. In the New Testament, we remember the words of Jesus when he upbraids the cities of Chorazin and Bethsaida: "Woe to you, Chorazin and Bethsaida, for if the mighty works done in you had been done in Tyre and Sidon, they would have repented long ago in sackcloth and ashes." See Matt 11:21 RSV.

The biblical roots for the imposition of ashes on Ash Wednesday are clear, and the New Testament shows that Jesus recognized the observance. In addition, the specific Scripture texts that are used in Ash Wednesday liturgies also illumine the practice. One text in particular comes from the prophet Joel, and is worth quoting at length:

> Even now, says the LORD, return to me with all your heart, with fasting, with weeping, and with mourning; and rend your hearts and not your garments. Return to the LORD your God, for he is gracious and merciful, slow to anger, and abounding in steadfast love. . . . Blow the trumpet in Zion; sanctify a fast; call a solemn assembly; gather the people. Sanctify the congregation; assemble the elders, gather the children, even nursing infants. Let the bridegroom leave his room, and the bride her chamber. Between the vestibule and the altar let the priests, the ministers of the LORD, weep and say, "Spare thy people, O LORD, and make not thy heritage a reproach, a byword among the nations. Why should they say among the peoples, 'Where is there God?'" Then the LORD became jealous for his land, and had pity on his people.[11]

This text is significant because Joel is describing an official, *public* day of fasting and prayer. All people of the covenant are called together to engage in a corporate act of repentance, so that God might have mercy on a sinful people. One of the reasons for this was so that people who had wandered from God might come back to covenant obedience. This explains why, through the centuries, the church has always proclaimed on Ash Wednesday: *Come back to God. Rend your hearts. Repent and return to Christ and the Church.* Wendy Wright observes:

> The trumpet blast of Joel's prophecy signals the beginning of the season of change. Gather the people—all of them. We need to be alerted to the reality of the situation in which we find ourselves. We would like to live in ultimate control. We would prefer to be able to predict our futures and sketch our own life designs. But, in truth, we are merely collaborators in a larger design which his neither entirely under our control nor of our individual making.[12]

There is an additional precedent for the church's Ash Wednesday practice in the Old Testament. It happened once a year on perhaps the most important day of the year. The day was *Yom Kippur*, the Day of Atonement.

11. Joel 2:12–18 RSV.
12. Wright, *Rising*, 20.

We read about it in Lev 16. On this day, every Jew was called upon to pray, and to fast, and to abstain from pretty much everything! The purpose of *Yom Kippur* was to effect individual and collective purification through the practice of forgiving the sins of others as well as by expressing sincere repentance for one's own sins before God.[13]

There is a sense, then, in which Ash Wednesday becomes the church's version of *Yom Kippur*. The reading from Joel serves to reinforce the public nature of the day. The season of Lent begins with a public, corporate call to prayer, fasting, and repentance.[14] It begins with the corporate recognition that scientific and technological advances are impotent to cure us of our moral sickness. Ash Wednesday calls on the church to undertake a communal examination of conscience, acknowledging our failure both personally and corporately to live faithfully to God and to one another. We confess our pride and self-reliance that create barriers between us and those whom God calls us to love and to serve.

While Ash Wednesday inaugurates the Lenten journey in this corporate and public way, the good beginning that this day helps us to make of the Lenten season also trickles down into our personal lives, reminding us of a twofold emphasis during Lent: the taking on of practices and disciplines that enhance the flow of God's grace in our lives, and the giving up of things that impede the flow of God's grace in our lives. This is necessary because we have arrived at that stage of the Christian Year where we are called to walk with Jesus toward Jerusalem where he will embrace the cross. As we do, we will hear his call and invitation for us to pick up and carry our own cross, to die to ourselves and to surrender to God all that is not God's best for us.

13. *Yom Kippur* was the only day of the year on which the high priest could enter the Holy of Holies, the inner sanctum, of the temple. There, he would perform a series of rituals and sprinkle blood of sacrificed animals on the Ark of the Covenant, which contained the Ten Commandments. Through this ceremony he made atonement and asked for forgiveness on behalf of all of the people of Israel.

14. These three practices are historically linked to the church's observance of Lent. They correspond to the temptations Jesus experienced prior to beginning his public ministry, and they correspond to the testing the children of Israel faced en route to the promised land (see Num 8). Where Israel failed the test, however, Jesus is victorious.

Chapter Thirteen

Innocuous Accumulation

The safest road to hell is the gradual one—the gentle slope, soft underfoot,
without sudden turnings, without milestones, without signposts.

—C. S. LEWIS

SUGGESTED READINGS

Isa 58:6–12; Rev 3:1–20; Heb 12:1–2

GROWING UP AS A kid in Nebraska, my grandmother had an annual ritual that she passed on to my mother, which in turn became a yearly event for our family. Perhaps you experienced something similar. I'm referring to the annual rite of spring cleaning. Everything in our house, it seemed, had to be washed and cleaned. All trash and any belongings you weren't using had to be thrown out or given away. Everything that remained had to be put in order. A place for everything, and everything in its place.

I never looked forward to this annual event. But once it was finished, I remember how good it felt to be in our house. I especially remember how it felt to be in my bedroom. My room became a pleasurable place to dwell once again, a place worth inhabiting.

It is no coincidence that the term "Lent" comes from the Old English word *lengten*, which means "spring." It calls to mind the lengthening of the days as spring arrives. From the earliest days of the church, Lent has been a time when Christians are called to get their lives in order, a time to prepare for the resurrection of Christ.

Enjoying a life that is well-ordered sounds wonderful because we muddle through much of the year with the painful awareness of how much our lives are *disordered*. We don't enjoy the intimacy with God we desire, which affects our intimacy with others. We are troubled by our sin, by things in our lives that we would like to change but seem powerless to control. We lack the will, the time, the energy, to live differently. And where we do desire to change, we often lack the necessary discipline to take meaningful action. So we put on a happy face and carry on as best we can. When friends ask how we are doing, we say, "fine." We *are* fine, if by fine you mean frenzied, insecure, troubled, and conflicted.

Why do we so easily find ourselves in this condition? One possible answer might be that in our affluent culture we allow our appetites to control us rather than controlling our appetites. We ask of God, but we cannot receive because our hands are already full of the things of this world. We pray for God to fill us, but there is no open space in our hearts to allow what God wishes to give us. We plead for God to comfort us, but we are already comfortable. What do we really expect God to do for us?

The writers of Scripture knew how easy it can be to allow our appetites to control us instead of us controlling our appetites. So did many of the ancient church fathers. A common theme in their writings involves subduing the bodily appetites as a necessary means to spiritual maturity.[1] Failure to do so results in disordered lives, inverted priorities, impure motives, unhealthy attitudes. We seek to follow Jesus, but we find it easy to stray from the straight and narrow path and to settle for convenient detours. Before we know it, we're traveling in the wrong direction.

In the fall of 1989, my wife and I packed all our belongings into a Ryder truck and headed north from our home in Kentucky bound for graduate school and new adventures in Canada. Our route took us to Buffalo, New York, where we would cross the Peace Bridge into Canada on our way to our new home in Toronto. With my map in front of me (before the days of smartphones and GPS) we arrived in Buffalo and made our way toward the Peace Bridge. But after several minutes, the Peace Bridge was nowhere in sight. I decided to stop at a gas station, since we needed fuel anyway. While inside the station, the man behind the counter asked, "Where you headed?"

---

1. Climacus, *Ladder of Divine Ascent*, 167.

"To Toronto," I responded. "As soon as we get to the Peace Bridge."

The man responded with mild amusement and laughter. "Buddy, you're never going to get to the Peace Bridge the direction you're driving now. You're going the wrong direction."

I was stunned. I was dead sure that I had been traveling in the right direction to arrive at the Peace Bridge. But I was dead wrong. Climbing back into the truck, I had to explain my mistake to Connie, who enjoyed a good laugh. We finally made it to the Peace Bridge and crossed the border into our new life in Canada.

The ancient philosopher Socrates was reportedly once asked how to get to Mount Olympus. He is said to have replied, "Make sure every step you take is in that direction." The season of Lent invites us and challenges us to reorient our lives in the proper direction. This turning, this change of direction, is described by the old- fashioned biblical word *repentance*. The term means "to turn," or "to change direction." When I was young, I often heard preachers speak about repentance in terms of godly sorrow for sin. Indeed it is that. But repentance involves much more. It involves a change in the direction of one's life, a deliberate turning away from all that keeps us from God's best for us.

Some may observe: "I've been a follower of Jesus for a long time. Why do I need to reorient my life? Why do I need to repent?" One answer to that question is that repentance is necessary because of the principle of *innocuous accumulation*.

Have you ever noticed that people who live in the same place for a long period of time tend to accumulate a great deal of stuff? My grandparents lived in the same house in Oklahoma for more than fifty years. The time came when my stepfather felt it was necessary to move them to Nebraska so that they could be cared for in their old age. In preparing for their move, my stepfather thought he would never finish rummaging through their belongings and cleaning that house.

I have lived in the same home now for more than twenty years. And the same phenomenon is alive and well where I live. With little to no effort at all, my closet grows fuller each year. My garage is shrinking to the point where it is hard to fit the cars into it. The storage space above my garage has swelled to the point where I sometimes worry that all of those things are going to collapse onto the cars. With little effort on my part, the passing of time yields itself to a slow, continuous growth of material things.

I call this the principle of *innocuous accumulation*. I've discovered that it operates in the spiritual life as much as it does in the physical life. Spiritual clutter grows and multiplies without requiring any effort on our part. In some ways, our lives are analogous to a stream. With the passing of time, a stream can become clogged through the buildup of sediment, tree limbs, debris, and other materials. The once vibrant flow of water slowly becomes a trickle.

Spiritually, our lives can experience a similar process. Our faith journey becomes marked more by routine than reflection. The activities of life and the cares of the world slowly accumulate until they begin to shift our focus and block the Spirit's activity in our lives. It happens subtly and does not call attention to itself. It is so innocuous that something external to us must force us to stop, to change directions. Something must make us aware that we need to engage in spiritual and material clutter removal. A Nigerian Christian describes his experience like this:

> God in heaven, you have helped me to grow like a tree. Now something has happened. Satan, like a bird, has carried in one twig of his own choosing after another. Before I knew it he had built a dwelling place and was living in it. Tonight, my Father, I am throwing out both the bird and the nest.[2]

The subtle, slow, consistent nature of innocuous accumulation in the spiritual life is precisely what makes it so dangerous. Unhealthy attitudes, motives, and actions can creep into our lives almost unawares. Our spiritual sensitivities can become dulled even though we never intentionally desire such a thing to happen.

An experiment I read about several years ago described placing a small frog into a large pot of boiling hot water. Upon placing the frog in the scalding water, it immediately hopped out. Nearby was a second pot of water which was not hot, but which was being heated by a mild flame. The frog was placed into this pot of water, and stayed there, swimming and moving about. Oblivious to the fact that the water was gradually being heated, the frog eventually died when the temperature reached a boiling point.

I am also reminded of Jesus's words to the church at Laodecia in John's *Apocalypse*, the book we know as *Revelation*. Although neither John nor Jesus use the phrase *innocuous accumulation*, Jesus does make it clear to this congregation that they have allowed other things to take the place of Jesus's supreme Lordship in their lives. The spiritual fire has cooled to a glowing ember. Jesus bluntly diagnoses their problem:

> I know your works: you are neither cold nor hot. Would that you were cold or hot! So, because you are lukewarm, and neither cold nor hot, I will spew you out of my mouth. For you say, I am

2. Slim, *Feast of Festivals*, 73.

rich, I have prospered, and I need nothing; not knowing that
you are wretched, pitiable, poor, blind, and naked.[3]

The cure that Jesus prescribes involves repentance and returning to the living vitality of their faith that characterized their relationship with Jesus at its inception. Priorities must be reexamined. The natural tendency of fire is to die out unless it is carefully nurtured. Lukewarm living is unhealthy.

Innocuous accumulation attempts to work its way into our lives both materially and spiritually. We become increasingly attached to *things*. Possessions become *possessors*. William Wordsworth was right in lamenting that the world and its values permeate our lives, often to an unhealthy degree. This imbalance in material things reveals an underlying spiritual atrophy that occurs when spiritual fires are not tended carefully. The end result, barring a change of direction, is that we end up losing sensitivity to the things of God and the needs of others. Our hearts fall spiritually out of tune, and we become tone deaf to this reality.

Lent is a time of focused and sustained vision. A time of repentance, of changing directions, of rejecting innocuous accumulation, both materially and spiritually. It is a season for reducing spiritual and material clutter, a time where we take to heart the admonition from the writer of the book of Hebrews:

> Therefore, since we are surrounded by so great a cloud of witnesses, let us also lay aside every weight, and sin which clings so closely, and let us run with perseverance the race that is set before us, looking to Jesus the pioneer and perfecter of our faith, who for the joy set before him endured the cross, despising the shame, and is seated at the right hand of the throne of God.[4]

Lent is about ongoing conversion in the life of faith. We place our lives under the searchlight of the Holy Spirit, seeking to become aware of the tentacles of innocuous accumulation that grip us and hinder the work of God's grace in us. The Lenten season provides us with fresh opportunities to amend our lives. Yes, we can and should spiritually grow throughout the rest of the year. But during Lent, we are challenged to take a deeper look at ourselves. We are invited to confront our patterns of behavior that may have become unfruitful or even sinful. As a result, a desire for change and for something greater can be born in us.

One practical approach to removing clutter during Lent involves simplifying your life. Starting with small changes to your physical living space

3. Rev 3:15–17 RSV.
4. Heb 12:1–2 RSV.

can often make a big difference. The clothes closet is often a good place to start. One friend I know begins each January by reversing the direction of the hanging clothes in his closet. After two months, any clothes on hangers that have not been worn are donated or given away. This works for all areas of our living space. The key is to simplify. When our physical living space becomes less crowded and messy, a corresponding peace in our spiritual lives settles upon us. It is perhaps no exaggeration to say that the easiest way to organize your stuff is to get rid of most of it. To unburden ourselves of the acquisitions that clutter both our outer and inner lives leaves us free to respond to God and to the needs of others more readily.

Another domain worthy of decluttering in our technologized day-and-age is our digital devices. The scientific data has been conclusive for some time now that our constant streaming of online gaming, social media scrolling, and internet searches is rewiring our brains and changing the way they function, and not for the better.

Author and businessman T. J. Burdick tells the story of his addiction to his cell phone in his book, *Detached: Put Your Phone in Its Place*. The book's title is revealing. Burdick fully recognizes the positive impact of technology and its potential to enhance our lives. His solution is not to offer simplistic or impractical formulas requiring the elimination of our phones or tablets. Where he attempts to help us is by exposing the dark side of this technology and our increasingly unhealthy attachment to it.

The underbelly of the enormous benefits of our phones and tablets is what Burdick describes as the "social normalization of technology addiction."[5] Instead of using technology to grow in our knowledge of God and nurture the life of holiness, we settle for mindless scrolling on social media and high-point scores on the latest gaming fad. Since the fall of Adam and Eve, we have been cursed with an incessant desire to do what is contrary to our own happiness. We take the path of least resistance. But the path of least resistance is usually a road that leads to nowhere.

This means that our cell phones can potentially become our proverbial kryptonite. They create within us what Buddhist teaching calls the "monkey mind," a term describing how our thoughts are unsettled, restless, indecisive, and uncontrollable. From a Christian perspective, it means that our screens act as catalysts toward sin more than virtue. They become the source of endless temptations. Borrowing from the work of Steven Pressfield's *The War of Art*, we might say that our phones can easily function as "resistance,"

---

5. Burdick, *Detached*, 37.

the negative force whose aim is to distract us and, in this case, to prevent us from pursuing our true calling of intimate relationship with God.[6]

Since the advent of the iPhone in 2007, persons have become addicted to this technology to the extent that they now believe that they cannot function without it. The term "nomophobia" was coined to describe the thoughts and feelings associated with not having our devices. One 2012 study from the United Kingdom found that 66 percent of adults struggled with nomophobia. That number increases in younger persons. Of those polled in the eighteen-to-twenty-four age bracket, seven out of ten persons suffered from it.[7] What this tells us is that this form of technology has become so ingrained in our lives that we live in fear of losing it. This is a telltale sign of behavioral addiction. I found it interesting to learn a few years ago that Steve Jobs, innovator of many of the phones that now shape our lives, refused to let his children own the very devices he created. This speaks volumes about the potential of our devices to distract us, to stifle curiosity and natural creativity, to function as "resistance" toward pursuing our higher calling. But let us be clear:

> Your phone isn't the devil. On the contrary, your phone has an immense potential for good, just as it has an equally immense potential for bad. Everything hinges on your ability to contemplate the good that can be produced through the use of your phone. The thing itself isn't the issue. It is how you choose to use it that makes screen time either a holy encounter or a self-destructive behavior.[8]

The solution is to create priorities in life that help us to regulate our devices. These priorities then help us to allow our phones and tablets a certain amount of daily time, and no more. Using the analogy of a freeway, we assign our phone its own "lane," and then force it to stay in its lane. When it comes to our digital lives, it behooves us to think seriously about what is really meaningful to us, and whether sites like Facebook or Instagram help us to achieve it. In addition, consider how much time you spend in solitude and prayer when compared to the time you spend using your digital devices. Then consider positive changes or adjustments that you can make in an effort to simplify this area of your life.

Lent is a season that reminds us that we are constantly faced with choices in life that require our discernment. In the early centuries of the

---

6. Pressfield, *War of Art*, 31–48.

7. Burdick, *Detached*, 124.

8. Burdick, *Detached*, 103. Burdick offers practical helps and advice for those who wish to become proactive in the use of this technology throughout his book

church a group of Christian ascetics known as the desert fathers and mothers withdrew themselves into the desert, convinced that following Jesus meant a radical transformation of their lives. Using Jesus's journey into the desert prior to the beginning of his public ministry as their analogue, they fled the "world" with its false values and went into the desert to do battle with the demons lodged in their own hearts. All of the false motivations that typically control us—pride, greed, lust, self-aggrandizement, the desire for power—were rooted out and were replaced by the spirit of Christ. Compassion, humility, and purity of heart became the controlling features of their personalities. The key to their transformation was solitude. In the quiet of the desert, these early followers of Jesus discovered the noisiness of voices raging within their hearts.[9] But as they persevered, they discovered that God's voice began to be heard from beneath that tumult of harmful competing voices.

Most of us are not able to withdraw ourselves completely from the world. Nonetheless, we *are* called to be attentive to the ways in which we allow the competing voices of the world to stifle the voice of the Spirit in our lives:

> Lent is a time for tuning our ears, for listening carefully, for discerning the texture and quality of our own demons, for attending to God's unceasing, creative plea amidst the noise of cultural pressures, the busyness of life, and our own self-limiting habits . . . it involves a radical and risky self-evaluation and a commitment to rethink and rework everything you know and are.[10]

During Lent we seek a greater focus and intensity with regard both to our inner and outer lives. The purpose of this heightened focus is not spiritual *scorekeeping*, but spiritual *housecleaning*. We take up arms against innocuous accumulation. We seek, through disciplined practices and the cultivation of solitude, to bring the disordered areas of our lives to God where his mercy and grace can heal us.

9. Wright, *Rising*, 32–33.
10. Wright, *Rising*, 32–33.

Chapter Fourteen

When God Weeps

Human beings have an inherent tendency towards violence both
towards their fellow human beings and towards the creation itself.
The Genesis Story tells us that this violence grieves God.

—ADAM HAMILTON

SUGGESTED READINGS

Gen 9:8–17; Ps 25:1–10; 2 Pet 3:18–22; Mark 1:9–13

DURING THE LENTEN SEASON, the story of salvation history is often recounted in public worship through a focus on the covenants God established with his people in the Old Testament. One of those important covenants is God's covenant with Noah and his sons. The backdrop to this covenant is Gen 1–11, which is the story of the origin and spread of human sin, culminating in the great flood which destroys the earth and its inhabitants.

The downward spiral begins in chapter 3, where sin creates disharmony between human beings and God, human beings and one another, and between us and the entire creation. By the time we arrive at chapter 6, the language of the text is raw and painful:

> The LORD saw that the wickedness of man was great in the
> earth, and that every imagination of the thoughts of his heart
> was only evil continually. And the LORD was sorry that he had
> made man on the earth, and it grieved him to his heart.[1]

We are barely into the introductory pages of the long story that is the Bible,
and we have gone from "and God saw that it was good" to "and God saw
and regretted":

> The grief in God's heart is the same word for the pain in the
> woman's womb. The curse has gotten into God. God's creatures
> are seeing and seizing. They are destroying the earth. Violence—
> hamas, a Hebrew word we know all too well—covers the earth.
> They cannot transcend their self-interest to care for each other.[2]

The sad words of Genesis tell us that God is grieved and deeply regrets his
human creation. God is vulnerable to the evil that human beings do. It gets
to him. And lest we think the Genesis story applies only to a day and time
long ago, consider what human beings have done to each other in recent
years. More than 800,000 Rwandans died because of tribal warfare. In the
land of Jesus's birth, retaliation continues to win the day as Israelis and
Palestinians continue to kill each other. Cruel tyrants who rule countries
continue to practice ethnic cleansing.

In wealthy North America, we continue to abort, euthanize, and ware-
house people. Humans are trafficked, and women and children are turned
into sex toys. We continue to exploit the planet of its natural resources with
little thought for those who come after us. Rivers of blood flow in the streets
of our cities because of gun violence. Thousands of people risk their lives to
make their way across our southern border as they flee violent gangs and
powerful drug cartels.

The Genesis text tells us that God's heart was so broken at the pain
and rebellion of his human creatures that he decided to pull the plug on the
universe. God acted on his regret. The God who blew the waters back in creation now holds his breath and lets them return in a great flood. But how did
God do this? Did God wipe out the entire creation and then just walk away?

---

1. Gen 6:5–6 RSV. It must be noted here that the writer of Genesis is projecting
human emotions onto God in order to explain the human experience of God from the
human perspective. These verses, and my subsequent material in this chapter, are not
an attempt to deny the traditional doctrine of God's impassibility. God is never passive.
God is never acted upon, but is always the Actor. God is all-powerful and all-sufficient
such that he is never compelled, coerced, or made to do anything. See Papandrea, *Reading the Church Fathers*, 15–18.

2. Boone, *Dark Side of God*, 944.

When my sister Becky was little, she was drawn like a magnet to mud puddles. If there was mud or a mud puddle within striking distance, she would find it. Not only would she find it, she would welcome it and befriend it. One day our family arrived home from a wedding in our nice clothes, and Becky made her way to a mud puddle near the house. When my mom came to check on her she found Becky covered from head to toe, dressed now not just in her finest, but in her muddiest.

Was my mom angry? Absolutely. But what did my mom do? Did she go into the bedroom and grab my father's handgun from the top of the closet and shoot Becky dead in the yard? No. She grabbed her daughter by the hand, led her into the bathroom, ran the tub full of water, and washed her clean of her muddy mess.

And when God saw that the thoughts of our hearts were continually evil, did he just blow up the whole creation and walk away? No. God cried an ocean full of tears from a broken heart, and he used those tears to drown what he had made with a bath so that a new beginning could be made. The whole creation was cleansed and given a new beginning, a chance to live once more in harmony with God.

In the story of the great flood, it was not just humanity or the creation that were the great losers. It was God who was the great loser. The flood waters that covered the earth were not merely God's judgment. They were the flood of God's tears, a torrential downpour of God's sorrow for a world gone terribly wrong.

Which brings us to God's covenant with Noah and his children. In reading this story, we must be attentive to the meaning of a covenant in Scripture. It can be easy to confuse a covenant with a contract. In a contract, there is an exchange of goods and services. I give you something, and you give me something in return. Contracts remain in force only for the time needed to fulfill their agreements.

A covenant, however, is an exchange of *persons*. It is an enduring family bond. In a covenant, I am yours and you are mine.[3] But God's covenant with Noah is one-sided, entirely God's doing. God enters into this covenant with Noah and with creation by pledging an oath to himself. God promises never again to destroy the creation with a flood. And as a sign of this promise, God places the rainbow in the sky.

I have often wondered why God chose the rainbow as the sign of his promise never to destroy the earth again with water. However, depictions of a deity armed with a bow and arrow are common in antiquity. Perhaps the sign of God's covenant here with Noah—the bow in the sky—is a bow

---

3. Hahn, *Father Who Keeps His Promises*, 24–30.

of battle. For God to "hang up" his bow in the sky, then, may be tantamount to his ceasing from battle. It is God's promise that destruction is now off the table when it comes to his plan to restore fallen humanity.

Ironically, the flood did not cleanse the human heart of sin. And yet God enters into covenant with us anyway. God is committed to seeking us out and restoring us to himself. But the rainbow in the sky that we see from time to time is a reminder to us that God has laid down his arms. God will no longer respond to violence with violence.[4] God's plan is to *love* us into restoration. How do we know this? The answer is simple: Jesus of Nazareth. Anyone who believes the tired cliché that the god of the Old Testament is a god of wrath and the god of the New Testament is a god of grace has not read carefully the story of the flood and God's covenant with Noah. For it is not just humanity who loses when we sin and rebel against God. God loses.

Many years ago a couple had a son named Matthew who loved comic books. His love was so strong that his parents limited his intake of comic books so that he would read something of greater quality. One day Matthew's parents discovered stacks upon stacks of contraband comics hidden in Matthew's room. The books were all from the public library, and had not been checked out, but stolen.

Matthew's parents lectured him about honesty and stealing and made him return the books to the library and confess what he had done. They hoped and prayed that this was the end of the story. But a year or so later, they discovered more stolen comics in their son's room. This time they learned that the items had been taken from a convenience store near the family's vacation cabin several states away. It wasn't realistic for Matthew to return the books, so this time his frustrated parents piled them all in a heap and burned them. They hoped and prayed that this was the end of it and that their son had learned his lesson.

But before long, they found yet more purloined comics in Matthew's room. His parents were now desperate to get through to their son. Matthew's dad took him into his office and gave the boy a spanking. Then he said to his son: "You sit here and think about what you have done and what will happen to you if you do not overcome this." Then he went outside, closed the door of his study, leaned against the wall in the hallway, and wept. He wept because of what he had done. And he wept because of what the future might hold for his son.

---

4. God's covenant with Noah may also illumine the discussion of the perennial question as to why God permits evil in the world. There was a time when God responded to evil by eradicating it. For those who persist in demanding that God justify why he allows evil, are we prepared for him to remove it by starting with us? In the covenant with Noah, God chose to respond to our brokenness in a different way.

Years later, Matthew had grown up and moved away. He returned home for a visit, and at one point the issue of his stolen comic books came up. Matthew's mom asked him about it, and he said: "You know, Mom, after Dad spanked me that time in his study, I never stole again."

She asked, "Was that because Dad spanked you?"

Matthew replied: "No. It was because after he left the room I heard him sobbing in the hallway. In that moment I knew I could never steal anything again."

The story of the flood is the story of a God who sits in the corridors of time and weeps at our brokenness and our failures. Anytime you or I fall into sin or choose misguided paths, God still weeps. When we hurt others or ourselves, God's heart breaks.

But the story does not end there. The story of the flood is about a God who, try as he might, cannot forget his creation. God does not have it in his character to blot us out and walk away. So the sign of the rainbow is God's sign to help him remember never to abandon us in our sins. The rainbow is a sign which reminds us of the lengths to which God is willing to go to save us. The rainbow is a sign to us and to all of creation that God's grace is greater than our sin. God's love is deeper than our rebellion.

In many traditions, on the first Sunday in the Lenten season a lengthy prayer known as *The Great Litany* is prayed. The prayer is a corporate and personal acknowledgment of the brokenness of our world, and of our culpability in that brokenness. It is a forthright confession of our personal and corporate responsibility for breaking God's heart through the ways we live and relate to one another. During the season of Lent, we are called to acknowledge in particular ways how we break God's heart with our sin and disobedience. We confess how we grieve his heart when we love things and use people. We acknowledge our culpability for the world's brokenness, both in terms of what we have done, and in what we have failed to do. Then we move from acknowledging our culpability toward concrete action where we seek to cooperate with God's grace to put things right, beginning with ourselves.

Chapter Fifteen

The Call to Radical Obedience

To find the Savior outside obedience is to lose him altogether.

—Saint Francis de Sales

SUGGESTED READINGS

Gen 22:1–14; Ps 16:5–11; Rom 8:31–39; Mark 8:31–38

One of the hidden blessings of the Lenten season is that it is a sustained time where we encounter the radical and all-encompassing nature of God's call upon our lives. A great example of this is found in the Old Testament story of Abraham and his son, Isaac.

Many years before Isaac was born, God called Abraham and promised him that he would have a family, that his descendants would become great, that they would occupy their own land and become a blessing to all peoples of the earth.[1] Part of this promise involved God calling Abraham to leave his home, to launch out in faith and to travel to a place where God would lead him.

1. Gen 12:1–3.

This is precisely what Abraham did. In spite of the fact that he and his wife Sarah were well advanced in years and childless, they stepped out in faith and responded to God's invitation. In the book of Hebrews, the writer says this about Abraham: "By faith Abraham obeyed when he was called to go out to a place which he was to receive as an inheritance; and he went out, not knowing where he was to go."[2]

As the years pass, there are numerous situations where Abraham's faith is less than stellar. He lies under pressure and tells the Egyptians and Abimelech that Sarah is his sister and not his wife. On another occasion, he sleeps with Hagar the Egyptian servant woman when he doesn't see evidence of God working things out to bring his promised son. But finally, after many years, Isaac is born. Abraham literally holds God's promise to him in his arms. He settles in the land of Beersheba where one would think that his physical and spiritual journey is pretty much over. Not so. More than twenty-five years after calling Abraham the first time, God visits him again. He asks him to take his only son—the very promise of God—to Mount Moriah and sacrifice him as a burnt offering.

Reading this story floods our minds with questions. These questions may actually hinder us from hearing the story on its own terms, but they are so compelling we must address them. We ask: Would God really ask for a human sacrifice? Is this consistent with the God revealed to us in the Scriptures? We also ask: Why would God deal patiently with Abraham for so many years, leading him to accept God's promise, and then take the promise back once it was finally in Abraham's hands?

These are significant questions. But they are not on the lips of Abraham, and they are not the heart of this story. This story may challenge our settled notions of God. But the central issue in this story is not the character of God but the *testing* of Abraham. The story proceeds on the premise that Abraham is being tested, and that God really is calling him to offer Isaac up as a sacrifice.

As the story unfolds, Abraham saddles the donkeys, grabs Isaac and some servants, and heads off for another distant place. Abraham may have thought to himself: "I spent the last twenty-five years traveling to an unknown place and to a future I don't understand. All I could do was trust God to show me the way and how to get there. If I did it once, I can do it again."

As Abraham and Isaac approach Mount Moriah, Isaac asks, "Father, we have wood and fire, but where is the lamb for the burnt offering?"

Abraham replies, "God will provide a lamb, my son."

This is a pivotal moment. The Hebrew word for "provide" is the word which means "to see." Abraham answers his son by saying, "God will see it

---

2. Heb 11:8 RSV.

[the lamb], my son." This notion of *seeing* is key to the story. In saying that God will "see" the lamb, Abraham affirms that God will see what is needed before Abraham sees it, and that God sees what Abraham does not see. Abraham's challenge at this point is whether he can trust in the character of God, not just what he can see and hold in his hands.

God is leading him in ways that seem threatening and even contrary to reason and experience. It even appears that God's leading in this situation contradicts everything that God has done in the past with respect to God's original promise. Abraham now faces a decision as to whether he will trust this God who acts in unexpected ways and who does not always fit into his settled categories. No matter how absurd the path appears, is Abraham willing to trust that God "sees" what he cannot see?

And here is where I locate myself in the story. I am very much like Abraham. I certainly want God's will in my life. But I want it on *my* terms, according to things I can see and control. I want a predictable God, one who would never call me into uncertainty, and who would certainly never ask me to give up something that I cherish.

I suspect that I am not alone. We want a safe God in a safe world that we can manage. We want a God who will fit within the confines of our finite thinking, where we construct the biggest theological words we can find to draw those boundaries for him. In our honest moments, we want a God who is domesticated and controllable.

But the God of Abraham is not that kind of God. One middle aged man, after hearing this story in church one Sunday morning, went to his pastor after the service. He said: "Pastor, my family and I will be looking for another church after this morning."

"May I ask why?" his pastor answered.

"Because when I look at that God, the God of Abraham, I feel I'm near a real god, not the sort of dignified, businesslike, Rotary Club god we chatter about here on Sunday mornings. Abraham's God could blow a man to bits, give and then take a child, ask for everything from a person and then want more. I want to know *that* God."

I find it compelling that at this early stage in the Bible, the question "What is faith?" is not answered with theological statements, a set of propositions, or even with admonitions to be faithful, but with a *story*. The story of a man who trusted God even when God appeared to be acting against his promise. The faith that Abraham shows—biblical faith—involves great risk, not in the sense of accepting certain beliefs, but the risk that comes from taking concrete action. It is easy to obey God and believe God in matters that do not test us or require much of us. It is easy to trust God when there is little sacrifice required on our part.

But Abraham's story reminds me that the motive for my faith must be constantly clarified and purified. I must be reminded that I do not believe because I always understand God's words completely or because of what I can gain by believing. As those who are pursuing God's will, we do not believe because it is easy, convenient, or fashionable. We believe because the God who reveals himself to us is not deceitful and is completely trust-worthy. Although I cannot probe into the mind of Abraham with certainty, surely it is fair to conclude that he did not understand fully why God was commanding him to sacrifice Isaac. Isaac was the tangible embodiment of God's promise. Everything was riding on Isaac. To lose Isaac would be to lose everything God has promised to Abraham.

Abraham understood fully why God had commanded such a thing only *after* he had obeyed God's word in faith to the very end. His story re-veals to us that the more we obey God in faith, the more we actually begin to understand God's ways in our lives. This reminds me of a statement of Jesus in John's gospel, where Jesus says: "If you continue in my word, you are truly my disciples, and you will know the truth, and the truth will make you free."[3] Abraham's story, and Jesus's words here, confirm for me an important truth: Our knowledge of God and our understanding of God's ways is the outcome of *obedience*. Everything else is just information.

It can be difficult in those moments of life where God asks something difficult, perhaps impossible, from us. For example, how do we respond when we hear these words: "If any of you would be my follower, you must put aside your selfish ambition, shoulder your cross, and follow me"?

The biblical faith demonstrated by Abraham is not defined by how we *feel* but by how we *act*.[4] It demands radical obedience, motivated by love, at any cost. God's call on our lives is total and all-encompassing. His love for us is such that he will not accept anything less than our full surrender.

But there is another dimension to this story that warrants our atten-tion. Abraham places great trust in God, but God also places incredible trust in Abraham. If this truly is a test of Abraham and not a charade, then a great deal depends on Abraham in this case. God calls him to make this journey, but finally it is he who must make it.

God has placed Abraham under the promise. But Abraham can reject it. There is no sense in the text that God has compelled or forced Abraham to accept the promise. In fact, the whole story depends upon the possibility of Abraham failing the test and rejecting the promise, otherwise it makes very

---

3. John 8:31–32 RSV.

4. Fred Craddock observes: "Scripture does not give psychological profiles of its characters but permits the reader to see them through action and conversation" in *Luke*, 55–56.

little sense. God chose Abraham, and then called on Abraham to choose God. But Abraham is free to reject what God has called him to do and be. In this sense, I wonder if the story is as much a test of God as it is of Abraham.

Once again, we can locate ourselves in the story. God calls each of us to covenant relationship with him. He calls us to a journey of faith, to step out into the unknown. Answering that call will almost certainly lead you into circumstances you cannot control. God may ask the impossible of you, and work on his timetable and not yours. The journey may take you into unspeakable tragedy. You may suffer incalculable loss. You will be tested. That testing will be an opportunity for you to ask yourself an important question: Will you live your life with faith that God sees what you cannot?

What makes Abraham's sacrifice remarkable to me is that he is asked to give up that which is dearest to him—his beloved son. This passage is one of the first instances in the Bible where the word "love" is used, and it is used with respect to a father's great love for his son.

How could Abraham do this? How could Abraham honor this request from God that seemed to make no sense? What perplexes me about this story is that because of the emotional response it produces in me, I want to know Abraham's emotional state. I want the text to put Abraham on the Psychiatrist's couch, to analyze Abraham and let me peek deep into his soul and to see the raging conflict that surely must be happening there. But the text doesn't do that. We are not told in this story how Abraham feels. We are only told how he *acts* and what he *does*. We are only told how he directs the course of his life.[5]

If you choose to follow Jesus, one thing you can be sure of is that Jesus calls you to radical obedience at every stage of your faith journey. At times the call to obedience will severely test your faith. And while the greatest tests of your faith will certainly involve your feelings, your choice to *take action* and to move your life in a specific direction will ultimately determine the outcome of the test. Will you trust God in the face of great risk? Will you take action when your feelings argue against it? Will you obey God when the going gets tough?

What gave Abraham the strength to obey God and to trust God in this situation? The answer may lie in the words of Saint Augustine, who is

---

5. When one reads this story of Abraham's testing, and notes especially the parallels between Isaac and Jesus, how Isaac is a type or prefiguring of Christ, the question of why God would demand of Abraham that he sacrifice his own son recedes into the background. The story reveals not a capricious God who demands human sacrifice, but rather a God of such profound love that he will sacrifice his dearly beloved Son for a sinful human race. Seeing this episode as a type or prefiguring of how God will act in Jesus is what makes the story intelligible.

thought to have said, "What seems hard, love makes easy." There is no question that Abraham loved Isaac. Isaac is his beloved son. But what enables Abraham to follow through in this story is that he loves God even more. And what seems hard, love makes easy. The impossible becomes possible in the face of overwhelming love.

In the eighth chapter of Mark's Gospel Jesus issues a radical invitation to those who would follow him. For any who would respond to Jesus, we face the same issues that confronted Abraham. It would be relatively easy for us to follow Jesus as he heals and performs mighty miracles. It would be thrilling to follow Jesus as he performs exorcisms and amasses great crowds and teaches with authority. It would be exhilarating to stand by his side as he puts all hostile forces in their place, subjecting them to his authority.

But what do we do when he calls on us to follow him to Jerusalem, to accompany him to his death and subsequently to lay down our own life? It is easy to believe in Jesus when nothing is required of us, when there is little or no sacrifice on our part. But what happens when you are asked to surrender your claim upon your own life?[6] What happens when you are summoned to put God's agenda ahead of your own, to follow a path you would not choose if you were doing the choosing? What could possibly enable us to respond to Jesus's call and actually surrender our lives totally to him? Like Abraham, where can we find strength for this kind of radical obedience?

Perhaps our strength lies in this: What seems hard, love makes easy. But it isn't so much our love for God but God's love for us that enables us to hear and answer Jesus's call. It is only by his supernatural grace that we can offer up our own radical obedience upon his altar.

The apostle Paul tells the Christians at Rome that God "did not spare His own Son, but freely delivered him up for us all."[7] What would cause God to do such a thing? When I consider my life, my sins, my rebellion, all the ways I have hurt God and others and myself—what would prompt God not to spare his own Son, but to deliver him up for me?

Only one answer comes to mind: That which is hard, love makes easy. God the Father loved his beloved Son. But he loved us so much that he gave his beloved Son to be born for us and to die for us. What is hard becomes possible in the face of great love. This is the testimony of the saints and martyrs throughout the history of the church. Their mantra: *radical obedience, motivated by love, at any cost.* This becomes the Spirit's call to us during the Lenten season as we journey with Jesus to Jerusalem.

6. See the testimony of Dietrich Bonhoeffer, the German theologian who was martyred for his resistance to Hitler and the Nazi regime during World War II, especially Bonhoeffer's famous dictum: "When Christ calls a man, he bids him come and die."

7. Rom 8:32 RSV.

Chapter Sixteen

The Privilege of Sharing Jesus's Suffering

The great tragedy of the world is not what people suffer,
but how much they miss when they suffer.

—FULTON J. SHEEN

SUGGESTED READINGS

Isa 43:16–21; Ps 126; Phil 3:8–14; 1 Pet 1:3–9; Luke 20:9–19

DURING THE SEASON OF Lent, many of the Scripture lessons reveal to us the God of the Exodus experience. In leading the children of Israel out of slavery in Egypt, the Old Testament lessons in particular show us a God who is faithful and whose faithfulness leads him to do great things. The psalmist captures this with his joyful expression: "The LORD has done great things for us, and we are glad indeed."

But while God's deeds in the past are amazing, even more amazing is what God promises to do in the future. Writing to the Philippians, the apostle Paul anticipates this future because of the death and resurrection of Jesus. Using language reminiscent of Matthew and other New Testament writers, Paul envisions the future in terms of a new Exodus. This new and greater Exodus has begun in the death and resurrection of Jesus. Through this new Exodus, Christ's resurrection has the power to lay hold of every one of us in the same way it touched the apostle Paul: "Forgetting what lies behind and straining forward to what lies ahead, I press on toward the goal for the prize of the upward call of God in Christ Jesus."[1] That goal toward which Paul strives is the last new thing God promises—the resurrection of the dead. It is the great Exodus in which we all hope to share, our arrival at last in the promised land of heaven.

It is also during the Lenten season when we are put in touch with the truth that reaching that goal and sharing in Christ's resurrection only happens as we share in Christ's *sufferings*. Our life as followers of Jesus is not centered on information about Christ. Our life is about *participation* in the life of Christ. And that means sharing in his sufferings.

Even a cursory glance reveals how Paul's language to the Philippians is participatory and experiential.[2] It reflects a mystical reality where Paul is able to experience in his own life the things that marked Jesus's life. The shape of Paul's life takes on the shape of Jesus's life, which was cruciform. It is a journey of death and resurrection. It is a journey marked by sacrificial love and by suffering. Following Jesus involves being united to him in his death, so that we might be united with him in his resurrection.

Paul is likely recalling the moments when he was shipwrecked and afraid for his life. Or perhaps he remembers when he was beaten and threatened for preaching the gospel. Perhaps he remembers when the churches he started had difficulty or wandered away from his guidance.

The apostle Peter sounds this same theme of sharing Jesus's sufferings in his first letter to Christians in Asia Minor. Peter writes to these believers that the resurrection of Jesus changes everything—not only in the present, but also in the future where a great inheritance awaits them. This produces an inexpressible joy that gladdens the heart.

At the same time, the people to whom Peter writes are learning through hard experience that the transformation brought about by Jesus's resurrection does not come about in typical or expected ways. Christ's resurrection does not exempt them from the trials and struggles of life. They are not immune from sickness and disease. They struggle with financial hardship. They are not guaranteed that their children will not rebel and become prodigals. They may face the prospect of losing their jobs. Some are

1. Phil 3:13–14 RSV.
2. Phil 3:8–14.

already struggling with the anxiety that comes when life falls down around them and all they have left is their belief in the One whom they cannot see.

It's almost as if these believers had communicated with Peter in some way before he penned this letter, saying to him: "Hey, Peter, if Christ has been raised, why is life trying to knock us to the canvas and put us down for the count? Where's the joy in that?" Peter's response: Be glad. Don't lose your joy. This all leads somewhere, even though right now things are tough for you.[3]

The thrust of both Paul's and Peter's words is to clarify for us the truth that the power of Jesus's resurrection is not a power that exempts us from suffering. To believe that the salvation Jesus brings exempts the Christian from suffering is to deny the truth of human experience. Further, it contradicts the explicit teaching of Scripture. Nonetheless, this misguided view holds sway among many Christians:

> There are two ways of looking at the relationship between the head (Christ) and the body (the Church) as it pertains to suffering. The first one—which is not found in the Bible—is that Jesus simply did everything for us. He suffered for us, he redeemed us, he intercedes for us, he shepherds us, he heals us, he guides us, he prospers us—he does everything, and all we do as the body of Christ is receive the benefits.[4]

It is true that Jesus suffered, died, and rose from the dead for us. He teaches us, he counsels us, he heals us. He meets our needs. But the view of Peter and Paul and the other New Testament writers is that Jesus, as the head of the body (the church) has chosen to share his mission with us. We're not mere spectators or recipients of his saving work. We're participants and cooperators. Like Mary, our hearts must be pierced for love of him who first loved us. The power of the resurrection is a power that works through our suffering and uses it to refine us and to conform us to the likeness of Christ.

I'm reminded of a story I once read about a woman who made an appointment with a silversmith so that she could watch him do his work. As she watched, the silversmith held a piece of silver over the fire and began heating it. The craftsman said to her, "In order to refine silver, you have to hold the silver precisely in the middle of the fire where the flames are hottest, so that all of the impurities can be burned away."

The curious woman asked, "Do you have to be present and sit with the silver in front of the fire the entire time you are refining it?"

---

3. 1 Pet 1:5–15.
4. Cavins, *When You Suffer*, 22.

His answer: "Yes, I do. It's important that I keep my eye on the silver the entire time it is in the fire. If the silver is left in the fire a moment too long, it will be destroyed."

The woman sat in silence, thinking. Then she asked, "So how do you know when the time is just right, when the silver is fully refined?"

The silversmith replied: "I always know the silver is fully refined when I see my image in it." As the head of his mystical body (the church), Christ shares his mission with us. He grants us a share in his sufferings in order to perfect us in love and to help us grow in holiness and to renew us in his image.

God granted me the privilege many years ago of meeting a woman who experienced firsthand the refining fire of suffering. Her name was Bev, and we were both attending a large Christian conference. She told me how she awoke one morning with pain in her legs. During the next few days the pain grew worse, and soon spasms racked her body. She became incapable of walking or moving. Specialists examined her and could not determine what was wrong. Within a matter of weeks Bev was curled up in a fetal position, unable to move, fed with a pump placed into her stomach. Her husband arranged for her to stay in their darkened bedroom because Bev was sensitive to light of any kind. He would sit with her, and friends from her church came to help. In time, neighbors and friends also came and offered what help they could. Many times the gift of their presence was all that they could offer her.

I said to her: "Bev, what did you do?"

She said: "I could not move, the pain was so severe. All I could do was pray and talk to God and listen for him to talk with me."

Looking at her in that moment, she looked perfectly healthy. I said to her: "This must have been terrible for you. How long did this last?" She paused. Then she looked at me and said, "Fifteen years."

I can assure you that if you desire to be a follower of Jesus, you will experience seasons where you will be tried and refined in the fires of harsh life experience. The question is not *if* we will suffer. The issue is how we respond to it. No experience in life has meaning unless we ascribe meaning to it. Discerning and attaching meaning to our suffering is the antidote to despair. And the key to understanding and finding meaning in our suffering is to understand Christ's suffering.[5]

Understanding Christ's suffering involves seeing that his suffering was *redemptive*. He suffered in obedience to his Father out of love for the salvation of the world. He embraced the cross, and invites his disciples to do no less: "If any man would come after me, let him deny himself and take up

5. Cavins, *When You Suffer*, 22.

his cross daily and follow me."[6] Christian faith is nothing less than *sharing* in the life of Jesus. As Paul says, "As we share abundantly in Christ's sufferings, so through Christ we share abundantly in comfort too."[7] Paul's words to the Corinthians remind us that we, as the church, share in both Christ's sufferings and his comfort. There is a sharing, a participation, a communion between Christ and his mystical body, the church. What the Head experiences the mystical body also experiences.

Perhaps this is the best way to understand the enigmatic verse from Paul to the Colossians, where he says, "Now I rejoice in my sufferings for your sake, and in my flesh I complete what is lacking in Christ's afflictions for the sake of his body, that is, the church."[8] Commenting on this verse, Jeff Cavins observes:

> Wasn't the suffering of Christ good enough to redeem the world? Yes, and it was good enough to transform our suffering into something of eternal value that participates in Christ's suffering. . . . St. Paul sees the sufferings of the body of Christ as part and parcel of the sufferings of Christ. The suffering of the Church is the suffering of the mystical body of Christ.[9]

The implications of Paul's words to the Colossians are staggering. Because we are joined to Christ as the body is to the head, we are united with him in our physical and moral suffering.[10] Our sufferings become one with his. Our suffering, when offered to Christ in obedience to his will, becomes laden with redemptive significance. It affords us the opportunity to love as Christ loves, to grow in holiness. Pope John Paul II observed that nothing was lacking in Christ's suffering, but in order for us to know the love of God more deeply Christ made room in his suffering for us to participate in it. Christ calls us to share in his suffering, through which all human suffering has been redeemed.[11] Christ calls and invites us to share in his mission whereby each of us, in our suffering, can share in the redemptive suffering of Christ:

---

6. Luke 9:23 RSV.

7. 2 Cor 1:3–7.

8. Col 1:24 RSV.

9. Cavins, *When You Suffer*, 77.

10. There are two kinds of suffering, physical suffering and moral suffering. Physical suffering is when the body is in pain and is the most familiar to us. Moral suffering is when the soul is in pain. It is often hidden and not as noticeable as physical pain. See Cavins, *When You Suffer*, 16.

11. John Paul II, *Salvifici Doloris*, 2.8.

> Those who share in the sufferings of Christ preserve in their own sufferings a very special particle of the infinity treasure of the world's redemption and can share this treasure with others.[12]

One person who discovered this truth firsthand was Allison Brown. Prior to her thirteenth birthday, she became seriously ill and confined to bed for long periods. Diagnosed with Chronic Fatigue Syndrome, by age sixteen Allison was barely able to function. She experienced fatigue, nausea, fainting spells, confusion and memory problems. As she grew into adulthood, the pain affected every joint, muscle, and bone in her body. The pain traveled to nerve endings, making it extremely painful even to wear clothing. In subsequent years, Allison was diagnosed with diabetes and kidney disease, and the mental confusion and memory problems grew worse. Making sense of her circumstances was difficult. She said:

> Over the years I would struggle immensely trying to understand what my purpose in life was. How could my life have any true meaning or purpose where all I could do was lay in bed, too sick to leave the house? I spent many years asking the question, "Why me?"[13]

In time, though, Allison came to see her suffering as a sharing in Jesus's suffering. She discovered that her suffering was an opportunity to pray for others. Her perspective changed:

> He has taught me to suffer joyfully. That when we suffer for God's will and in accordance with his plan, we are working with him, alongside him for the eternal salvation of the world. . . . To know I can unite myself with Jesus through my own cross gives me great strength and joy. . . . This joy brings me hope and this hope turns my suffering into a purpose that is served for God and for others.[14]

You may be experiencing suffering in your life right now. If so, remember that the key to understanding your trial is to understand Christ's suffering. By joining your suffering to Christ's, your experience becomes redemptive, and has redemptive potential for those you love. Through the help of the Holy Spirit, your experience of suffering can expand your capacity to love God and others and to conform you to the image and likeness of Christ. You can, through Jesus, find meaning and purpose to your life and to

---

12. John Paul II, *Salvifici Doloris*, 5.27.
13. Brown, "Chronic Illness," para. 12.
14. Brown, "Chronic Illness," paras. 15, 17.

your suffering. It is through the depth of your suffering that God most fully reveals himself and draws you into union with Christ.

When we learn to accept suffering as an act of love in obedience to God's will—as Jesus did—we begin to experience firsthand Paul's enigmatic words to the Colossians. And, by God's grace, we find ourselves seeing a hard thing turned into glory.

Chapter Seventeen

The Gospel according to Judas

And what does anyone know about traitors, or why Judas did what he did?

—JEAN RHYS

SUGGESTED READINGS

Isa 52:13—53:12; Ps 22:1–11; Heb 10:1–25; Matt 27:1–10

THROUGHOUT THE COURSE OF human history there have been a number of
infamous traitors. There was Marcus Brutus, the Roman statesman and military general, who helped to assassinate Julius Caesar. He met with twenty
others who were friends of the Caesar, and when he entered into the Roman
Senate they all stabbed him to death.

Then there was Alger Hiss, a longtime state department employee
who was convicted of perjury and treason in 1950 for giving away military
secrets. Or we might think of Julius and Ethel Rosenberg, who gave away
atomic bomb secrets to the Soviets during the days following World War II.
President Eisenhower refused pleas for clemency twice, and the Rosenbergs
were executed in Sing Sing Prison in 1953 in the electric chair.

In the world of sports, there was "shoeless" Joe Jackson, who allegedly
was part of a scheme to "throw" the 1919 World Series while he played for

the Chicago White Sox. Jackson is considered by some to be among the greatest baseball players who ever played. Born in Greenville, South Carolina, he played on mill teams as a boy. There has been growing consensus through the years that Jackson was innocent and that he should be in the Baseball Hall of Fame.

One might also think of the Japanese emissaries who sat with President Roosevelt in December of 1941, and while they sat and talked conditions of peace the bombers were moving across the South Pacific to attack Pearl Harbor in what President Roosevelt came to call a day that would live in infamy.

Then there was Judas Iscariot, arguably the most infamous of all. His name is a synonym for disloyalty and betrayal. He was one of the members of the inner circle, one of the apostles, one intimately close to Christ. He was present with the others in the upper room. For only thirty pieces of silver he arranged to lead the authorities to Jesus in a city which had swelled to upwards of a million pilgrims who had come to celebrate Passover. The authorities would have never found Jesus among all those people unless someone knew where he was. Judas did, and he led the authorities to Jesus—for just thirty pieces of silver.

Why did Judas do this?

We could speculate as to a number of possible reasons. Perhaps, as the only non-Galilean, Judas felt like an outsider. He didn't feel as though he was truly a part of the "old boys club," and it finally overcame him. A person can go to extreme measures, perhaps even throw his or her life away, from a perceived lack of acceptance.

Perhaps another reason why Judas betrayed the Master was that he was simply turning states' evidence. He knew the simmering conflict between Jesus and the religious and political leadership was coming to a boil. The situation was coming to an end, it was obvious. The Jewish religious authorities, cooperating with the Roman government, *were* going to get Jesus. It was only a matter of time. So maybe Judas thought, "I'll just turn him in and get it over with, and maybe the authorities will go easy on me. There's nothing wrong with looking out for yourself."

Or maybe Judas was just greedy and simply wanted the money. The old cliché opines that every man has his price. How much would it take to buy *you*? How much would it take for you to compromise your ideals, to betray what you know is right and true?

Or maybe Judas just resented Jesus because Jesus knew what Judas was all about. Jesus knew the darkness in Judas's heart. Jesus knew Judas's thoughts. Or maybe Judas was an infiltrator, a plant belonging to a group of terrorists planning to overthrow the Romans and free themselves of its bondage. If they could get Jesus on their side, it would further their cause in a big way.

None of these reasons is ultimately satisfying to me. For Judas believed in Jesus. He believed that Jesus was the Christ. He was one of the twelve. He wanted Jesus to show his heavenly power sooner rather than later. Perhaps, he thought, if he could just get Jesus started on the road to the cross, surely he would show his power and take control and inaugurate God's kingdom. Things would come to their proper conclusion. Judas was proactive. It is possible he was doing the wrong thing for the right reason.

But now the deed has been done. The authorities drag Christ before a nighttime court. The soldiers have beaten and bloodied him and left him exhausted from all that has gone before. Now at the break of day in the early morning mist while history hangs heavy in the air, the chief priests and elders of the people take counsel against Jesus to put him to death. They lead him away and hand him over to Pilate the governor.

When Judas sees that Jesus has been condemned, he is seized with remorse and returns the money to the chief priests and elders. "I have sinned," he says. "I have betrayed innocent blood." In the early morning hours while Peter weeps over his own betrayal of Jesus, Judas sees the immensity of *his* deed. In an attempt to undo what he has done, he takes a number of steps. He tries to fix it. His heart is breaking, his eyes have left him with an indelible image of a man who has done nothing but treat him with kindness. And his deed has now brought him to the lowest point in his life. When Judas sees that Jesus has been condemned, he realizes that what he has done cannot be undone. Things have gone too far. He is gripped to the depth of his soul.

It can be a watershed moment in your life when you summon the courage to acknowledge to yourself what you have done to hurt others. When you peel back the layers of self-deceit and come face to face with who you are and what you have done, you realize that you have grieved the heart of God. And in that moment, your own heart is grieved with remorse.

It seems that the world in which we live is in short supply of remorse. Our culture is awash with people who act brazenly and feel no remorse for anything. Judas felt remorse. Everything had gone awry. But he didn't merely feel remorse. He acted. He realigned his priorities. He brought the money back. He was penitent. He wanted to make amends.

As Matthew tells it, I wonder if Judas, when he was initially conspiring to betray Jesus, did not envision and certainly did not intend that it would lead to Jesus's death. It's like the petty thief who never intends that his burglary will lead to murder, or like most of us who never imagine how one disobedient decision can lead us down paths we never could anticipate with consequences we could never envision.

The text from Matthew gives us a glimpse into both Judas's heart and his actions. As to his heart, we are told that he was "filled with remorse." The dictionary defines remorse as "deep and painful regret over wrongdoing." This is the very thing we are called to as followers of Jesus. What is required of anyone who would leave a life of sin and come to Christ? The answer: *repentance and contrition*. Repentance involves a complete change of mind. Contrition involves godly sorrow for our sins. If Judas does not meet these requirements, who does?

Kind David did, of course. He confessed and acknowledged, "Against you, you alone have I sinned and done what is evil in your sight." Simon Peter was also filled with remorse and wept bitterly at his betrayal of Jesus. But Peter and King David were both restored. So what is the difference between them and Judas? As far as I can tell, simply this: *Judas lost all hope that he could be forgiven and restored.* I'm no expert on suicide. But surely one of the chief reasons people end their lives must be that they have lost hope. They see no way forward.

The consequences of our sin most assuredly affect other people. Judas knew it. But what else could he do? He couldn't turn back the clock, so he gave back the thirty pieces of silver. He did what he could. He came to the chief priest, and he said: "I know what I've done!" He came to his sin.

The great need in our world today is for us to take personal responsibility, to get to the root of our sin, and to repent. It's the great need in our marriages, in our homes, in our workplaces, and in our churches. Like the younger son in Jesus's famous parable, we must come to that moment in life where we "come to ourselves," where we acknowledge that *we* are to blame for the mess we have made of our lives. We are rebels. We desperately need God's mercy and forgiveness.

Judas came to himself. He accepted his personal responsibility for what he had done to Jesus. He did not play the victim card. He didn't blame the unfairness of the disciples, or the jealousy they may have had for him because of his position. He didn't blame Christ. He said, "No, this is about what *I* have done." He accepted personal responsibility for his actions.

The tragedy in this story is not merely Judas's betrayal of Jesus. The tragedy is that Judas came to every single person *but* Jesus to try to put things right. The weight of his sin diminished his hope in God's mercy. He may have felt that it was impossible for him to be forgiven. So Judas did what many of us do when we have sinned against God's grace. We withdraw from Jesus in the very moment when we should flee to him. We fail to see that contrition for our sin and confidence in his mercy are not mutually exclusive. The grief caused by our sins can co-exist with confidence in God and the peace of God in our souls. A heart broken into pieces by sorrow can also experience undiminished confidence in God's mercy. Saint Therese of Lisieux discovered this truth firsthand:

> This I know very well: although I should have on my soul all the crimes that could be committed, I would lose none of my confidence; rather, I would hasten, with my heart broken into pieces by sorrow, to cast myself into the arms of my Savior. I know how greatly He loved the prodigal son; I have marked His words to Mary Magdalen, to the adulterous woman, to the Samaritan. No, no one could make me afraid, because I know to whom to cling by reason of His love and His mercy. I know that all this multitude of offenses would disappear in the twinkling of an eye, as a drop of water cast into a roaring furnace.[1]

If we could rewrite history, how would we tell Judas's story? Let us imagine the cross and the bleeding, broken Christ hanging upon it. Let us picture this pitiful broken man Judas, who has committed no legal crime. He falls to the foot of the cross that runs red with the blood of the Christ. He says, "I've gone to everybody but you. Jesus, would you forgive me?"

Had he done that, I am convinced that our New Testament would contain a twenty-eighth book. Somewhere between Matthew and Mark and Luke and John you would find *the Gospel according to St. Judas*, and it would be the greatest story of grace that you've ever read.[2]

The Gospel according to Judas. It could have happened. It didn't. But the good news is this: It can still happen for us. God's mercy and compassion are boundless, and Jesus stands ready to forgive us for the messes we've made and the pain we've caused. An old hymn says,

> There's a wideness in God's mercy like the wideness of the sea;
> There's a kindness in His justice which is more than liberty.
> For the love of God is broader than the measure of man's mind,
> And the heart of the eternal is most wonderfully kind.[3]

We desperately stand in need of the Savior's forgiveness. But sometimes in life we come to believe that we have gone too far, that we have made such a mess of things that there is no possible way that Christ could forgive us for

---

1. Martinez, *Worshipping a Hidden God*, 39–40.

2. This was the subject of a sermon delivered by the Rev. Chuck Millhuff in September, 1993, at College Church of the Nazarene in Olathe, Kansas. This chapter is indebted to Rev. Millhuff's sermon.

3. Frederick William Faber, "There's a Wideness in God's Mercy," public domain.

what we have done. We come to believe that the best years of our lives have been wasted, that Jesus could not find anything in us that is worthwhile. This may especially be the case where others have shunned us or written us off because of our past mistakes. You may be reading this and thinking the same thing and asking the question: Why me? Why would Jesus forgive me? What possible good could he see in me?

A marvelous answer to that question is found in John 4, the story of an encounter between Jesus and a woman at Jacob's well near Sychar. John tells us that the woman was a Samaritan, known as bitter enemies of the Jews because of their mixed heredity.[4]

The fact that Jesus would initiate a conversation with a woman, and a Samaritan woman at that, violated all customs of the day. There is quite a subtext here. We must remember that in Jesus's day, singles' bars had not been invented. Instead, the primary gathering places were often wells. Wells were the original "watering holes" where folks gathered, especially women, because drawing water was considered women's work. When Jesus's disciples are perplexed that Jesus is talking to this woman there is reason for their concern, because in that day wells were often places where betrothals occurred. In the Old Testament, for example, two of Israel's patriarchs—Isaac and Jacob—found their wives at wells. So did Moses.

Given the underlying dynamics at work in this encounter between Jesus and this woman, it was interesting to me to discover that historically the church has looked on this story and found a romance in it. It sees Christ in search of his bride, the church. When Jesus says, "Give me a drink," it is not merely a request for water. It is the Bridegroom searching for his lover. God is thirsty for sinners.

This is demonstrated by the additional context of the story. This Samaritan woman was at the well *alone*, at around noon, during the heat of the day. The customary time of day when women went to draw water from wells was either early in the morning or early in the evening, when it was cooler. And women usually went to draw water in groups, not alone.

Why, then, is this woman here at the well at the warmest time of the day, alone? It is likely because of her life circumstances. She has had five husbands, and the man she currently lives with is not her husband. While that may not cause anyone to blink twice today, in the first century it was scandalous. And the rather public nature of her lifestyle came with the corresponding public shame and stigma. When the New Testament refers to

---

4. The Samaritans were Jews who had intermarried with gentiles from the Northern territories of Israel after the Assyrian invasion during the sixth century BC.

Jesus eating with "tax collectors and sinners," the word "sinners" described people like this woman.

So it is possible that this woman is at the well alone in the heat of the day because she is trying to avoid the shame and condescension aimed at her by those who looked down on her because of her circumstances. Noon would be the time of day when you were least likely to encounter others at the well. Some ancient sources even referred to noon as "the devil's hour." And yet, here sits a Jewish man resting at this well in the noonday heat. Of all people, why was this half-breed "sinful" woman the one so privileged to have this life-changing conversation with Jesus?

The answer is simple if we are willing to see it. The reason this woman was privileged to encounter Jesus is the same reason Jesus seeks you and me: Because he loves us and wants to pour his grace and mercy out upon us. He thirsts for relationship with us. He seeks us out to give us a gift that we can never merit. Notice what Jesus says to her: "If you knew the gift God has for you and who I am, you would ask me, and I would give you living water."[5]

When the woman fails to understand the full import of these words, Jesus continues:

> People soon become thirsty again after drinking this water. But the water I give them takes away thirst altogether. It becomes a perpetual spring within them, giving them eternal life.[6]

It isn't water and food that Jesus is seeking. He's hunting for people who, without even knowing it, are seeking for him. His hunger and thirst are satiated by the faith of sinners. The Bridegroom rejoices in his bride.

Consider all the metaphorical wells that modern people find themselves at today, searching for meaning and purpose in their lives. Some find themselves at the well of drugs and alcohol, seeking meaning or relief in a bottle or pill. If only they knew the gift of God, they could ask of him, and he would give them what they truly seek.

There are countless ones today who are at the well of online addiction, seeking fulfillment that only a God-ordained relationship can give them in the counterfeit of pornography. If only they knew the gift of God, they could ask him, and discover the true fulfillment they seek.

There are untold numbers of people today who are at the well of money and material things, thinking that those things can satisfy the deep thirst in their souls. If only they knew the gift of God, they could ask him, and satisfy their thirst through his love that cannot be bought or sold.

---

5. John 4:10 NLT.
6. John 4:13–14 NLT.

And others today are at the well of prestige and recognition, seeking to "be somebody." If only they knew the gift of God, they could ask him, and discover their true identity in the One who appeared at Jacob's well.

If only we knew the gift of God. We may have made a mess of life. We may have hurt ourselves and others in terrible ways. We may have betrayed those close to us, and in so doing have betrayed Jesus. We wonder how and why Christ could ever forgive and restore us. But Jesus believes in lost causes. Jesus thirsts for sinners, broken people like you and me who have spurned his love and betrayed his friendship. Pope Francis reminds us that Jesus demonstrates his pity toward us chiefly in showing mercy:

> Your loving gaze freed Zacchaeus and Matthew
> from being enslaved by money;
> the adulteress and Magdalene from seeking happiness
> only in created things;
> made Peter weep after his betrayal,
> and assured Paradise to the repentant thief.
> Let us hear, as if addressed to each one of us,
> the words that you spoke to the Samaritan woman:
> "If you knew the gift of God!"[7]

We cannot go back and rewrite history. We cannot undo Judas's tragic actions. But we can learn from him. We learn from Judas that the only difference between his betrayal and Peter's betrayal was that Judas apparently lost hope that he could be restored and forgiven. If only he knew the gift of God, the mercy that poured forth from Jesus as he hung on the cross on Good Friday. There's a wideness in that mercy that extends all the way to us.

7. See "Year of Mercy Prayer."

Easter

Chapter Eighteen

On Finding and Being Found

I have wandered all my life, and I have also traveled; the difference between the two being this, that we wander for distraction, but we travel for fulfillment.

—HILAIRE BELLOC

SUGGESTED READINGS

Acts 9:1–19; Ps 33:1–11; Rev 5:6–14; John 21:1–14

THE ANCIENT CHURCH FATHER Tertullian is said to have remarked that the blood of the martyrs is the seed of the church. Perhaps this was because the manner in which many Christians died for their faith actually served to increase the growth of Christianity rather than suppress it.

Indeed, Tertullian's words have been proven true historically, dating all the way back to the first century and the book of the Acts of the Apostles. The pattern can be seen beginning in Acts 7. There, a man named Stephen holds the religious leaders accountable for Jesus's death and is stoned to death by a violent mob as a young man named Saul watches on and approves.

Stephen's death becomes the catalyst for a great persecution that erupts against those who believe in Jesus. At the center of this storm is a young man named Saul from Tarsus. He is hell-bent on tracking believers down and punishing them. We are told at the beginning of chapter 8, subsequent to Stephen's death:

> But Saul laid waste the church, and entering house after house, he dragged off men and women and committed them to prison.[1]

In chapter 9, we learn more of Saul's activity:

> But Saul, still breathing threats and murder against the disciples of the Lord, went to the high priest and asked him for letters to the synagogues at Damascus, so that if he found any belonging to the Way, men or women, he might bring them bound to Jerusalem.[2]

This story dramatically portrays Saul's murderous pursuit and arrest of Christians. However, if we look more closely, we discover that this is not just a story of Saul pursuing and arresting Christians. *This is a story of Christ pursuing and arresting Saul!* Saul, in his zeal to hunt down followers of Jesus, discovers on the Damascus Road that Jesus is hunting *him*! Eugene Peterson translates the text like this:

> When he [Saul] got to the outskirts of Damascus, he was suddenly dazed by a blinding flash of light. As he fell to the ground, he heard a voice: "Saul, Saul, why are you out to get me?"
>   He said, "Who are you, Master?"
>   "I am Jesus, the One you're hunting down."[3]

The irony is palpable. The stoning of Stephen and Saul's zealous pursuit of Christians launched a great persecution that forced believers to flee from Jerusalem and spread out to Judea and Samaria. Forced to leave home base, the Christians all became missionaries. And now, Jesus is going to use the very man whose persecution started the spread of the gospel outward from Jerusalem to be a vital part of continuing that message. He will be the one who will take the message to gentiles, and to kings. Saul's zealous pursuit of Christians becomes the zealous pursuit of the upward call of God in Christ Jesus, as he sees that the One whom he pursued was actually pursuing him!

What is true of Paul is also true of each of us. Evangelical Christians often speak of "coming to Christ," or "finding Christ," or "accepting Christ." But if we learn anything from Saul of Tarsus, we learn that we don't actually "find" Christ—Christ finds *us*. We do not come to Christ—Christ comes to

---

1. Acts 8:3 RSV.
2. Acts 9:1 RSV.
3. Acts 9:3–5 MSG.

us. The only sense in which we find Christ is in response to his relentless pursuit of us.

There is another illustration of this in chapter 10 of John's Gospel. Jesus engages the Pharisees in a conversation that perplexes and upsets them. Using the image of a shepherd, Jesus observes, "Truly, truly, I say to you, he who does not enter the sheepfold by the door but climbs in by another way, that man is a thief and a robber."[4] John then says that the Pharisees don't understand what Jesus means, so Jesus continues: "I am the door of the sheep; all who came before me are thieves and robbers, but the sheep did not heed them."[5]

At this point, the Pharisees are not the only ones who need help understanding Jesus. We can partly understand that Jesus is the Good Shepherd, but what does he mean by saying that all who came before him are thieves and robbers?

The answer is found by traveling back to the Old Testament. In this case, we must return to the prophet Ezekiel. Midway through his ministry, the prophet speaks a harsh word of rebuke to the priests of Israel, who had become corrupt. He says:

> Thus says the LORD God: Ho, shepherds of Israel, who have been feeding yourselves! Should not shepherds feed the sheep? You eat the fat, you clothe yourselves with the wool, you slaughter the fatlings; but you do not feed the sheep. The weak you have not strengthened, the sick you have not healed, the crippled you have not bound up, the strayed you have not brought back, the lost you have not sought, and with force and harshness you have ruled them. So they were scattered because there was no shepherd; and they became food for all the wild beasts. My sheep were scattered . . . over all the face of the earth, with none to search or seek for them.[6]

When Jesus says that all who came before him were thieves and robbers, he is speaking about the priests under the Old Covenant who became corrupt and who did not nurture the spiritual lives of God's people. As a result, the sheep were scattered. They were taken into exile by the Assyrians and Babylonians and wound up being dispersed throughout the world. This displeased the Lord greatly. So God decided to take action. Here is how Ezekiel describes it:

4. John 10:1 RSV.
5. John 10:7–8 RSV.
6. Ezek 34:2–6 RSV.

> For thus says the LORD God: Behold, I, I myself will search for
> my sheep, and will seek them out. As a shepherd seeks out his
> flock when some of his sheep have been scattered abroad, so will
> I seek out my sheep; and I will rescue them from all places where
> they have been scattered on a day of thick clouds and darkness.[7]

The priests under the Old Covenant failed in their duty to shepherd
God's people. Their corruption created a spiritual wasteland which led to
sin and disobedience. Sin and disobedience led to captivity, and the people
were scattered abroad. So, says Ezekiel, God himself is going to come looking for them. God himself is going to rescue them on a day of thick clouds
and darkness.

Wait a minute. Day of thick clouds and darkness? What's that all about?

Well, a few hundred years after Ezekiel delivers his prophecy, there
came a day where darkness covered the earth from the sixth hour to the
ninth hour. Do you remember that day? It was the day a man cried out, "My
God, my God, why have you forsaken me?"

When God spoke through Ezekiel and said that God himself would
come and seek out his scattered sheep and rescue them on a day of thick
clouds and darkness, he wasn't kidding:

> I myself will be the shepherd of my own sheep, and I will make
> them lie down, says the LORD God. I will seek the lost, I will
> bind up the crippled, and I will strengthen the weak. . . . And I
> will set up over them one shepherd, my servant David, and he
> shall feed them; he shall feed them and be their shepherd. And
> I, the LORD, will be their God, and my servant David shall be
> prince among them. I, the LORD, have spoken.[8]

In his discussion with the Pharisees in John's Gospel, Jesus takes the
words of the prophet Ezekiel and applies them to himself. He is the loving
Shepherd sent from God to rescue God's scattered people. He is the One sent
from God to gather in the twelve tribes of Israel who have been dispersed.
He is the true Son of David, the loving Shepherd sent to rescue God's people
and to lead them to New Covenant pastures of abundant life. When he hangs
on a cross outside Jerusalem and the earth turns dark, Ezekiel's prophecy is
fulfilled and their rescue is set in motion. The loving Shepherd who comes to
lead God's people is not just the Messiah, it is God himself in the flesh.

But there is more. Just a few verses after this passage in John's Gospel,
Jesus says that he has "other sheep not of this fold" that he must bring into his

---

7. Ezek 34:11–12 RSV.
8. Ezek 34:15–16, 23–24 RSV.

care also. This describes all of us. The Good Shepherd seeks out not just the lost sheep of the house of Israel, but all lost sheep everywhere! The apostle Peter alludes to this in his epistle to Christians in Asia Minor. Writing to people converted out of paganism, he says, "For you were straying like sheep, but have now returned to the Shepherd and Guardian of your souls."[9]

This is supremely good news. As the Good Shepherd, Jesus shows us the heart of God that pursues us and seeks us out in order to bring us into his fold and restore us to relationship with him. He pursues us not to devour us, but to bind up our wounds, to carry us in his arms, to heal what is broken in us. He pursues us in order to help us to lay aside our counterfeit substitutes for peace and happiness and exchange them for the real thing. He pursues us, not merely to give us life, but to share his life with us.

Francis Thompson experienced this truth firsthand. Thompson was the son of a British doctor who grew up in a Roman Catholic home. In many respects, his early life appeared to be one failure after another. He studied for the priesthood but did not complete his studies. He joined the military but was quickly released. He studied medicine but failed his medical exams. Depressed, ill, and poor, he became addicted to opium.

During this time, Thompson submitted two poems for publication to Wilfred Meynell, a London magazine editor. Meynell recognized Thompson's literary talent and published the poems, which won the commendation of Robert Browning.

In one of his poems, Thompson tells the story of a fugitive sinner seeking to escape the relentless pursuit of God's love in his life:

> I fled him, down the nights and down the days;
> I fled Him, down the arches of the years;
> I fled Him, down the labyrinthine ways
> Of my own mind; and in the midst of tears
> I hid from Him, and under running laughter,
> Up vistaed hopes I sped;
> And shot, precipitated,
> Adown titanic glooms of chasmed fears,
> From those strong feet that followed, followed after,
> But with unhurrying chase,
> And unperturbed pace,
> Deliberate speed, majestic instancy,
> They beat—and a voice beat
> More instant than the feet—
> "All things betray thee, who betrayest Me."[10]

9. 1 Pet 2:25 RSV.

10. Thompson, quoted in Comfort and Partner, *One Year Book of Poetry*, May 8.

The poet speaks autobiographically, and we recognize in these words the famous "hound of heaven."

I love this story, and this poem. I love it because I suspect that most of us are less like the apostle Paul and more like the disciples immediately following Jesus's resurrection. We don't have any lingering vendettas against Jesus. We're not angrily pursuing an agenda to bring Jesus down. We're more like Peter, James, John, and the others who have failed Jesus, and our sense of guilt and shame and fear drives us to the place where we feel that our only option is to return to old ways of being and doing. At times, we run because we fear that God wants to rob us of our happiness and freedom.

We remember bygone days when we heard Jesus calling us, inviting us to walk with him on his journey. We felt the rush of what it was like for him to pursue us. But after trying and failing so many times and in so many ways, we wonder whether Jesus has left us behind and moved on to other things. As we ponder these questions, we find Jesus waiting for us. He is the Good Shepherd. He cares for every sheep that becomes lost. His pursuit of us is relentless. His grace reaches lower than our worst mistakes. His love runs faster and farther than our ability to run away.

This is the Easter message. Wherever you are, wherever you have been, whatever direction your life has taken, the secret to life isn't about "finding yourself." The secret to life is in *being found*. And the One who pursues you is Jesus, the Living One.

As you are reading this, perhaps you have been brought to a pivotal moment in your life. You've been running from God, perhaps evading Christ's loving call to you for years. The reasons are many. But in this moment filled with grace, none of them make sense anymore. His love is here to catch you, to embrace you, to forgive you. His mercy is bringing healing to you in this moment, giving you a new start. Stop running. Turn your heart toward home. Repent, and believe the gospel.

Chapter Nineteen

When God Lets You Down

Sometimes the only way God can gain access to our hearts is to break them open.

—Fulton Sheen

SUGGESTED READINGS

Acts 2:14, 36–47; Ps 116:10–17; 1 Pet 1:17–23; Luke 24:13–35

THE STORY IN THE twenty-fourth chapter of Luke's Gospel is unique to Luke and reveals a fascinating encounter between Jesus and two of his disciples several hours after Jesus's resurrection. It happens on the road to Emmaus, a village about seven miles from Jerusalem. This story has become one of my favorite stories in the New Testament.

The narrative unfolds in four parts. On the Sunday after Jesus's crucifixion, two disciples of Jesus find themselves walking the long road from Jerusalem to Emmaus, sad and dejected. Trapped in the tragedy of Good Friday, they keep playing the events of that day over in their minds as they travel.

As they walk, they are joined by a man who engages them in conversation. We know it is Jesus, but they do not. Their eyes are kept from recognizing him. They are blinded by despair. When Jesus inquires as to the nature of their conversation, they are shocked at his question. What is *everyone* in

Jerusalem talking about? Cleopas, one of the men, says to Jesus: "Are you the only visitor to Jerusalem who does not know the things that have just happened there?"

The humor in this exchange should not be lost on us. We are allowed to see the situation from God's perspective. The two disciples think that the man walking alongside them is clueless, but Jesus was the only one who had a clue! "Are you the only one who does not know?" Actually, Jesus is the only one who *does* know. He is the only one who understands the events in their proper context, in the long sweep of salvation history. Jesus sees that despair has darkened the intellects of these men, so he addresses the situation. He speaks bluntly and clearly: "O foolish men, and slow of heart to believe all that the prophets have spoken!"

This brings the men to attention, but Jesus is not finished. He then "interprets to them in all the Scriptures the things concerning himself." He takes them on a tour through their Scriptures in order to show them the necessity of a suffering Messiah. Then, while they are seated at table in Emmaeus, he reveals himself to them in the breaking of the bread. This propels the two disciples back to Jerusalem with burning hearts.

One of the reasons this story is so endearing to me is because of how it resonates with my own life experience. I love this story because of four little words that are sandwiched at its midpoint: *But we had hoped.*

So much is said in these four little words that can describe our lives today. They may speak of a deeply longed for future that is not to be. They may speak of a dream that energized us and created enthusiasm but did not materialize. They may speak of a promise that created faith but proved to be false. They speak of a future that is now closed off, irrelevant, dead. And few things are more tragic than a dead and hopeless future.

Ernest Hemingway was once challenged to create a short story in six words. He is said to have written, "For sale: baby shoes, never used." Sometimes in life, it's not just the tragedy of what *happens* to us that hurts. Sometimes the pain comes from the gaping wound created by all that *could have happened* but won't. *We had hoped.*

In addition to death and taxes, disappointment is inevitable in life. No matter how carefully and intentionally we plan our course and pursue our goals, life often turns in a different direction. In the words of John Lennon, life is what happens to us while we're making other plans. Life happens to us, often in the form of loss, tragedy, and heartache.

As I write this, a mother and father in my hometown are laying to rest their fourteen-year-old son who died tragically in an automobile accident. His older brother was driving the vehicle and sustained life-threatening injuries and has undergone multiple surgeries. The vehicle the boys were in crashed head-on into a car driven by a woman on her way to work who was only weeks from retirement. She was life-flighted to an urban hospital, where she underwent multiple surgeries and suffered the loss of her left leg. For both of these families, life changed in the twinkling of an eye.

When things happen to us in life that seem unfair and inexplicable, our disappointment is often directed at God. How could this happen? Why me? Where is God in this mess? Author Phillip Yancey spent several years interviewing people and learning of their painful experiences. The fruit of his research became his popular book, *Disappointment with God*. Yancey wrote the book, he says, "for victims of overwrought promises and dashed expectations."[1] The book is a lengthy tour through sacred Scripture in an attempt to explore God's perceived silence and unfairness in the midst of life's trials and painful circumstances.

The insights Yancey shares are worthy of serious reflection, but he acknowledges that ultimately God will always seem unfair to us mortals who are trapped in time and who do not see things from God's point of view, what Yancey describes as the view "from above." God stands outside of time and sees what we cannot see. We would prefer that God roll up his sleeves and step into our lives and into the world with visible power. We would prefer that God not stay so hidden and silent, that he work in less mysterious ways. But a quick reading of the Old Testament would prove to us that even were God to do so, all is not solved, because his direct intervention in the lives of people there did not automatically lead to faith and obedience.

In a similar way, there is no possible explanation that God might offer that would satisfy us when we suffer life's defeats and disappointments. This is because God's definitive response to the question of unfairness was not with words, but with a *visit*, an incarnation. In Jesus, God entered into the vagaries of our human existence and suffered the ultimate unfairness. God responds to life's unfairness not by answering it, but by taking it into himself. Such is the stuff of mystery. Yancey observes:

> We remain ignorant and many of our questions of God go unanswered, not because God enjoys keeping us in the dark, but because we do not have the faculties to absorb so much light. Faith means believing in advance what will only make sense in reverse.[2]

In the wonderful story of the Emmaus Road, Luke tells us that the risen Jesus comes to two heartbroken disciples and walks alongside them

---

1. Yancey, *Disappointment with God*, 160.
2. Yancey, *Disappointment with God*, 223.

on the road. Astonished that they don't see as they ought, he opens and explains the Scriptures to them to help them understand their disappointment by placing it in its proper perspective. He helps them to see things from God's point of view, from above. He reveals his presence to them through bread and wine. And then he gets them back up on their feet and sends them back into the world with hearts that are on fire.

This is what Jesus seeks to do with all of his disciples each week as the church gathers for worship. Jesus comes alongside the gathered community, patient with us when we don't see as we ought to see. He teaches us the Scriptures and reveals himself through bread and wine so that we might be sent forth back into our neighborhoods and workplaces with hearts that are alive and on fire.

This incident on the road to Emmaus leads to a question: Could we be a people who could do for others what Jesus did for these disciples? Could our churches be clinics that are equipped to treat peoples' broken hearts? Could we be a people whose hearts are sensitive and whose ears are ready to listen when people say to us: *We had hoped*? Could our churches be places where persons are allowed to share their disappointment that the cancer has returned, the beloved has died, the addiction is persisting, the children have walked away, the job did not materialize, the family has rejected them, and that people in the church have hurt them instead of helped?

In the experience of these two brokenhearted men I see myself, and I realize that quite often in my life my heart has first been *broken* before it could *burn*. These two disciples needed permission to grieve a future that would never materialize in order that they might hear and receive the future God had created and prepared for them. In their disappointed state they could not envision the joy and happiness that awaited them on the far side of their heartbreaking circumstances.

When I read the story of Joseph in the Old Testament, I cannot help but wonder whether Joseph experienced similar disappointment and sadness as a result of what happened to him at various places in his journey. His brothers actually contemplate killing him but end up throwing him into a pit instead because of the foresight of Reuben, one of the brothers. As a caravan of Ishmaelites passes by, they sell Joseph to them for twenty sheckels of silver. What began as an innocent trip to check on his brothers as they pastured the flocks near Shechem ends with Joseph enslaved in Egypt to Potiphar, an officer of Pharaoh.

God is with Joseph in the midst of this mess, however, and soon Potiphar puts Joseph in charge of his entire household. As Joseph seeks to make the best of what has happened to him, Potiphar's wife tries to seduce him. When he refuses her advances, she accuses him of raping her, which lands him in prison. I wonder if he thought to himself in prison: "I had hoped that things were improving in my life, but I guess not. I thought that God was helping me, but here I am in prison for doing the right thing."

Soon after Joseph is put into prison, the butler and baker of the king of Egypt are thrown into prison with him. When they experience dreams but cannot discern their meaning, Joseph interprets the dreams for them. The butler is released and restored to his position. Joseph does what you and I would do in this situation: he asks the butler to remember him before Pharaoh, to speak kindly about how Joseph has helped him. But when the butler is released and restored to his position, he forgets Joseph. It would be two long years before the butler would finally remember Joseph to Pharaoh. I can't speak for Joseph, but those years would have been a time of profound disappointment for me, a time where I likely would have felt abandoned by God.

As we read Joseph's story, we have the benefit of seeing it "from above," from the perspective of the God who was orchestrating events in Joseph's life not merely for his benefit but for the salvation and deliverance of many. Joseph's temporal vision may not have been able to see (at least immediately) how God was present with him as he was sold into slavery, wrongly accused and imprisoned, and forgotten by those who could have helped him. Viewed "from below," it was a most discouraging picture. The view "from above," however, revealed a much different reality. God was orchestrating events and bringing good from Joseph's calamitous situation. I'm not sure at what point in his painful and trying circumstances God allows Joseph to see what has happened to him "from above," but by the end of the story Joseph has been graced with this perspective, as he states to his brothers:

> Do not be distressed, or angry with yourselves, because you sold me here; for God sent me before you to preserve life . . . it was not you who sent me here, but God; and he had made me a father to Pharaoh, and lord of all his house and ruler over all the land of Egypt. . . . Fear not, for am I in the place of God? As for you, you meant evil against me; but God meant it for good, to bring it about that many people should be kept alive, as they are today.[3]

When we are disappointed and disillusioned, it is hard to trust that God is orchestrating the events of our life in a meaningful way. When we are living the painful events, when we are in the eye of the storm, it is hard to see beyond that. We don't yet have the benefit of hindsight that gives us the needed perspective to see those events in a larger context. Our painful

3. Gen 45:5–6, 8; 50:19–20 RSV.

circumstances trap us into seeing only "from below." But with time and distance, we begin to see "from above." As we do, we are able to add a "but God" to the narrative. Joseph's insight becomes our insight. The painful and messed up experiences of the past come into sharper focus with the benefit of time and God's supernatural grace acting upon us.

When we were first married, my wife Connie enjoyed working on counted cross-stitch pictures. Some time after our children were born, she decided to make a cross-stitch Christmas stocking for each member of the family. The project was very labor-intensive, consuming vast amounts of time as the stockings were quite large and the pattern on each was very detailed. I watched with fascination as each stocking took shape. When the first one was almost finished, Connie handed me the large hoop stretched tightly around the fabric. As I took it, I was looking at the underside of the fabric. It was a jumbled, intricate, and by all appearances a haphazard mess. But when I turned the hoop right-side up, the picture was stunning. I was captivated by the detail and the handiwork. The view from the underside, "from below," was an incoherent, tangled mass of thread. But the view "from above," from the top side, was a beautifully crafted work of art.

There are times in life when our view "from below" is almost incoherent. Times when tragedy strikes out of nowhere. Times when relationships fall apart, when disease robs us of health in the prime of life. Times when everything we touch turns to dust. Times when we can't seem to catch a break. Times when the very foundation crumbles, when everything we trust in for security is taken from us.

In such times, know this: God isn't finished writing your story. Weeping may endure for the night, but joy comes in the morning. You may be knocked down, but by God's grace, you cannot be knocked out. God is at work in the details of your life, even when you don't see it. When you love him and are seeking to do his will, he works in every situation to bring good from it. This was Joseph's testimony when, by faith, he saw the events in his life "from above" and was able to tell his brothers, "What you meant for evil, God meant for good." With the help of the Holy Spirit, we can view our circumstances as Joseph viewed his—with tenacious trust that God has the final word, and that he is bringing our story to a good and gracious end. This is the powerful and life-changing truth of Easter.

Chapter Twenty

Notes in the Mailbox

Pursuing the will of God ultimately means pursuing God Himself.

—Jack Hayford

The Lord does not give us grace for our lives before we live them.
He promises sufficient grace, not perpetual assurance.

—Michael Scanlon

SUGGESTED READINGS

Acts 4:23–31; Ps 100; 1 John 3:1–8; John 10:11–16

ONE OF THE MOST prominent images used of Jesus in the New Testament is that of the shepherd. The fourth Sunday of the Easter season is known as "Good Shepherd" Sunday in many traditions, and many of the Scriptural lessons for that day focus on the image of the shepherd and on God's shepherding role in our lives.

The picture we see in Ps 100, John 10, and numerous other passages like Ps 23 and Isa 40, is a picture of a shepherd gently leading his sheep, and it evokes emotional images of God's leading and direction in our own lives. As nice as these images are, they have also been the source of much frustration for me, especially at times where I have struggled to discern God's specific will and direction for my life. I know that Ps 23 talks of the shepherd restoring the soul, making us lie down by quiet waters, and leading us in paths of righteousness for his Name's sake. But I stopped counting long ago the number of times in my life where I said, "If the Good Shepherd is leading me, then why do I feel like I don't have a clue where I'm going?"

Several years ago an informal book club in my congregation met to discuss William Paul Young's book *The Shack*. In the book, the protagonist receives a note from God in his mailbox summoning him to a life-altering weekend where he confronts the pain in his life that resulted following the tragic murder of his young daughter. At one point in our discussion one of the members spoke up and said, "I wish God would put a note in *my* mailbox, because I want to do what God wants, but it's hard to know what that is."

I suspect that many followers of Jesus might empathize with that sentiment. It seems that life would be so much easier if, after praying to God for guidance or assistance, we could hear his answers directly. While there are undoubtedly times in life where God provides clear and direct impressions of what should be done in a given situation, in my experience those occasions are rare.[1] Often, discerning God's will in specific cases involves a process of deciding between numerous and at times competing options which are good or morally neutral. We listen for God, hoping to hear his voice in a powerful wind, in an earthquake, or in a blazing fire. But instead, we hear only a tiny whispering wind (1 Kgs 19:11–13). So I'm not immune from asking: Wouldn't it be nice if God would tell us directly what to do regarding specific and important decisions in our lives? How nice it would be to wake up in the morning, trundle out to your mailbox, and find a note that said

* Pursue *this* job or vocation
* Marry *that* person
* Live in *that* city or country
* Pursue *this* opportunity

---

1. I concede that examples of direct revelation are found in Scripture, such as when Moses spoke with God face-to-face (Exod 33:11), or when the apostles were able to inquire of Jesus directly about various and sundry issues. And I acknowledge that saints and mystics have testified to having direct and immediate encounters with God, such as John of the Cross and Theresa of Avila. But in the normative course of things, each of us is called to choose between several paths when discerning God's will. The key is not having a direct line to God, but in being obedient to his will once we discern it. See Esper, "Seek the Lord's Will."

I readily admit that more than a few times in my life I have looked up to heaven, exasperated, and said: "God, please just tell me what to do, and I'll do it." I know that doing God's will is of utmost importance. I agree with Saint Ambrose, who is said to have remarked, "The will of God is the measure of all things." So if God's will is of paramount significance, why isn't it clear and easy? Why do I often feel so lost?

Reading numerous texts from both the Old and New Testaments makes me wonder if maybe the problem is not with God as much as it is with how I think about God's leading in my life. For instance, in John's Gospel Jesus says,

> To him [the true shepherd] the gatekeeper opens; the sheep hear his voice, and he calls his own sheep by name and leads them out. When he has brought out all his own, he goes before them and the sheep follow him, for they know his voice. A stranger they will not follow, but they will flee from him, for they do not know the voice of strangers.[2]

When I think about God's leading in my life I typically think about Jesus leading me by being *out in front* of me and calling on me to follow. But this is not the only way that shepherds lead their flocks. Dr. Laura Mendenhall tells a story of her experience living in West Texas, and of a friend of hers who is a rancher and a real shepherd. His name is Tom. Speaking of her friend, the shepherd, she says:

> Tom treats his sheep like family. Tom does not usually shout to his sheep about anything. Sometimes he sings to them. They follow him, not because of his authoritative directions, but because they trust his voice. Tom is not usually out in front of them, but rather behind them.[3]

Dr. Mendenhall then continues:

> We may sometimes be frustrated when we are unable to see Jesus. But most of the time, Jesus is leading from behind, picking us up when we get into trouble, encouraging us to go ahead and trust what we know. We are just as vulnerable as the sheep, and Jesus leads us through our challenges [from behind].[4]

Reading these words was an epiphany for me. I often struggle with God's leading in my life because I want Jesus to be *out ahead* of me. I want a direct

---

2. John 10:3–5 RSV.

3. Mendenhall, "Led from Behind," 38.

4. Mendenhall, "Led from Behind," 39.

order about specific decisions I need to make. I want a note in the mailbox. But God often has something else in mind. Jesus often chooses to lead me *from behind*. The proper path for my life is found not in having him dictate to me specific answers to specific questions, but in cultivating a relationship with him and learning to hear his voice.[5] The context of John 10 makes this clear, as does real-life shepherding.

In ancient Palestine, when night came shepherds needed to construct makeshift sheepfolds based on the materials they had available to them in their given location. They often looked for rock formations that formed an enclosure, but when that wasn't possible the shepherds would scour for brush and pile it up in a "U" shape. Then they would find thorny bushes and pile them on the top of the enclosure to prevent the sheep from trying to jump out and to make it harder for thieves to jump over the wall to steal them.

Once the enclosure was constructed the only way in and out of the fold was through a space the shepherd would leave open. When the sheep were safely enclosed the shepherd would lie across the opening, becoming the "door" or the "gate" in and out of the sheep fold. At night, many flocks of sheep would often come together and share the same fold. In the morning, each shepherd would take a position and begin calling his sheep out of the fold. The sheep would respond not so much to the words, but to the distinct *tone* of their shepherd's voice.

It is human nature for us to want Jesus to lead us and guide us by taking the lead, by being *out ahead of* us and saying, "Come here, go there, do this, do that." But God often declines to lead us this way. It is more often necessary for Jesus to lead us *from behind*, to allow us a measure of freedom to explore, to think, to choose, even to make mistakes.

Author Stacey Sumerau discovered a clue to how God works in these moments. Reflecting on her own experience, especially her frustration at why God wouldn't put a note in her mailbox, she says:

> The truth is, God wanted me to stay close to Him but choose for myself. He loves me like His child, not His servant. I would often ask God to just tell me His will. Instead, He would answer, "Do you know how much I love you?"[6]

The key here lies in the truth that God loves us as his children, not servants. He often refuses to dictate to us what to do because he wants us to choose

---

5. See Scanlon, *What Does God Want*, 95. See also Willard, *Hearing God*, 81–82. Willard correctly notes that when we try to force God to tell us something we encounter problems, because we cannot force a conversation. In a true conversation, we respect and wait and listen.

6. Sumerau, "Discerning Vocation," para. 13.

for ourselves, even if this means we follow a long, meandering path to do so. We can trust him either to speak to us or to let us figure things out for ourselves, according to what is best for us. Dallas Willard observes:

> With respect to many events in our future, God's will is that we should determine what will happen. What a child does when not told what to do is the final indicator of what and who that child is. And so it is for us and our heavenly Father.[7]

Jesus is concerned not just with individual choices we make, but with our desire to hear his voice amidst the clamor of so many other voices that would call to us. When Jesus leads from behind, it's our *relationship* with him that's critical. Individual choices are borne from the relationship. Jesus leads us and guides us and shepherds us from the heart of this relationship where he not only knows our names, but where he lays down his life for us. As he says earlier in John's Gospel, "The thief comes only to steal and to kill and to destroy. I came that they may have life, and have it abundantly."[8]

In leading us to abundant life, Jesus often shepherds us from behind. It is guidance borne from love, not coercion. But make no mistake. He *is* leading us. A passage from the prophet Isaiah recently reminded me of this. Isaiah informs disobedient Israel that punishment in the form of exile awaits them unless they repent and turn to God in renewed obedience. In spite of this, the promise of hope underlies Isaiah's message:

> Therefore the LORD waits to be gracious to you; therefore he exalts himself to show mercy to you. For the LORD is a God of justice; blessed are all those who wait for him. Yea, O people in Zion who dwell at Jerusalem; you shall weep no more. He will surely be gracious to you at the sound of your cry; when he hears it, he will answer you. And though the Lord give you the bread of adversity and the water of affliction, yet your Teacher will not hide himself any more, but your eyes shall see your Teacher. And your ears shall hear a word behind you, saying, "This is the way, walk in it," when you turn to the right or when you turn to the left.[9]

I have read this passage many times, but the prophet's announcement that "your ears shall hear a word *behind* you" made me sit up and take notice, especially in view of John's discussion of Jesus as the Good Shepherd and the method of many shepherds to lead their sheep from behind. Without

---

7. Willard, *Hearing God*, 82.
8. John 10:10 RSV.
9. Isa 30:18–21 RSV.

pressing Isaiah's image too far, when the voice of discernment is behind you it implies that you are being guided and led *from behind*, confirming and correcting your choices as you go along.

Jesus is our Guide, our Guardian, our Shepherd. And images from the Gospels and life experience remind us that all of our individual decisions in life are best made not when we look for a note in the mailbox, but when we listen closely for the sound of a voice. Consider Abraham. Abraham had been walking with the Lord and listening to his voice for decades before he took his son Isaac and set off for the three-day journey toward Mount Moriah. This was no harebrained scheme that came to Abraham on the spur of the moment in his head because it seemed "spiritual." Abraham was a man who knew the voice of his Lord. He had been listening to that voice and tuning his life to its frequency for years.

We, too, can learn to know that voice. But sometimes we struggle because we want to know specific details about our life and our future. We want to know in advance how things are going to work out for us. Sometimes God gives us some of the details, but most times he does not. God keeps his promises to us, but our life following Jesus doesn't usually unfold in the ways we imagine that it will. God's will in our lives will always be a beautifully progressive revelation. Jesus doesn't fill in many of the blanks. He doesn't reveal too much of what lies ahead on our road of faith. He simply promises to bless us with his presence if we step out in faith and follow him. In fact, I would go so far as to say that if you think you are convinced of the will of God for your life in some long-range, highly detailed plan that stretches out into the future, you should reconsider whether you have discerned the will of God. On the other hand, if you have an insistent sense that the next, very hesitant step beyond which you can see nothing is in fact the step that must be taken, that step is most likely the will of God for you.[10] The words of Saint John Henry Newman may be relevant here:

> Lead, kindly light, amid the encircling gloom,
> Lead Thou me on!
> The night is dark, and I am far from home—
> Lead Thou me on!
> Keep Thou my feet; I do not ask to see
> The distant scene—one step enough for me.[11]

Further, learning to discern God's voice is a daily venture. The path is not always predetermined or clear-cut. God's will is not a puzzle to be solved but a mystery to be lived into. It is a mystery whose contours emerge as we

10. Wright, *Rising*, 35.

11. Newman, "Pillar of the Cloud," stanza 1.

move forward in faith and journey onward.[12] It is discovered in the process of walking day by day and listening for the sound of Jesus's voice. Sometimes in our desire to know God's will we are so focused on getting to the "aha!" moment where everything falls into place that we miss the importance of *now*. But the truth is that if we are loving the people God has placed in front of us right now, we are in the right place and in his will. Our big milestones and major decisions grow and arise from these daily, smaller acts of love and obedience.

This means that each day we are faced with the question "What does God want from me *today*?" This question is not merely for those who are younger and whose lives are still out in front of them. Those of us who are older must remember that there is a place in the will of God for us at any age. Remember that Abraham was seventy-five years old when God tapped him on the shoulder. Moses became the leader of the nation of Israel at age eighty. Caleb was eighty-five when he was summoned to lead a great military expedition. The prophet Haggai was ninety when he proclaimed his powerful word from the Lord to rebuild the temple following the Babylonian exile. The aged Simeon held the infant Jesus in his arms and predicted the rising and falling of nations near the end of his life.

We may feel limited by our advancing years and our perceived weaknesses and inadequacies, but God is not limited by any of those things. The key for all of us is to listen to him daily, to train ourselves to discern our Shepherd's voice in the midst of numerous other competing voices crying out for our attention. One simple, but overlooked, method of training ourselves to hear Jesus's voice is the cultivation of silence in our lives. Work schedules, family responsibilities, and recreational activities crowd our days and leave precious little time for us to be alone with ourselves and with God. For decades now, we have inhabited a society where we are intent on amusing ourselves to death,[13] a phenomenon that has grown exponentially in the last decade with the expansion of new technology. It is increasingly difficult for us to abide silence, as demonstrated by the intentional avoidance of it in many services of worship.

Discerning God's will is difficult when our lives are so full of noise that we have no room to listen to him. The wisdom of the church through the ages reminds us that contemplation—learning to think and see like God—is best developed through silence. It is through silence that God's voice is often made known to us, most often in an inaudible way through a mental connection, a unique thought, or a sense of peace. When you are linked to God

12. Wright, *Rising*, 36.

13. See Postman, *Amusing Ourselves to Death.*

through consistent and contemplative prayer, you will be given the grace of clarity regarding what you are supposed to do with your life.[14]

When I was a student at Asbury Theological Seminary, I had the privilege of interviewing Dr. Dennis Kinlaw, then-president of Asbury University, as part of a course I was taking on preaching. Dr. Kinlaw was a respected Old Testament scholar and in high demand as a preacher. In the interview, I asked Dr. Kinlaw what, in his opinion, was the most essential ingredient in becoming an effective preacher. Without hesitating, he replied, "Every great preacher or communicator I have known has enjoyed great swatches of silence in his or her life." This wisdom is sound advice not only for preachers, but for all disciples of Jesus who strive to discern God's will and to do it faithfully.

14. Burdick, *Detached*, 75. See also Sarah, *The Power of Silence*.

Chapter Twenty-One

Friendship with Jesus

*Friendship marks a life even more deeply than love. Love risks
degenerating into obsession, friendship is never anything but sharing.*

—ELIE WIESEL

SUGGESTED READINGS

Acts 17:22–31; Ps 148:7–14; 1 Pet 3:8–18; John 15:1–17

I'VE HEARD MANY SERMONS from John 15 and preached a few myself. I've
preached about Jesus's familiar words, "abide in me." And I've preached
about Jesus's well-known command, "Love one another, as I have loved you."

However, I have never fully explored the latter portion of this text
where Jesus says, "I no longer call you *servants*, because a servant does not
know his master's business. Instead, I have called you *friends*, for everything
that I learned from my Father I have made known to you." I have always
steered clear of these words of Jesus. I'm not sure why, because it seems like
such an attractive and pleasant text. To be called a friend of Jesus seems like
an incomparable gift.

Perhaps my reluctance to pursue this text more earnestly stems from
something that happened many years ago while I was a graduate student.

173

I encountered part of a sermon given by an elderly African-American preacher. His text was Jas 2:23, which says "Abraham was a friend of God." I remember the preacher saying: "Abraham was a friend of God—but I'm sure glad *I'm* not a friend of God." The preacher captivated and confused me at the same time. In view of Jesus's words in John 15, why would anyone say that? When Jesus says, "I no longer call you servants, but friends," why would anyone bristle at that? Isn't going from a servant to a friend a step up, a promotion of sorts? Think of it: Out of the cabin and into the big house. Off of the floor and into the big bed. No more, "Tote that barge, lift that bale." Instead, the words "Come, friend, let us walk together."

Jesus says, "I do not call you servants any longer, because the servant does not know his master's business." There is much truth in that. I read a story once of a man who had spent most of his life as a servant to a wealthy landowner and businessman. He recounted that his whole experience of working for this man involved doing what he was told. He never knew what his boss was thinking. He did not know what went on in the boss's house, for he slept in the servant's quarters. The deals and trades, profits and losses, were all the responsibility of his boss, not him. He did not know about his boss's business—job one for him was to mind his own.

But here in John's Gospel when Jesus tells his disciples, "You're no longer servants, but friends," that sounds very much like a promotion. It signals a change in the relationship, a change very much for the better.

Indeed, it is. Jesus says, "I have called you friends, because I have made known to you everything that I have heard from my Father." It appears from Jesus's words here that friends of his now share in the knowledge of *what* God is doing, and *how* God is doing it. God is creating a family, a community of love that is to embrace all people. A *friend* has experienced this love and extends it to others.

But this change in status comes at a price. The world that does not know God will hate the friend of Jesus, as it hated Jesus, for practicing this love. Jesus paid the full price for loving in this way, and friends of Jesus will not be exempt from the same fate. When Jesus brings people into his inner circle and shares with them what God is doing, *those friends now share the responsibility of that knowledge.* If the servant becomes the friend of the master, then the master's burdens become the servant's burdens. Friends of Jesus are no longer free of the duty to bear fruit and to pay the full price of love. It is a wonderful thing to sing the old hymn, "What a Friend We Have in Jesus." But the notion of "What a Friend Jesus Has in Me" can start to feel a bit burdensome. Are we sure that becoming a friend of Jesus is really a promotion?

Jesus says, "You are now my friends, because I have made known to you everything that I have heard from my Father." I'm not sure I'm ready for that. Seriously, do I really want to know everything? In some areas of my life, I prefer to remain deliberately ignorant. As a child I carried images in my mind of General George Washington with his troops at Valley Forge, braving the brutal winter conditions. Stories of men dying in the extreme cold were part of the lore. Then I remember what I felt like when I learned that Washington was quartered in a large, comfortable farmhouse nearby while these soldiers were freezing and dying. I'm not sure I want to know absolutely everything. Some time ago I heard a speaker describe how thirteen million children in America go to bed hungry every night, over ten million children don't have health insurance, and every thirty minutes a child is shot in the United States. Honestly, there are some things I prefer *not* to know.

But to be a friend of Jesus is to be brought into the inner circle, to be made aware of what God is doing, to participate *with* God in what God is doing. And with that comes the uncomfortable truth that carries with it an unavoidable duty—the duty to love, to lay down my life. In the hymn "One There Is Above All Others," Jesus is described as the friend of sinners, as one whose love is costly, pure, and knows no end. His was a sacrificial love that laid down his life in order to save others, something that is rare in the realm of human friendship.

Recently I read, however, the story of a human friendship that embodies this type of sacrificial love revealed to us in Jesus. When Art Garfunkel began his college studies at Columbia University, he met a fellow student at freshman orientation named Sandy Greenberg. The two became roommates and fast friends and bonded over their shared love of literature and music. In their youthful idealism, they promised to be there for each other regardless of where life took them.

Soon after starting his studies, Sandy began experiencing vision problems. The initial diagnosis of conjunctivitis proved wrong as Sandy's eyesight grew worse. After some time, a specialist gave him the news that severe glaucoma was destroying his optic nerves. This young man with a promising life ahead of him would soon be completely blind. The news sent Sandy spiraling into depression. He relinquished his dream of becoming a lawyer and moved home to Buffalo, worried that he might become a burden to his financially strapped family. He severed contact with his old friends, refusing to answer their letters or return their calls.

One day, to Sandy's surprise, his friend Art showed up unannounced at his front door. He had purchased a ticket and flown to Buffalo. He convinced Sandy to give college another try, promising him that he would stay by his side to make sure he didn't fall—literally or figuratively. And he kept that promise. He faithfully escorted Sandy around campus, firm in his desire that even though Sandy had been plunged into a world of darkness, he should never feel alone. Art actually started calling himself "Darkness" to demonstrate his empathy with his friend. He would say things like, "Darkness is going to read to you now." Art set his needs aside and organized his entire life around helping Sandy.

One day as Art was guiding Sandy through a crowded Grand Central Station, he suddenly told his friend that he had to go, leaving Sandy petrified. Sandy stumbled, bumped into people, and fell at one point, cutting his leg. After a few horrific hours, he finally managed to board the correct subway train. When he exited the station at 116th Street, he bumped into a man. When the man apologized, Sandy recognized the voice of his friend. Art had followed him the entire way home, making sure he was safe. In the process, he had given Sandy the priceless gift of independence. Sandy later said, "That moment was the spark that caused me to live a completely different life, without fear, without doubt. For that I am tremendously grateful to my friend."[1]

Sandy graduated from Columbia and then earned graduate degrees from Harvard and Oxford. He married his high school sweetheart and became a successful entrepreneur and philanthropist. While at Oxford, Sandy received a call from his friend Art. This time Art was the one in need of help. He had formed a folk-rock duo with his high school pal Paul Simon, and they desperately needed $400 to record their first album. Sandy and his wife Sue had exactly $404 in their bank account, but he didn't hesitate to give his friend what he needed.

Art and Paul's first album was not a success. There was, however, one song on the album that became a number one hit a year later. The opening line of the song echoed the way Sandy always greeted Art: "Hello Darkness, My Old Friend." We know that song, of course, as "The Sound of Silence." Simon and Garfunkel went on to become one of the most beloved musical acts in history. The two friends from Columbia University remain best friends. Art Garfunkel said that when he became friends with Sandy, "my real life emerged. I became a better guy in my own eyes, and began to see who I was—somebody who gives to a friend." For his part, Sandy describes himself as "the luckiest man in the world."

Reading this story reminded me that true friendship brings with it a huge responsibility—the responsibility to love, to sacrifice, to lay down one's life. This is especially true in the case of friendship with Jesus, because Jesus brings us into God's inner circle where we are called to cooperate with him

1. Greenberg, *Hello Darkness*, 91–97.

in saving and healing a world mired in pain and brokenness. We are called to walk alongside those who are struggling, those broken by the effects of their sinful choices and bowed low by the effects of circumstances beyond their choosing. As the Light who has come into the world, Jesus calls us his friends and summons us to enter a world of spiritual blindness, to give ourselves away by helping those who struggle.

I remember the first time I ever saw the inside of a pulpit. The pulpit in the church I attended as a teenager was a carved wooden pulpit made from mahogany. It was a stunning piece. But I remember the first time I was given the opportunity to preach and saw the pulpit from the backside and what was inside it. There was an old hymnal missing its cover. Beside it rested an open book of matches, and some individual matches already burned. There were some old, marked-up sermon notes. There was a smattering of coins, a couple of AA batteries, a stump of a candle, and an empty coffee cup. Needless to say, the view from the pew was much more attractive to me than where I now sat. In that moment, I did not feel like I had been given a promotion. Since that day, there have been additional days where being a servant has seemed more attractive than being a friend.

Jesus says, "I no longer call you servants, but *friends*, because I'm bringing you into the inner circle of what God is doing." But we must honestly ask ourselves: *Are we prepared for what that might mean?* In the chapter prior to this one in John's Gospel, Jesus says that in his Father's house there are many rooms. I had a rather strange dream some time ago, and in that dream I was invited to spend a night in God's house—the "big house."

I was so excited. It was my first visit to the house of many rooms. When I arrived, angels greeted me and showed me around and answered all of my questions. The food was incredible, the atmosphere indescribable. Then at one point I was escorted to my room. With a "Good night, sleep well," I was left to be alone.

The excitement of the day finally turned into weariness, and weariness into rest. My bed was a cloud. I slowly drifted off to sleep. But sometime during the night I was awakened, and I could hear strange sounds coming from the room next to mine. I did not know who was in that room, but whoever it was he or she was having a very bad night.

I could hear what sounded like agonizing moaning. At times, there was what sounded like violent tossing and turning, and at times I thought I heard what sounded like footsteps pacing the floor. I got up and put my ear to the wall, but I was afraid to call out, because I didn't want to add to the person's discomfort, and I didn't want to wake anyone else. So I laid awake in my bed until the morning, trying to snatch a bit of sleep here and there.

At daybreak I heard the person next door move about the room and then step out into the hall. I quickly got up and went to my door. I wanted to see who it was, and if possible, to express my regret for the night going so badly. When I opened my door and peeked out into the hall, I could not believe my eyes. There, looking back at me, was God. I was shocked. Isn't God the One who gives peace that passes understanding? Isn't he the One who blesses and calms even a whimpering child? Yet there he was, restless, unable to sleep. God said, "I'm sorry if I disturbed your sleep. I know my groaning was a disturbance. But I can't get my mind off of all my hurting children down there."

What a wonderful privilege and blessing to be called Jesus's friend. But I'm still haunted by the words of that African American preacher. He concluded his sermon with these words: "If you find yourself being drawn into Jesus's inner circle, being called a friend of God, you are incredibly blessed and fortunate. But pray for the strength to bear the burden of it."

Chapter Twenty-Two

Up, Up, and Away

At his Ascension our Lord entered heaven, and He
keeps the door open for humanity to enter.

—OSWALD CHAMBERS

SUGGESTED READINGS

Acts 1:1–11; Ps 110:1–5; Eph 1:15–23; Luke 24:49–53

FORTY DAYS AFTER JESUS'S resurrection, he ascends to the Father. The scene is recorded by Luke in the Acts of the Apostles. The ascension is celebrated as one of the principal feasts of the church year. It is important. But many may wonder: What is the significance of the ascension for me? What are its practical connections to daily life?

To answer that question, we must start in Ps 110, the psalm typically assigned for Ascension Day. The psalmist, writing about the coming Messiah who would be a king in the line of David, writes: "The LORD has sworn and he will not recant: 'You are a priest forever after the order of Melchizedek.'"

The name "Melchizedek" means "king of righteousness." Melchizedek was the king of Salem, which in Hebrew is *shalom*, meaning peace. He was a priest-king whose kingdom was a kingdom of peace. He first appears in

Gen 14, where he comes to give a blessing to Abraham who has just rescued his nephew Lot from Canaanite kings who had taken Lot hostage. As part of the blessing, Melchizedek brings Abraham bread and wine. Abraham, in turn, pays tithes to Melchizedek.

It is important for us to know that the New Testament writers—especially the author of the book of Hebrews—see Jesus as the fulfillment of Psalm 110. Melchizedek was a *type*, a foreshadowing, of Christ. And Melchizedek's priestly ministry was a foreshadowing of Christ's priestly ministry.[1] The central theme of the book of Hebrews is that the New Covenant brought by Christ brings to completion the Old Covenant. And the way that this happens is through the priesthood of Christ, whose priesthood is like Melchizedek's and not the Levitical priests of the Old Covenant.

Under the Old Covenant, priests were from the tribe of Levi. One became a priest by birth, by physical descent. But Jesus was not born from the tribe of Levi. He was a descendant of Joseph. So Jesus would not qualify to serve as priest under the Old Covenant.

But the writer of Hebrews says that Jesus's priesthood derives from a different and superior lineage. He is a priest according to the order of Melchizedek. Interestingly, in Genesis, which is a book of genealogies, Melchizedek has no genealogy. He simply appears. There is no record of his beginning or ending. In a similar way, Christ is priest of a different order, an eternal order, one that has no beginning or end.

The Old Covenant priesthood was an earthly and imperfect "copy" of what was to come. Under the Old Covenant, the priests offered sacrifices daily in the temple, and once a year the high priest would take the blood from the sacrificial lambs and move into the Holy of Holies, the inner sanctuary. There, on the Day of Atonement, he would offer sacrifice for the sins of the people.

But as the mediator of the New Covenant, Christ himself is the High Priest. And Christ enters not the *earthly* temple, but the *heavenly* temple. The writer of Hebrews says it this way:

> But when Christ appeared as a high priest of the good things that have come, then through the greater and more perfect tabernacle (not made with hands, that is, not of this creation) he entered once for all into the Holy Place, taking not the blood of goats and calves but his own blood, thus securing an *eternal redemption* (emphasis mine).[2]

And just a few verses later, the writer continues:

1. For a fascinating study of Jesus and his relationship to Melchizedek, see Ybarra, *Melchizedek and the Last Supper*.

2. Heb 9:11–12 NLT.

> For Christ has entered, not into a sanctuary made with hands,
> a copy of the true one, but into heaven itself, now to appear in
> the presence of God on our behalf. Nor was it to offer himself
> repeatedly, as the high priest enters the Holy Place yearly with
> blood not his own; for then he would have had to suffer repeat-
> edly since the foundation of the world. But as it is, he has ap-
> peared once for all at the end of the age to put away sin by the
> sacrifice of himself.[3]

Now we are starting to get at the heart of Jesus's ascension. In his ascension to heaven, Jesus isn't merely returning to the Father in order to sit
at the Father's right hand and assume his royal throne. In his ascension into
heaven, Jesus enters the heavenly sanctuary or temple not made with hands
in order to offer the sacrifice of himself once for all time!

It might be easy for us to think that Jesus's earthly sacrifice that began
in the upper room on Holy Thursday and climaxed on the cross on Good
Friday was the end of it. But that is not the end of it. Jesus's ascension brings
to completion what occurred during Holy Week. Jesus's saving work did
not end with the empty tomb or his appearances to the disciples over forty
days. Jesus's saving work has a liturgical consummation. He is the great high
priest, where he still has to ascend to the *heavenly* Jerusalem, there to celebrate the Paschal feast in the true Holy of Holies.

This is precisely what the writer of Hebrews is telling us. With Jesus's
ascension, Jesus brings his glorified and resurrected body into the heavenly
temple, *where he now offers himself as a sacrifice to the Father, not in time,
but in eternity; not on earth, but in heaven.* It is not Jesus's resurrection, but
his ascension, that is the climax of God's saving work in our lives.

To see this, return with me to Holy Week. During Holy Week, on earth,
Jesus fulfilled the feast of Passover by showing himself to be *the* very Passover Lamb, slain from the foundation of the world. As the New Covenant
Passover Lamb, Jesus brought the Old Covenant Passover to its fulfillment
in the true sense of the word, i.e., he "filled it full." When Jesus establishes
the New Covenant, he does not abolish the Old Covenant in the sense of
setting it completely aside in order to move in a completely new direction.
He *fulfills* the Old Covenant. He invests the features of the Old Covenant
with greater capacities. Think of a piece of music transposed to a higher key.
The music is the same, but elevated to a higher plane. Jesus did not come to
replace something bad (the Old Covenant) with something good (the New
Covenant). He came to take something already great and holy and bring it

---

3. Heb 9:24–26 NLT.

to divine completion. The Old Covenant did not die out, but came to new and fuller life with the New Covenant of Jesus.

With his ascension to heaven, the writer of Hebrews tells us that Jesus fulfills the Old Covenant Day of Atonement. Whereas the Old Covenant high priest would enter the earthly temple into the Holy of Holies, now Jesus has entered the heavenly temple, carrying not the blood of bulls and goats but his very own blood. And unlike the Old Covenant Priest, Jesus's sacrifice in the heavenly temple is needed only once. And from the heavenly temple, Jesus now exercises his high priestly ministry continually. The writer of Hebrews says,

> He [Jesus] holds his priesthood permanently, because he continues forever. Consequently, he is able for all time to save those who draw near to God through him, *since he always lives to make intercession for them.*[4]

In his ascension, Jesus takes his sacrifice at Calvary—offered once in history—into *eternity*, into the heavenly sanctuary.

It might be easy to think that Jesus's high priestly ministry was finished on Calvary. Not so. For the offering of himself that occurred in history, at Calvary outside of Jerusalem, has become a perpetual and eternal offering through his entry into the *heavenly* temple. Christ now permanently exercises his priesthood from the heavenly temple, taking his sacrifice for us 2,000 years ago in a far-off place and making it eternally *present*. His sacrifice is "once-for-all" not in the sense of "one and done," but in the sense of *never-ending*. It stands outside of time. He is a priest according to the order of Melchizedek, whose priesthood is eternal.

The lectionary readings from Acts and the gospel of Luke for the Feast of the Ascension shed further light on this truth. In Acts 1, Luke writes that just before Jesus ascends he lifts up his hands and "blesses" the disciples. As he is blessing them, he is carried up into heaven.

This act of blessing is very significant. Blessing was something familiar to every first century Jewish man and woman. Each day at 9:00 a.m. and 3:00 p.m., as commanded in the law, the Jewish priests celebrated what was known as the *tamid*, or "perpetual offering" in the temple.[5] One group of priests placed a lamb, a cake of bread, and wine on the altar. Another group of priests led the people in reciting the Ten Commandments. They would then sing the Psalm designated for that day of the week.

---

4. Heb 7:24–25 NLT, emphasis mine.

5. Exod 29:38–41.

The *tamid* concluded with the priests gathering on the steps of the Holy Place (the Holy of Holies), extending their arms out toward the people and invoking the blessing of the Lord originally entrusted to Moses and Aaron:

> The Lord bless you and keep you; the Lord make his face to shine upon you, and be gracious unto you; the Lord lift up his countenance upon you and give you peace.[6]

When the apostles see Jesus ascend into heaven *while in the very act of blessing them*, they understand that he is climbing the steps of the true Holy of Holies, the heavenly temple. Only one Jewish priest was allowed to enter the Holy Place at the time of the *tamid*. The only person who could enter that room was the high priest, and he did so only once a year on the Feast of *Yom Kippur*, the Day of Atonement.

When the apostles see Jesus disappear into a "cloud"—the Old Testament symbol of God's presence[7]—they understand that Jesus has now entered into God's *heavenly* throne room, the reality to which the temple and the earthly Holy of Holies pointed. Jesus continues to offer himself to the Father, in his glorified humanity, just as he has from all eternity in his divinity.

In fact, Hebrews and Revelation portray Jesus, the Lamb of God, offering himself perpetually to the Father in the heavenly sanctuary.[8] Jesus draws all of heaven, the angels and saints, into this great perpetual heavenly liturgy. *It is this same liturgy that breaks forth to earth, upon the altars of our churches, in the Eucharist.* The bread and wine we offer are the fulfillment of Israel's *tamid*, and we receive Christ in the Eucharistic communion, the same Christ who bodily entered into the glory of the Father. It is Jesus's ascension that makes all of this a reality.

When Jesus ascended, he did not merely return to heaven to sit at the Father's right hand and exercise his rule and authority until the Father might decide it's time to bring history to an end. At his ascension, Jesus entered into the heavenly temple, bringing his resurrected and glorified body that he offered up *in history* and offering it up in *eternity*—so that what happened on Calvary is as present as right now because it is the sacrifice that never ends. In the liturgy of the church, heaven comes to earth and earth is drawn up to heaven. Worshippers are mystically drawn into the realm where the heavenly liturgy is ongoing and stands outside of time, where Jesus is still

---

6. Num 6:24–26 NLT
7. Exod 13:31–32; 24:16–18; Num 9:15–23.
8. Heb 7:25; 9:24; Rev 5:6–14.

mediating a New Covenant, feeding his people with his body and blood and constantly interceding for them as their great high priest.[9]

Many modern people struggle to accept or understand Jesus's ascension because they mistakenly believe that the ascension is about where Jesus went *spatially*. But as we've seen, that is not the focus of the church's historic teaching. When seen through the lens of the church year, the ascension of Jesus powerfully demonstrates that *God finishes what he starts*. He is faithful in bringing about his saving purpose for the world. Jesus—our great high priest—has ascended into the heavenly temple, the heavenly Holy of Holies. There, as both Priest and Victim, he offers himself to the Father, and his intercession for us is continual.

---

9. This is the historic teaching of what occurs in the Roman Catholic mass.

Chapter Twenty-Three

When Turning the Page Is Difficult

Ascensions into heaven are like falling leaves, sad and happy all
at the same time. Going away isn't really sad, especially when
your going enables a new kind of presence to be born.

—ERNEST HEMINGWAY

SUGGESTED READINGS

Acts 1:1–11; Ps 110:1–5; Eph 1:15–23; Luke 24:49–53

I AM A PERSON who is not particularly fond of goodbyes. Saying goodbye can sometimes be a difficult and emotion-laden thing to do. If you are not convinced, go to an airport and sit in an obscure spot and observe people for a few minutes, or watch persons from the armed forces as they prepare to board a ship or a plane and leave their families behind. Saying goodbye is not easy.

Perhaps you remember the first time you left home and said goodbye to your parents. Perhaps when you embarked for college, or were ready to be married, or were entering the service of your country. Most parents vividly recall saying goodbye to their children when they left the nest to begin college or career or a new life somewhere else. I remember taking our firstborn to begin her university studies. After the eight-hour drive, we spent hours unloading her things into the dormitory, attending orientation workshops, discovering schedules, getting acclimated to the university. But after two days, the moment came when we had to say goodbye to our child and to return home. Parting was difficult, but the full weight of that goodbye did not come until I returned home. The lawn needed mowing, so I started the mower and proceeded on my horizontal back-and-forth journey across the front yard. After two or three passes, without warning I was overcome with the magnitude of the life transition we were experiencing. My relationship with my daughter was changing. Life as I had known it with her for eighteen years would never be the same. Suddenly, my feet could not move to push the mower. I walked up to the house next to the garage, sat down and pulled my knees up to my chest, sobbing and shaking.

Saying goodbye is not easy. But in all of these situations, saying goodbye can also be like saying hello. The closing of one chapter in our lives makes possible the beginning of another. Through the sadness and bittersweet taste of goodbyes, relationships have a chance to grow and change and evolve to another level. In a sense, those relationships become something new by ceasing to be what they were before. To gain by losing. To hold fast by letting go. To become something new by ceasing to be what we were before. These truths are at the heart of the gospel. And perhaps nowhere is this more true than in the story of Christ's ascension.

Jesus spoke often to his disciples about the fact that he would leave them. But they treasured his presence so much that they couldn't imagine his departure. This had to be compounded by the fact of his appearances with them for six weeks after his resurrection. They were now completely convinced that he was the Messiah, and who could blame them for thinking that he was going to restore the Davidic kingdom and to exert earthly power? How disheartening, then, when Jesus begins to tell them that he must go away, that he is no longer going to be present with them in the way he is with them now. How confusing it must be when he tells them that he is going away, but that they must not go back to "business as usual." Rather, they are to wait in Jerusalem for what comes next. Forty days of being with the resurrected Jesus could easily lead them to want to hold on to Easter and its victory. And yet their risen Lord is calling them to let go and to look to the coming Spirit as the One who will lead them into the future.

Although we have not had the privilege of being with the earthly or risen Jesus, we can empathize with the disciples. We understand all too well the challenges that confront us when God wants to start a new chapter in our lives and calls on us to let go of the comfort zones we have built around us and to open ourselves to an uncertain future. God is faithful to us in these seasons of change and transition, even as he was with the disciples as they faced their transition. What is hard for us is that we, like the disciples, must wait on God to clothe us with the Spirit and to empower us for whatever it is that he is leading us to do.

Do you remember Clark Kent, who would transform himself into Superman? Every time Clark Kent would become Superman, he would go into a phone booth and strip off his ordinary business suit, revealing his official Superman costume. Amazingly, Clark Kent could only stop locomotives and lift skyscrapers when he was properly clothed in the outfit that revealed his true identity.

In a similar way, I think this is what Jesus is trying to do with his disciples prior to his ascension. They are so used to Jesus being with them that they do not see that God's plan is not complete, that there is more to be done, that an unsettling transition is necessary. Jesus is trying to show them that the Father's plan must move forward, but the disciples will only be able to share in that plan if they wait on God and are clothed with the power of the Spirit. For it is the Spirit who will give them their true identity and enable them to do the tasks that lie ahead.

In the words of the Apostles' Creed we say of Jesus, "He ascended into heaven, and is seated at the right hand of the Father, from whence he shall come to judge the living and the dead." As we have seen, God's plan for the world did not end with the resurrection of Jesus from the dead, as wonderful as that is. And Jesus's plan for his disciples didn't end there, either. There was more to be done. But in order for that to happen the disciples were being called to let go of Jesus as they knew him, to trust him when he said that God would lead them into an uncertain future.

And so it is with us. God's plan for us does not end with Jesus's resurrection. There is more to be done, and God calls on us to be involved. Jesus may be physically *absent*, but that does not mean he is not *present* with us. For the Spirit comes to empower us and give us what we need, so that in some mysterious and mystical way the church can become the continuing presence of Jesus in the world.

This is a little unsettling, especially as the truth of it trickles down into our personal lives. It sometimes can require of us that we let go of our comfortable ways of knowing Jesus so that God can move us into the next phase of his work in us. As we consider this, an important question arises: *In what situation that confronts you right now are you being called to let go of your comfortable way of knowing Jesus so that the Spirit may guide you forward in your life?* Whatever that situation may be, God is faithful. He promises you grace to empower you to let go of your comfortable ways of knowing Jesus.

That grace enables you to reach out in faith to follow him into an uncertain future. It is the grace that helps us to turn the page into a new chapter of life when turning the page is difficult.

The goodbye of Jesus's ascension was one of the most difficult transitions his disciples experienced. For when Jesus left them, he would never again be with them in the same, recognizable way. But Jesus's goodbye to the disciples—bittersweet though it was—was in a sense also a "hello," for the special relationship they enjoyed with him now took on a new character and shape. On the one hand, the disciples had to say goodbye to the Christ who was *before* them and *beside* them. It's very hard for us to comprehend how difficult this must have been. They have rubbed shoulders with the divine, with the very Son of God. They have seen him do amazing things right before their very eyes. They have walked with him and talked with him and known him in a way we could never imagine. No doubt saying goodbye to Jesus was hard. And maybe this is why much of the New Testament is preoccupied with looking for Jesus's imminent return once he ascended. After all, when you've spent so much time with Jesus *before* you and *beside* you, it's natural to want him back before you and beside you after he is gone.

But saying goodbye to the Christ who was *before* them and *beside* them made it possible for the disciples to say hello to the Christ who was to come to dwell *within* them through the power of the Spirit filling the church. And in time, it dawned on the disciples that the divine presence for which they were waiting was already with them. They had inherited Christ's mission, and with his ascension to glory his power was now with them. Saying goodbye had made possible a new hello.

Goodbyes are bittersweet for us also, which is why the Ascension is something we should ponder often. Our lives are full of "letting go" and "beginning again." This happens when we begin a new job. It happens when we graduate from school and transition to the next chapter in our lives. But perhaps nowhere is this more true than when we lose a loved one. When we lose someone we love, there is an emptiness in our hearts. So God sends his Holy Spirit, and we cling to the church. God comforts us for present and past pain and channels our sorrow into sincere prayers and gracious acts. He gives us grace so that even these painful goodbyes can be preparation for joyous "hellos" which will come in their appointed time.

Yes, saying goodbye can be difficult and bittersweet. But what is it, really, to say goodbye? Centuries ago, English-speaking Christians parted by saying, "God be with ye." In time, it became "God be w' ye," and then finally "Good-bye."

Jesus's ascension fills the phrase "goodbye" with the full power of its meaning. In his ascension, "Goodbye" truly means "God be with you." It means that God *is still with us.* One day, perhaps sooner than we imagine, this same Jesus who said goodbye and rose into the clouds will return on the clouds with great glory. In that moment, every loss will be turned to gain, every rough place will be made smooth, every tear will be wiped dry, and justice will be done in all the earth.

In the meantime, let us resolve to be witnesses to his love and power. Let us throw our lot in with the people of God, the church, and continue to explore this relationship which was made possible through the saying of a painful goodbye. And as we do, let us always remember our Lord's words to his disciples: "I am with you always, even to the end of the age."

Pentecost

Chapter Twenty-Four

Pentecost Sunday

When Jesus talks about fire, he means in the first place his own passion,
which was a passion of love. Jesus does not come to make us comfortable.
Rather, he brings the great living fire of divine love, which is what the
Holy Spirit is, a fire that burns, yet this is not a destructive fire but
one that makes things bright and pure and free and grand. Being a
Christian, then, is daring to entrust oneself to this burning fire.

—POPE BENEDICT XVI

SUGGESTED READINGS

Acts 2:1–11; Ps 33:12–22; 1 Cor 12:4–13; John 20:19–23

GROWING UP IN NEBRASKA we sometimes experienced weather that scared me as a kid. Storms could quickly roll in, where the wind could blow at forty-to-fifty miles per hour. The sky turned greyish black. Flashes of lightning exploded from the top of the sky quickly to the earth, followed a few seconds later by thunder that would rattle the windows of the house and shake the foundation. The raw power of nature was awe-inspiring and frightening.

The way Luke describes it, the pilgrims gathered on the day of Pentecost must have felt something like that. Thunder, wind, fire, storm. The explosive arrival of the Holy Spirit. Jerusalem has swelled with people from every race and nation. As Parthians try to speak and make sense of it in their native language, Persians hear and understood them in *their* native language. Diverse languages all around, yet everyone hears and understands.

The feast of Pentecost is a prime example of how Christian forms of worship had their origins in ancient Jewish practices. The word "Pentecost" is from the Greek word that means "fifty," or "fiftieth." In Hebrew the word is *Shavuot*, meaning "feast of weeks" because it occurred on the day following a week of weeks (seven times seven days), counting from Passover.[1]

Although Pentecost was an ancient Jewish feast, the earliest references to Pentecost as a Christian observance come at the end of the second century. The Christian observance differed from Jewish practice in that it consisted of a fifty-day period beginning on Easter Day rather than a feast on the day of Pentecost alone.[2] The entire fifty-day period celebrated Jesus's resurrection and ascension, the bestowal of the Holy Spirit, and also anticipated Christ's return in glory.[3]

Pentecost is thus regarded as the culmination of the Easter season, and the Eastern Church has historically emphasized this in its liturgies. In the West, however, the tendency has been to make Pentecost an independent feast day with a primary focus on the sending of the Holy Spirit.[4] In any event, the Christian observance of Pentecost becomes more widely attested by the fourth century. The Spanish Council of Elvira (AD 305) insists that all should celebrate the feast, and the Council of Nicea (AD 325) refers to some who kneel on Sundays and on the day of Pentecost.[5]

To understand Pentecost fully, we return to its celebration as a major festival for the children of Israel in the Old Testament. In the books of Leviticus and Deuteronomy, God instructed the people to bring him special offerings from the harvest. At the beginning of the harvest, they were to bring him some of the firstfruits which were often the first figs or dates that ripened. This usually happened near Passover. Then seven weeks after the firstfruits appeared, the people were to bring God special offerings from the completed harvest. Thus, Pentecost was also known as the Feast of Weeks because it occurred seven weeks after Passover.

1. Lev 23:15–16.
2. Bradshaw and Johnson, *Origins of Feasts*, 70.
3. Whalen, *Seasons and Feasts*, 70–73.
4. Chittister, *Liturgical Year*, 89.
5. Chittister, *Liturgical Year*, 72.

Passover was also the celebration of God's deliverance of the people from Egypt. Each year, part of the Passover celebration involved offering to God the sheath in preparation for the Spring harvest which would come fifty days later. On Pentecost, the firstfruits of the Spring harvest would then be offered to God, consisting of sacrifices and offerings in the temple. For the Jews, there were three feasts that were so important that all adult males were required to attend them each year. Pentecost was one of those feasts.

This explains Luke's comment in Acts 2:5: "Godly Jews from many nations were living in Jerusalem at that time." From the time of the Babylonian captivity, Jews had been dispersed throughout the world. In the first century, these persons were dispersed throughout the Roman Empire. But because Pentecost was an important feast, multiple thousands of pilgrims were in Jerusalem to observe it and give thanks for the harvest.

This occasion is ripe, then, for the fulfillment of prophecy that one day God would send the Messiah who would gather dispersed Jews and bring them back to Jerusalem to participate in God's reign. Listen, for example, to the prophet Micah's words:

> In the last days, the Temple of the Lord in Jerusalem will become the most important place on earth. People from all over the world will go there to worship. There he will teach us his ways, so that we may obey him. For in those days the Lord's teaching and his word will go out from Jerusalem.[6]

On the day of Pentecost, Jewish persons from all over the Roman Empire are gathered in Jerusalem to celebrate both the firstfruits as well as the completion of the harvest. They are gathered to celebrate God's giving of the law and making them his covenant people on Sinai. As Passover recalled the exodus of the children of Israel from Egypt, so fifty days later the feast of Pentecost marked that great event at Sinai where Moses received the law of God and renewed God's covenant with his chosen people. Thus, by the end of the first century the Jewish people came to see Pentecost as the completion of Passover. What God had begun in Egypt, God sealed by the giving of the law on Mount Sinai.

With signs and wonders very reminiscent of Sinai, the Spirit of God descends on the people in Jerusalem. Those witnessing this event realize that the harvesting of God's family is now underway and that it includes people from all walks of life, not just a select few. Red, yellow, black, and white; rich and poor; educated and uneducated; professionals and blue-collar workers;

---

6. Mic 4:1–2 NLT.

young and old; male and female; Jew and gentile—the promise is for all and the Spirit is poured out upon all.

An amazing feature about the powerful display of the Spirit on Pentecost was God's power to transcend and overcome differences among people. There were 120 people gathered in an upper room. They had rearranged their lives, their schedules, their priorities, in order to wait for something that Jesus promised. In a group that large there would be vast cultural and ideological differences. A group of diverse people that size—together in the same small space for several days—would be a formula for relational stress, to say the least.

Yet on the day of Pentecost this group of 120 persons was all together, waiting in anticipation for the fulfillment of a promise. And when the Spirit descended, a crowd of thousands began to gather to see what all the commotion was about. That crowd included Greeks, Arabs, Romans, Africans, Asians, to name just a few. And each person in that crowd was able to understand the conversation and witness what was happening in his or her own language! It was a miraculous undoing of Babel.[7]

On that day, the Spirit of God transcended multiple distinctions and differences among people in bringing about God's purpose. That day was the beginning of the biblical promise that from many parts would come *one* body. That day was proof that God's Spirit has the power to overcome every division among people and to transcend every hostility that separates people from one another.

All of this is in the background on Pentecost. Luke tells us that thousands of Jews who lived in distant lands (Luke lists them here from East to West) fulfilled their duty by traveling to Jerusalem. The city's population swelled with persons who were ethnically Jewish but culturally and linguistically gentiles after more than five hundred years of being dispersed in the middle East.

Meanwhile, at the same time, the apostles are gathered in Jerusalem, waiting in quiet expectation. They know something significant is about to occur because Jesus promised as much when he took leave of them at his ascension. As the disciples wait in the upper room, Luke describes the scene: "All of these with one accord devoted themselves to prayer, together with the women and Mary the Mother of Jesus, and with his brothers."[8]

As Acts 2 unfolds, the sound of a rushing mighty wind comes from heaven, filling the house. Tongues of fire descend and rest on those gathered and they are all filled with the Holy Spirit and begin speaking in other languages

7. Gen 11:1–9.
8. Acts 1:14 RSV.

as the Spirit enables them. These physical manifestations would have instantly reminded those present of the giving of the law at Sinai:

> Then Moses brought the people out of the camp to meet God, and they took their stand at the foot of the mountain. And Mount Sinai was wrapped in smoke, because the LORD descended upon it in fire.[9]

Here, on the anniversary of Sinai, once again the LORD descends in fire and with the rush of a mighty wind. All of this causes quite a disturbance and people gather to see what's happening. In response, Peter stands up to preach, quoting the prophet Joel:

> And in the last days it shall be, God declares, that I will pour out my Spirit upon all flesh, and your sons and your daughters shall prophesy, and your young men shall see visions, and your old men shall dream dreams.[10]

As he preaches, Peter describes the "last days" of Joel in terms of what is happening *now* on this very day of Pentecost. The Spirit has been poured out, and the effects are visible. As God once gave the Old Covenant law to Moses on tablets of stone, so now he writes his New Covenant law on peoples' hearts. Pentecost, then, is no isolated event or random occurrence. What is happening on this day is very much connected to the stream of salvation history that began with our observation of Advent and continued through Holy Week where Jesus sat with his disciples in the upper room.

Throughout this book we have learned that Jesus was the new Moses who had come to lead God's people on a new Exodus, an Exodus not from slavery in Egypt but from slavery to sin. As the original Passover culminated in the giving of the law of God on stone tablets at Mount Sinai, so also the New Covenant Passover is culminated by the writing of God's law on human hearts through the pouring out of the Holy Spirit and the harvesting of people from every nation and language into the church, the New Covenant family of God. Just as God's descent on Sinai meant the formation of Israel as a nation, the descent of the Holy Spirit on Pentecost involves the formation of Jews and gentiles into the church, the *new* Israel.[11]

Pentecost, then, is the new Sinai. The church becomes the visible and physical manifestation in the world of the New Covenant even as Israel was the visible and physical manifestation of the Old Covenant. The church becomes the *new* Israel, empowered by the Holy Spirit to invite all people to

9. Exod 19:17–18 RSV.
10. Acts 2:17–18 RSV.
11. Gal 6:16.

become part of a New Exodus under the leadership of a New Moses who is the Lamb of God who takes away the sin of the world. The church, empowered by the Spirit, is the continuing incarnation of Jesus in the world until he comes again in glory to receive her to himself.

What began all the way back in Advent now reaches its apex at Pentecost. All of the promises to those under the Old Covenant that a New Covenant would come have been realized in Jesus. The new Moses has come. The new Exodus has been inaugurated. And the new Israel—The New Covenant people of God—has received God's law through the Holy Spirit. And that same Spirit—speaking through the church—invites men and women of every nation and boys and girls of every language into its loving embrace by calling on them to repent and to be reborn through baptism.[12]

Beginning with Peter and the apostles at Pentecost, the message of the church continues through the ages. The church continues to call all people to repent, to undergo a profound change in their inmost being. The church summons people to be buried with Christ in baptism and to rise again as the Holy Spirit fills them and works a radical change in their hearts and lives. The church invites persons everywhere to be renewed in the image of God, to share in God's divine life, to become God's beloved sons and daughters.

And the Holy Spirit gives to each of us a gift, a *charism*, which is like a fingerprint. Our charism is the unique way that the Spirit uses us edify others and build up the body of Christ. The Spirit grants some the ability to *discern*, and others the ability to *prophecy*, and others the ability to exercise great overcoming *faith* and even to work *miracles*. Some are granted unique *wisdom*. Some are able to *heal*. The Spirit bestows these gifts *not* for the benefit of the individual, but to build up the church so that Christ's high priestly prayer in John 17 may be realized, giving the church's witness to the world credibility. The Spirit of Pentecost engenders the undoing of Babel, enabling members of Christ's body to speak the same language—the language of love. In this way the church fulfills her mission.

The celebration of Pentecost forms a pivot which signals a transition to the second half of the church year known as Ordinary Time, or Kingdomtide. The liturgical color for this season is green, symbolizing the long season of growth as the church contemplates and lives into its mission as the continuing incarnation of Jesus in the world. To explore all of the possible themes of Ordinary Time would require another book. We will limit our discussion to a few key emphases, to which we now turn.

---

12. Acts 2:38–40; Rom 6:3–4; Col 2:11–12; Tit 3:4–7; 1 Pet 3:18–22.

Ordinary Time

Chapter Twenty-Five

Trinity Sunday

*The [Christian] teaching about God as Father, Son, and Holy Spirit
. . . is the single most practical truth available to human beings.*

—THOMAS JOSEPH WHITE

SUGGESTED READINGS

Gen 1:26—2:3; Exod 3:1–6; Isa 6:1–8; Ps 29; Ps 93; Matt 28:16–20; Rom
8:12–17; 2 Cor 13:5–14

THE HEART OF CHRISTIANITY involves a God who engages us and relates to
us personally, a God who comes to us in love and who invites us to love him
in return. It is important to know *who* God is because you cannot love what
you do not *know*. In all human relationships, persons want to be known and
loved for who they are in themselves, not merely what they do. In a similar
way, the God whom we worship deserves to be loved and worshiped not just
for what he has *done*, as wonderful as that is. God deserves to be worshiped
because of *who* he is. Christian faith teaches that God is *triune* in nature: one
God, revealed in three coequal and coeternal Persons.

The observance of Trinity Sunday in the liturgical year comes on the
first Sunday after Pentecost, at the beginning of Ordinary Time, or in some

traditions, Kingdomtide. The celebration has been observed as a solemnity in the Roman Church since the fourteenth century, but there is evidence that elements of what later became the feast of Trinity Sunday are found as early as the tenth century.[1] The timing and placement of Trinity Sunday is intentional. Beginning with the first Sunday of Advent at the beginning of the church year, the lectionary readings and ritual observances move us through the history of the one Life that changes all our lives. Christianity is a religion with a footprint over human history. God has revealed himself to humankind in time and space. This revelation was progressive, occurring in stages.

The formation of the nation of Israel revealed that there was no other god in heaven or on earth beside YHWH, the God who entered into a covenant with flesh and blood people to make them his own. The history of Israel revealed, however, how God's people often failed to keep faith with him. The coming of Jesus in the flesh revealed that God has a Son whom he sent to deliver Israel and all of humanity from our weakness. Jesus's resurrection and ascension demonstrated that the Son was successful in his mission. Pentecost revealed that the purpose of the Son's work of deliverance was to form a new humanity, born not of the will of flesh but of God. When the Son ascended to the Father's right hand, God sent the Holy Spirit upon the apostles to initiate them into the New Covenant—to live with God forever, in the same way that the Father and the Son abide together. Immediately the apostles began to extend to others what they had received, and the church was born.

The first half of the Christian year immerses us in the historical revelation of God. That historical revelation is now complete. We do not know all that we want to know about God, but we know all that we *need* to know. As the second half of the church year begins, it does so by calling the church to contemplate the mystery of the God who has acted decisively in history to save us and to make us God's covenant people. It calls on us to ponder the foundational doctrine of Christianity—the mystery of the Trinity.

The word "Trinity" is not found in Scripture. It is a Latin term that means "three in one." It points not merely to the biblical teaching about one God revealed in three Persons, but to the reality behind the teaching. In Scripture, God is revealed as the transcendent Creator, as the incarnate Son, and as present in and among the lives of believers through the Holy Spirit. Christians worship *one* God in *three* Persons, neither confounding the Persons, nor dividing the substance.[2]

---

1. LaCugna, "Making the Most of Trinity Sunday," 256–57.

2. This language comes from the church's creeds, particularly the Nicene and

Part of what makes the doctrine of the Trinity so complex is that it is a revealed truth that transcends finite human wisdom.[3] As such, there are no fully adequate analogies in human experience to explain it. The Eastern Orthodox tradition comes close by using the word *perichoresis*, from the words "circle" and "dance." God is not solitary, but is a loving communion of mutual love, respect, honor, and joy. Trinity means that shared life is the nature of God.

Joseph Ratzinger (later Pope Benedict XVI) similarly explains that the three Persons of the Trinity might be understood as a musical pattern. The Persons of the Trinity are not three separate beings, separate substances standing over against one another like three human persons meeting one another across a table. The persons of the Trinity are a *community* where each person is constituted by its relationship to the other two.[4]

This truth has enormous practical implications for disciples of Jesus. The Trinity is a *family* bound together by love. God is revealed as a Father who is creating a family. God's purpose is not merely to save us *from* sin and hell, as wonderful as that is. God's purpose is to save us *for* divine sonship and daughtership. One of the most compelling images of the church in the New Testament is the image of the church as the family of God. We are created in God's very image (Gen 1–2). God's purpose is that we become his children not merely in a spiritual or metaphorical sense, but in a real sense.

Theologians use the term "divine filiation" to describe this. God's purpose for us is that we become his sons and daughters by sharing in the divine life of the Trinity through the Holy Spirit. John speaks about this in his gospel in terms of mutual indwelling. Jesus calls his disciples to *abide* or *remain* in him, to dwell in him even as he dwells in the Father and the Father dwells in him. In John 17, Jesus prays that his followers will so intimately

---

Athanasian creeds. The creeds are summary articulations of the church's belief as the church grew in its understanding of divine revelation and as it was forced to address heretical teachings that contradicted the early apostolic witness to the faith.

3. While this is true, the explication of the Trinity as it developed in the history of the church also has at times made it difficult to make the doctrine pastorally relevant by showing how God personally relates to us in salvation history. From the fourth century on, the church's need to refute heresy caused many church leaders and theologians to focus on God's nature *in himself*, i.e., the Immanent Trinity. This focus was helpful in showing how the Persons of the Godhead relate to each other but did not address how God relates to human beings in salvation history, i.e., the Economic Trinity. Trinitarian theology became more a description of God *in himself* and less a description of God *for us*, which was prevalent prior to Arianism and other forms of heresy. LaCugna describes this as a transition from soteriology to ontology. See "Making the Most of Trinity Sunday," 257.

4. Barron, *Exploring Catholic Theology*, 10–11. For a thorough theological explication of the Trinity, see White, *Light of Christ*, 47–83.

share the love of he and the Father that they will reflect the unity of relationship within the Trinity.

In the apostle Paul's writings, the theme of divine filiation is found in Paul's frequent use of the expression "in Christ." In baptism, we are buried and raised up with Christ, Paul says. The word for baptism that Paul uses means "to plunge" or "to immerse." Paul is saying that baptism immerses us into God's divine life, like a fish in water.

John Wesley understood God's loving purpose of divine filiation to be at the heart of the apostle Peter's words to churches in Asia Minor:

> [God's] divine power has given us everything we need for life and godliness through our knowledge of Him who called us by his own glory and goodness. Through these he has given us his very great and precious promises, so that through them you may participate in the divine nature and escape the corruption that is in the world caused by evil desires.[5]

The triune God is a *family*: the Father, Son, and the interpersonal love that perfectly binds them together, who is the Holy Spirit. We were created to become part of this family in more than a spiritual or metaphorical way. We were created to share in the divine life of the Creator God. We were created to become by *grace* what God is by *nature*.

The apostle Paul, writing to the church at Rome, further explains this in terms of our being "fellow heirs" or "joint heirs" with Christ. Paul uses the Jewish imagery of the firstborn son who received a double portion of the earthly father's inheritance. In this analogy, Christ is the firstborn Son of God the Father. But with the Spirit given to us in baptism, we become not merely believers in God—we become sons and daughters of God who are now fellow heirs with Christ. We are Christ's younger brothers and sisters! From all eternity God is a Father who is fathering a family, beginning with his eternally begotten Son. In his love God adopts us into this family, and we share Christ's inheritance.

We might wonder: What is Christ's inheritance? Paul answers by telling the Christians at Rome that Christ's inheritance consists of the kingdom of heaven, namely, a life of glory with Christ.[6] Paul then makes it clear how believers claim their inheritance:

> When we cry "Abba! Father!" it is the Spirit himself bearing witness with our spirit that we are children of God, and if children,

---

5. 2 Pet 1:4 NLT.

6. See Paul's discussion in Rom 8.

then heirs, heirs of God and fellow heirs with Christ, provided we
suffer with him in order that we may also be glorified with him.[7]

We have a glorious inheritance as younger brothers and sisters of Christ,
but to claim that inheritance we must suffer with him![8] To be adopted into
the family of the Trinity is to be drawn up into a life of suffering love. As
our elder brother said more than once, "If you wish to be with me, you must
deny yourself, take up your cross, and follow me." In God's family, we learn
obedience through suffering. It's the family dynamic. It's what this family is
all about—total, complete, self-giving love.

The Trinity is not an esoteric and impenetrable doctrine, even though
it is a profound mystery. The Trinity is a Father who begets children. He
begets his Son in eternity, then in time by being born of a woman. He adopts
us as his sons and daughters through new birth in baptism. We become
Christ's younger brothers and sisters. We become by *grace* what Christ is by
nature, sharing in the Father's divine life through the Holy Spirit:

> God is a God of loving involvement and ongoing fidelity to the
> covenant; God draws us into the circle of divine life so that we
> may be sons and daughters of God, and brothers and sisters to
> each other.[9]

Christianity is the only religion in the world where its adherents are
privileged to call God *Father*. As a Father, God shares his very life with us.
He shares his life with us through earthly matter—water, wine, bread, oil, the
laying on of hands. And so we can say with the apostle John, "To those who
received him, he gave power to become children of God, who were born,
not of blood nor of the will of the flesh nor of the will of man, but of God."[10]

But the practical implications of the Trinity are not limited to our individual lives. There are implications for the church as well. The apostle Paul
describes this in his writings. Let us return for a moment to the analogy of
perichoresis and the notion of the Persons of the Trinity "dancing" together
in a relationship of mutual love. In Paul's correspondence, it's almost as if he
is giving congregations "dance lessons." That is, the church is to reflect the
reality of the Triune Godhead in its human relationships. Those relationships are to be characterized by mutuality, reciprocity, and peace. Christian
brothers and sisters are to practice forbearance, to honor one another in

7. Rom 8:15–17 RSV.

8. See also 1 Pet 1:6–7; 2:20–22; 3:13–17; 4:12–19. Sharing Jesus's suffering is a
prominent theme of 1 Pet.

9. LaCugna, "Making the Most of Trinity Sunday," 261.

10. John 1:12 NLT.

love, to maintain the unity of the Spirit in the bond of peace. They are to be united in heart and mind. They are to live humbly, placing the needs of others before themselves.[11] As those who have been brought to share in God's divine life, our relationships in the church should be a reflection of that divine life.

Our sharing in God's life—our participation in the life of the Trinity—does not occur primarily through mystical, subjective, inward experience. We become partakers of the divine nature through the sacraments that Christ instituted. Baptism gives us familial birth into this new life, and the Eucharist feeds and nurtures and grows us up into it. Marriage has a sacramental character to it as a sort of icon of the Trinity, where the self-giving love of a husband and a wife bears fruit in a third person who is distinct, yet of the same substance.

To this point, our discussion of the Trinity has been primarily confined to the realm of concrete, interpersonal knowledge. We learn of the Trinity through the concrete experience of being drawn up into God's divine life as adopted children. It is a knowledge of the heart through lived experience. It is knowledge in the sense that we might know a friend or family member.

But there is another way to know of the Trinity which is more theological and philosophical. If the first kind of knowledge involves the knowledge of a *friend*, this second way to approach the Trinity involves reflection on the nature of *friendship*. We might also distinguish the two approaches as the difference between a living participation in the mystery and a conceptual knowledge of it. Both ways of knowing are important.

For instance, author Dorothy Sayers, in her provocative 1941 study *The Mind of the Maker*, explored the nature of the Trinity through the lens of the human mind's creative process. She argued that the church's creedal statements about the Trinity—originally crafted to refute heresy—are not arbitrary claims about God that are irrelevant to day-to-day life. On the contrary, they are a witness to the truth about the nature of the human mind as it engages in the act of creative imagination. Sayers observes:

> For every work [or act] of creation is threefold, an earthly trinity to match the heavenly. First, [not in time, but merely in order of enumeration] there is the Creative Idea, passionless, timeless, beholding the whole work complete at once, the end in the beginning: and this is the image of the Father. Second, there is the Creative Energy [or Activity] begotten of that idea, working in time from the beginning to the end, with sweat and passion,

---

11. Eph 4:1–6; 25–31; 5:21–33; Phil 1:27–28; 2:1–11; Rom 12:3–11; 1 Cor 1:10–17; 2 Cor 13:5–14.

being incarnate in the bonds of matter: and this is the image of the Word. Third, there is the Creative Power, the meaning of the work and its response in the lively soul: and this is the image of the indwelling Spirit. And these three are one, each equally in itself the whole work, whereof none can exist without other: and this is the image of the Trinity.[12]

For Sayers, a creative work such as a novel corresponds to her concept of Idea, Energy, and Power, by being Book-as-Thought, Book-as-Written, and Book-as-Read. When we experience a work of art, we know something of the maker of it. We know something of Dostoevski from the profundity of his writing. But there is more to Dostoevski than the sum of his works. In the same way, we glimpse something of the nature of God by observing what God has made, but the mystery still remains. In art, the Trinity is expressed as the Creative Idea, the Creative Energy, and the Creative Power—first the imagining of the work, then the making incarnate of the work, and finally the meaning of the work. What is conceived in the imagination must be brought into being and made manifest. Extending this line of thinking further, Sayers posits that human beings are Book-as-Read; the universe is Book-as-Written; and that it is in the universe because it is God's idea about the universe (Book-as-Thought).

In any event, the church's need to understand the Trinity theologically and philosophically is rooted in history. From the time the church was born and in the first few centuries of its growth, it faced challenges when persons introduced teachings or doctrines that did not come from Christ or from the apostles on whom Christ bestowed his authority. As early as the end of the first century, the apostles began to appoint bishops to oversee local congregations in order to safeguard the deposit of faith that had come from Christ to the apostles. This oversight was given in order to preserve unity in doctrine and worship.

Early in the fourth century, a presbyter (from which we get our word "priest") from Libya by the name of Arius began teaching that if Jesus was God's begotten Son, that meant that Jesus was a creature, that there was a time when Jesus did not exist. Jesus was not the preexistent Son of God and was not of the same substance as God. Within a short time, Arius's teaching spread like wildfire. A catchy tune was even written and began to "go viral." People far and wide were singing, "There was a time when the Son was not."

In AD 325 the Emperor Constantine—newly converted to Christianity—saw what was happening and took action. He called for a council of bishops to gather at Nicaea in Northwest Turkey so that the issue could be

---

12. Sayers, *Mind of the Maker*, 37–38.

settled. More than three hundred bishops gathered to address Arius's teaching. The council of bishops declared Arius to be a heretic and condemned his erroneous understanding of the nature of Christ. The principal bishop who championed the correct understanding that Christ was of the same substance as God and that God was *one* God revealed in *three* Persons was a priest named Athanasius.

In many churches on Trinity Sunday, the creed that bears Athanasius's name is recited, replacing the Nicene Creed that is typically recited on the remaining Sundays of the year. Although the Nicene Creed is explicitly Trinitarian, the Athanasian Creed is somewhat more detailed in its attempt to reflect theologically and philosophically on the Godhead. It explicates in great detail God's nature as a *procession* of Persons who share an identity of *essence* within a *unity* of operation.[13] It corrects Arius's heretical teaching, a teaching which Arius forcefully and persuasively argued from Scripture.[14] Even though forms of Arianism persist to this day, without Athanasius's efforts (and that of his fellow bishops) at Nicaea, the distinctively Trinitarian shape of Christianity would have been eroded or possibly lost altogether.[15]

Athanasius is counted as one of the four great Doctors of the Church in the Roman Catholic tradition. In Eastern Orthodoxy, he is labeled as the "Father of Orthodoxy," because he was one of the first persons to argue for the divine inspiration of the twenty-seven books that became our New Testament. We are indebted to Athanasius and his fellow bishops. His heroic efforts remind us that Trinitarian faith is not a secondary aspect of Christianity. The light of the Trinity illumines everything.

13. See White, *Light of Christ*, 78.

14. The word "heresy" comes from a Greek word that means "to choose." It usually involves a selective picking and choosing, leading ultimately to impoverishment. Arius, and countless others before and after him who taught erroneous doctrine, all argued their positions from Scripture. Adjudicating these disputes could not, and cannot, be done by appeals to Scripture alone. A living voice of human authority is necessary in order to settle these disputes. See D'Ambrosio, *When the Church Was Young*, 73.

15. For a detailed examination of the life of Athanasius and his role in safeguarding correct Trinitarian teaching, see Bennett, *Apostasy That Wasn't*, 90–152.

Chapter Twenty-Six

All in the Family

In his holy flirtation with the world, God occasionally drops
a handkerchief. These handkerchiefs are called saints.

—Frederick Buechner

I believe . . . in the communion of saints.

—The Apostles' Creed

SUGGESTED READINGS

Neh 9:7–14; Ps 149; Rev 7:9–17; Matt 5:1–12

The Autumn season culminates the lengthy season of Ordinary Time
and brings the liturgical year to a close by turning our attention to last
things. Our focus turns to the end of time and the end of life. We come face-
to-face with the *telos* or end goal of God's creative and salvific work. We look
backward at the year, at our lives, at our deep shared history as Christians.
And we look forward to next year, to the next life, to the future hope that
weaves together the threads of our separate lives.[1]

1. Wright, *Time Between*, 207.

In Jesus's great High Priestly prayer recorded in John's Gospel, Jesus willed that those who believe in him should form an inner moral unity with one another, a unity modeled on his own unity with the Father.[2] The strength of this union transcends the boundary of physical death. It derives its strength from the unbreakable love of God, who in Christ has broken the power of death. The unity of the church surpasses the physical confines of this life.[3]

Since the earliest days of Christianity, the church has given special honor to men and women of heroic virtue. In the beginning this honor was reserved for martyrs who were celebrated on specific feast days, but gradually expanded to include any persons of exemplary holiness. In time, the number of holy men and women grew so large that a special feast day originated in order to recognize them. Thus, the feast of All Saints was born. Celebrated on November 1, the feast celebrates the great multitude of every nation standing before the Lamb on the heavenly throne recorded in the book of Revelation. Wendy Wright observes,

> [On all Saints] we lean with longing into the proffered vision of a new heaven and a new earth. We remember with gratitude all the saints . . . whose hearts have been opened wide enough to receive the sweetness of that longing. We remember those who have walked hand in hand with us into the promise that this life, these longings are the very pathways by which we will, at the completion, come face-to-face with God.[4]

It is commonly believed that the celebration of All Saints originated in the eighth century under the papacy of Gregory III, but in fact the feast dates to the mid-fourth century in the Eastern Roman empire. The feast is mentioned in the sermons of John Chrysostom in Constantinople, as well as Basil of Caesarea and Ephrem the Syrian, from AD 370–73.[5] There is a long and varied history in the church of honoring those who witnessed to Christ in extraordinary ways, often losing their lives in doing so. The Greek word "martyr" is translated to English as "witness."

Pope Paul VI, who served the church from 1963–78, once remarked, "Modern man listens more to witnesses than teachers."[6] The dictionary defines "witness" as "An individual who personally sees or beholds something."

2. John 17:21.

3. Campbell, *Feasts of Christendom*, 246.

4. Wright, *Time Between*, 224.

5. Campbell, *Feasts of Christendom*, 249, 266. Pope Gregory changed the date of the feast from May to November 1, but its origins date to the fourth century.

6. Paul VI, *Evangelii Nuntiandi*, 41.

The word also describes a person who bears witness or gives testimony, as in a court of law.

I believe that what Paul VI meant, in part, was that the world needs to see persons who have had a personal and life-changing encounter with Jesus Christ. Christianity is not an ideology or a philosophical system. Christianity is about Jesus Christ, who comes to reveal the love of God for the world *in person*. The modern world will never be convinced of the truth of Christianity through logical argumentation alone.

What the world needs is people who have encountered Jesus and who have been profoundly changed by the encounter. John Wesley would agree and is reported to have said, "If you catch fire for God, people will come to watch you burn." The apostle John, in the first of three of his short epistles, said it like this:

> From the very first day, we were there, taking it all in—we heard it with our own ears, saw it with our own eyes, verified it with our own hands. The Word of Life appeared right before our eyes; we saw it happen! And now we're telling you . . . that what we witnessed was this: The infinite Life of God himself took shape before us. We saw it, we heard it, and now we're telling you so you can experience it along with us, this experience of communion with the Father and his Son, Jesus Christ.[7]

Our world desperately needs witnesses who are willing to say with their lives and with their voices: "The Word of Life appeared to me, and my life has never been the same!" People like the man born blind in John's Gospel who said, "I'm not sure what the theologians and philosophers say about Jesus, but this I can tell you for sure: I was blind, and now I can see!"

History has seen its share of witnesses to Jesus who are well-known to us. We know of the apostles, most of whom were killed for their testimony. We know of persons who learned from the apostles, like Ignatius of Antioch who was torn apart by wild beasts, and Polycarp of Smyrna, who was burned at the stake. We know of people like Maximilian Kolbe, Edith Stein, and Dietrich Bonhoeffer, who bore witness to Jesus in the face of the atrocities of Naziism. In America, we are aware of people like Elizabeth Ann Seton or Martin Luther King Jr., whose encounter with Jesus led him to pursue justice and equality for all citizens of our nation.

America has no shortage of teachers and preachers. But she has a paucity of witnesses. On any given day, millions of Christians around the world profess their belief in the "communion of saints" as they recite the Apostles'

---

7. 1 John 1:1–4 MSG.

Creed. Few, however, recognize the importance of this phrase. What, exactly, is the "communion of saints?"

Understanding the communion of saints begins with taking seriously the New Testament's description of the church as Christ's *body*. The apostle Paul and other New Testament writers teach that membership in Christ's body involves a personal relationship with Jesus and, through him, with all Christians. Paul tells the church at Rome:

> For as in one body we have many members, and all the members
> do not have the same function, so we, though many, are one
> body in Christ, and individually members one of another.[8]

As members of Christ's body, we share a connection, a continuity, a special relationship with all Christians, including those who have gone before us in the life of faith. Jesus has just one body, not one in heaven and another on earth. All Christians, including those in heaven, are members of that one body. Paul further teaches that because of Christ's victory over death—a victory in which all Christians share—natural death cannot separate Christians from Christ or from each other.[9] Since death has no power to sever the bond of Christian unity, the relationship between Christians on earth and those in heaven remains intact.

The apostle Paul speaks of this communal relationship among believers in his letter to the Ephesians using the image of an inheritance. He prays for the Ephesians, that they might know the hope to which they have been called, and that they might know what a rich and glorious inheritance God has given to his people.[10] The KJV renders this verse "How rich is God's glorious inheritance in the saints."

Ordinarily we might think of an inheritance in terms of money, or property and possessions, or valuable family heirlooms. But the inheritance Paul speaks of is an inheritance comprised of *people and relationships*. Paul is saying that there is a vast depository of blessing and wisdom and encouragement—a spiritual, mystical inheritance—available to us in the lives of those who have preceded us precisely because our communion with them is not broken by death.

One special witness to the faith who is a part of our great inheritance is a man named Bernard. Some may know or recognize this great man of God by the name of a new monastery he was asked to lead in the early twelfth

---

8. Rom 12:4–5 RSV. The image of the church as the body of Christ is a prominent New Testament teaching. See 1 Cor 10:16; 12:12–27; Gal 3:28; Eph 1:22–23; 3:4–6; 4:4, 15, 25; 5:21–32; Col 1:18; 3:15; Heb 13:1–3.

9. See 1 Cor 15:25–26, 54–56; 2 Cor 2:14; 2 Tim 1:10; Rom 8:35–39.

10. Eph 1:18.

century—Clairvaux. Starting with twelve men, including his own brothers, Bernard led the monastery as its abbott, which grew to over 130 monks.

Bernard was an amazing, spirit-filled man. One historian has said that he "carried the twelfth century on his shoulders."[11] He was a gifted communicator and had a remarkable ability to bring schismatic and disputing parties in the church together and to effect reconciliation. He served as counsel to numerous popes and bishops, and under his leadership sixty-eight additional monasteries were started by brothers who had been with him at Clairvaux. He is recognized as one of the Doctors of the Church, and many of his writings still remain influential. He is also the author of the Hymn, "Jesus, Thou Joy of Loving Hearts."

Bernard reflects the teaching of the church through history that the saints in heaven serve not only as *exemplars*, but also as *intercessors*. Communion with another, or with others, involves relationship, and no relationship is possible without some basis of communication. Saint Bernard understands that those who have died in the faith are alive to God, in fact more alive now than ever. There are not two churches, one earthly and one heavenly. God does not segregate his finished, heavenly elite from us ordinary folks who warm our earthly pews. The church is at once heavenly and earthly. Those in heaven constitute the Church Triumphant, while those on earth comprise the Church Militant. The saints in heaven form what the writer to the Hebrews describes as the great cloud of witnesses who even now surround us on our journey of faith.[12] Since death cannot sever the bond of Christian unity, it is entirely appropriate for Christians on earth to ask for the intercession of those who are in heaven.

The New Testament gives us glimpses that this is precisely what the saints in heaven are doing. In the book of Revelation, the saints stand before the throne of the Lamb and before the altar in the heavenly sanctuary. They sing hymns of praise and offer up the prayers of the saints on earth which rise like billowing clouds of incense.[13] The saints in heaven are perfected in God's love. Because of this, they are filled with love for God's people, which leads them to intercede for us. Patrick Madrid notes:

> Heaven would be a very strange place indeed, and God a very strange Father, if Christians in heaven were prohibited from intercessory prayer. Why would God command intercessory prayer by Christians on earth but prohibit it by Christians in heaven?[14]

11. Hello, *Studies in Saintship*, 82.

12. Heb 11.

13. Rev 5:8; 8:3–4.

14. Madrid, "Any Friend of God," para. 24.

In addition to their role as intercessors, Saint Bernard shows that we enjoy communion with the saints in heaven as ongoing examples of the life of faith. They lived and died as heroic witnesses for Christ, and their lives inspire us to emulate them. Our hearts should be set on fire by their example, and we should desire to be reunited with them in heavenly fellowship. And we should seek their prayers in order that we may be prepared for Christ's return in glory:

> When Christ comes again, [though], his death shall no longer be proclaimed, and we shall know that we also have died, and that our life is hidden with him. The glorious head of the Church will appear and his glorified members will shine in splendor with him, when he forms this lowly body anew into such glory as belongs to himself, its head. Therefore, we should aim at attaining this glory with a wholehearted and prudent desire. That we may rightly hope and strive for such blessedness, we must above all seek the prayers of the saints. Thus, what is beyond our own powers to obtain will be granted through their intercession.[15]

We have inherited something far more precious and valuable than money, property, or family heirlooms. We have inherited the special relationship we have with all those who've gone before us in the faith—a glorious inheritance in the saints. And this relationship is so valuable, so strong, so precious, that not even death can sever or destroy it. Our communion with the saints in heaven hurls us out into the infinity of eternal life even though for a the time being we are still on earth. All Saints is the day in the church year when we crack open the family album and affirm that the veil separating earth and heaven is razor thin, when we give thanks for the great crowd of witnesses who surround us on our continued journey. Their faithful lives inspire us, and their intercession unites us as members of Christ's mystical body.

15. *Liturgy of the Hours*, 6:1527.

Chapter Twenty-Seven

Christic the King

Christ has dominion over all creatures, a dominion not seized by
violence, nor usurped, but his by essence and by nature.

— CYRIL OF ALEXANDRIA

SUGGESTED READINGS

Dan 7:9–14; Ps 93; Col 1:11–20; John 18:33–37

THE LAST SUNDAY OF the Christian year finds the church celebrating the reign of Christ over all things. We celebrate Christ as King, not only of our lives but also as Lord over all rival powers and kingdoms.

In the history and development of the Christian year, the celebration of Christ the King is the latest and most recent addition. It was added to the liturgical calendar in 1925 by Pope Pius XI. The timing was providential. The horrible effects of World War I (1914–18) were still playing out on the world stage. The "war to end all wars" had not brought the peace and tranquility that many thought it would. England and continental Europe were devastated, and the Russian Revolution had created great problems and suffering in Russia. Governments were suffering economic chaos.

Unemployment was rampant. The stability of the old political and social orders was crumbling.

The Treaty of Versailles included unreasonable reparations from the defeated Germans, which created a sense of anger and helplessness among its people. The time was ripe for the rise of tyrants, and rise they did. The festering philosophies of Fascism, National Socialism (the Nazis), and Communism produced the likes of Mussolini, Adolph Hitler, and Joseph Stalin. In their distress, the people gravitated to anyone who could provide them hope and a sense of direction. The dictators who emerged on the world stage provided that hope for many, but they also sought to exclude God from everyday life.

In this climate, the historic moral teachings of the church began to be seen as out-of-date for modern society. Modern thinking allowed that Christ might be King in the private lives of individuals, but he had no place in the public sphere. Some political regimes sought to banish Jesus from both the family and society. As nations were reborn, policies and laws were fashioned without regard to Christian principles.

In this environment, Pope Pius XI saw that people were denying Christ in favor of a lifestyle dominated by secularism and the false hope offered by political tyrants. He realized that he needed to address the political and economic forces that were crowding out the kingship of Jesus. He dedicated the beginning of his pontificate to "the peace of Christ in the reign of Christ."

In 1925, the church celebrated the 1,600[th] anniversary of the Council of Nicaea, which gave us the Nicene Creed that millions recite each week. Throughout that anniversary year, Pope Pius repeatedly emphasized the kingship of Christ that we declare in the creed when we say, "His kingdom will have no end." In December, the Pope issued an encyclical adding the celebration of Christ the King to the liturgical calendar. Its purpose was to remind the faithful of the supremacy of Jesus Christ over all men, nations, and earthly allegiances. In it the Pope said:

> Christ, who has been cast out of public life, despised, neglected and ignored, will most severely avenge these insults; for his kingly dignity demands that the State should take account of the commandments of God and of Christian principles, both in making laws and in administering justice, and also in providing for the young a sound moral education.[1]

Originally, the celebration of Christ the King was held on the last Sunday of October. Coming just before All Saints, this day reminded people that Jesus is not only King of this world who reigns among nations today;

---

1. Pius XI, *Quas Primas*, 32.

He is also the eternal King, glorified by the saints in heaven, who will one day come to judge all mankind.

In 1969, Pope Paul VI took steps to further enhance the celebration of Christ the King Sunday. He changed the date of the celebration to the last Sunday of the liturgical year in order to emphasize more strongly the connection between Christ's kingship and his second coming to judge the world.

Today, these many years later, peace still eludes us. Social, political, and economic orders are shaking at the foundations. Nations continue to reject the light of the gospel. The rejection of individuals and states against the authority of Christ continues to produce horrible consequences. We can be grateful, then, for the chance to celebrate each year the kingship of Christ. Now, more than ever, the world needs our witness to his rule over all things.

Yet for many North Americans and others in the world, the image of Christ as King is not one which they readily affirm. They see the image too easily linked to triumphalist understandings of the church, or to colonial ideologies focused on domination and control. But what exactly are we witnessing to when we confess Christ as King? Over what kind of kingdom does he rule? On Christ the King Sunday in 2009, Pope Benedict XVI answered that question definitively:

> [Christ's power consists] not in the power of the kings or the great people of this world; it is the divine power to give eternal life, to liberate from evil, to defeat the dominion of death. It is the power of Love that can draw good from evil, that can melt a hardened heart, bring peace amid the harshest conflict and kindle hope in the thickest darkness. This Kingdom of Grace is never imposed and always respects our freedom.[2]

Any concerns that images of Christ as King tend toward an unhealthy triumphalism are mitigated when that image is seen in the light of other images, such as Jesus riding a donkey into Jerusalem, the vulnerability of a baby in a manger, or the humiliating self-emptying of a man hanging on a cross, helpless and abandoned.[3] As Pope Benedict notes, Christ's kingdom is never imposed and always respects our freedom.

Admittedly, there is a sense in which the celebration of Christ as King seems a bit incongruous. We may feel like the writer of the epistle to the Hebrews, who writes that Christ has been placed in authority over all things, but at present it doesn't seem that way. On the surface of things, it appears that Jesus is not placed in authority over anything. But we should not be deceived, nor should we lose heart. Instead, as the writer says, we have need

---

2. Benedict XVI, *Angelus*, para. 2.

3. Wright, *Time Between*, 223.

of endurance. We need grace to persevere, to press on, and to fix our eyes on Jesus, the Author and Perfector of our faith. His kingdom is within us, it is coming to us, it is present in his church, and it will have no end. In this way, the celebration of Christ as King brings the liturgical year to a close as God's people acknowledge him as the King of kings and Lord of lords who will come again in power and glory to judge the world and inaugurate God's reign in its fullness.

Conclusion

IN OUR EXAMINATION OF the seasons of Jesus's life as embodied in the liturgical year, we have seen how our lives are drawn up into his life through the church's distinctive way of marking time. We discover that we are born not merely for earth and for time, but for heaven and eternity. Discovering how God has acted in time to save us and to fit us for eternity invests our lives with meaning and significance. We are immersed into a narrative that is larger than our individual lives. Through the liturgical year our lives are saturated with *kairos* time, moments where God continues to act in Christ for our salvation and where Christ seeks to make us whole through the church and its sacraments.

We began our examination of the challenges and joys of following Jesus in Advent, preparing for the arrival of a King. We end where we began, proclaiming Jesus as King of kings whose kingdom, in the words of the Creed, will have no end. Sandwiched between these two comings are our lives in all of their brokenness and beauty. Christ our King comes from God not merely to subdue us and treat us as servants, but to make us the Father's beloved sons and daughters, cooperators with God in his saving and healing work. Through the gift of supernatural grace, we discover that the abundant life that we seek comes through sacrifice, suffering, and radical obedience. True freedom comes not from self-determination or clinging to our autonomy, but surrendering our hearts, minds, and wills to Christ. We place ourselves as subjects under the Lordship of the One who began his rule from an unorthodox throne of a manger, who sits now at God's right hand, and who will come in glory to usher in God's kingdom in its fullness.

Christ's kingly reign is a reign of love. He is the Beloved One who comes to show us that we are destined to be God's beloved sons and daughters. We discover this and, more importantly, we *live into it* as we travel together through the seasons of the liturgical year. We learn what it means to be the church, the mystical body and continuing incarnation of Christ in the world. We discover that ordinary moments and days are made holy as all time is infused with divine grace:

> If I walk in the world on a path hollowed out by generations of persons who too have found their way on the road that wends from Bethlehem to the empty tomb by way of Calvary, I can only think of this road as a royal one. . . . Our lives are such a road, if only we would know the mystery at their heart.[1]

This book has been my attempt to put a frame around the mystery at the heart of our lives. At the beginning of our study we learned from Bernard of Clairvaux of Christ's threefold coming to us at Christmas. In his first coming he comes as our redemption. In his second coming he will appear as our life. But in between those comings he comes to us as *rest* and *consolation*. This rest and consolation is like a road, says Bernard, a road on which we travel from Jesus's first coming to his final coming.

Perhaps author Wendy Wright had Bernard in mind when she wrote above that the road that begins at Calvary and ends at the empty tomb is indeed a royal road, a road of rest and consolation. Rest and consolation are periodically necessary on this road because it is the *via Crucis*, the way of the cross. If this book has in some small way encouraged you to count the cost and to embark upon this royal road, or to become more intentional in traveling it, I am grateful. It is an ideal path to travel because the authentic life we all seek is only found in relationship to our Creator. Saint Augustine was right. Our restless hearts will never be at peace until they beat as one with the heart of Jesus. When, by God's grace, we discover this truth, every season of life becomes worth living.

1. Wright, *The Time Between*, 224.

Bibliography

Adam, Adolf. *The Liturgical Year: Its History and Meaning after the Reform of the Liturgy.* Collegeville, MN: The Liturgical, 1981.

Aquinas, Thomas. "Adoro te Devote." Translated by Gerard Manley Hopkins. https://www.ewtn.catholicism/library/adoro-te-devote-4528.

———. *Catena Aurea: Commentary on the Four Gospels, Collected Out of the Works of the Fathers.* Oxford: Parker, 1841–45.

Barber, Michael. *The True Meaning of Christmas: The Birth of Jesus and the Origins of the Season.* San Francisco: Ignatius, 2021.

Barron, Robert. *Exploring Catholic Theology: Essays on God, Liturgy, and Evangelization.* Grand Rapids: Baker, 2015.

———. "Zechariah and the New David." *Word on Fire* (podcast), June 30, 2020. https://www.wordonfire.org/videos/sermons/zechariah-and-the-new-david/.

Beale, Stephen. "Advent and Holy Saturday: The King Sleeps." *Catholic Exchange* (blog), November 26, 2018. https://catholicexchange.com/advent-and-holy-saturday-the-king-sleeps/.

———. "The Deeper Meaning of Advent in Latin." *Catholic Exchange* (blog), December 1, 2021. https://catholicexchange.com/the-deeper-meaning-of-advent-in-latin/.

Benedict XVI, Pope. *Angelus.* https://www.vatican.va/content/benedict-xvi/en/angelus/2009/documents/hf_ben-xvi_ang_20091122.html.

Bennett, Rod. *The Apostasy That Wasn't: The Extraordinary Story of the Unbreakable Early Church.* El Cajon, CA: Catholic Answers, 2015.

Bernard of Clairvaux. "Sermon 5." In *The Liturgy of the Hours,* 1:188–90. 4 vols. New York: Catholic Book, I:169.

Biffi, Inos. *An Introduction to the Liturgical Year.* Grand Rapids: Baker, 1995.

The Book of Common Prayer and Administration of the Sacraments and Other Rites and Ceremonies of the Church: Together with the Psalter or Psalms of David. New York: Seabury, 1979.

Boone, Dan. *The Dark Side of God: When God Is Hard to Explain.* Oklahoma City, OK: Smashwords, 2012.

Bradshaw, Paul F., and Maxwell E. Johnson. *The Origin of Feasts, Fasts, and Seasons in Early Christianity.* Collegeville, MN: The Liturgical, 2011.

Brown, Alison. "How Chronic Illness Brought Me Closer to God." *Catholic Exchange* (blog), May 9, 2022. https://catholicexchange.com/how-chronic-illness-brought-me-closer-to-god/.

Browning, Elizabeth Barrett. "From Aurora Leigh." In *The Oxford Book of English Mystical Verse*, edited by D. H. S. Nicholson and A. H. E. Lee, 150–52. Oxford: Clarendon, 1917.

Burdick, T. J. *Detached: Put Your Phone in Its Place*. Huntington, IN: Our Sunday Visitor, 2018.

Campbell, Phillip. *The Feasts of Christendom: History, Theology, and Customs of the Principal Feasts of the Catholic Church*. Grass Lake, MI: Cruachen Hill, 2021.

Cavadini, John C. "The Fatherly Heart of Saint Joseph." *Church Life Journal* (blog), January 26, 2021. https://churchlifejournal.nd.edu/articles/the-fatherly-heart-of-saint-joseph.

Cavens, Jeff. *When You Suffer: Biblical Keys for Hope and Understanding*. Cincinnati, OH: Franciscan Media, 2015.

Chesterton, G. K. *Orthodoxy*. New York: Dodd, Mead, 1908.

Chittister, Joan. *The Liturgical Year: The Spiraling Adventure of the Spiritual Life*. Nashville, TN: Nelson, 2009.

Climacus, John. *The Ladder of Divine Ascent*. Translated by Colm Luibheid and Norman Russell. New York: Paulist, 1982.

Comfort, Phillip, and Daniel Partner, comps. and eds. *The One Year Book of Poetry*. Wheaton, IL: Tyndale, 1999.

Craddock, Fred. *Luke: A Bible Commentary for Preaching and Teaching*, Ed. James Luther Mays. Louisville: John Knox, 1990.

Cyril of Alexandria. *Commentary on the Gospel According to St. Luke*. Translated by R. Payne Smith. Oxford: Oxford University Press, 1859.

D'Ambrosio, Marcillino. *When the Church Was Young: Voices of the Early Fathers*. Cincinnati, OH: Servant, 2014. Kindle ed.

Dictionary.com. "Presume." https://www.dictionary.com/browse/presume.

———. "Complacency." https://www.dictionary.com/browse/complacency.

Dix, Dom Gregory. *The Shape of the Liturgy*. New ed. London: Bloomsbury T. & T. Clark, 2015.

Driscoll, Jeremy. *What Happens at Mass*. Rev. ed. Chicago: Liturgy Training, 2011.

Eliot, T. S. *Collected Poems, 1909–1962*. New York: Harcourt, Brace, 1963.

Esper, Joseph M. "Seek the Lord's Will, Even in Uncertainty." *Catholic Exchange* (blog), May 18, 2020. https://catholicexchange.com/seek-the-lords-will-even-in-uncertainty/.

Ewing, Jeannie. "When You Feel Like a Thing Thrown Away: A Reflection on Psalm 31." *Catholic Exchange* (blog), June 8, 2022. https://catholicexchange.com/when-you-feel-like-a-thing-thrown-away-a-reflection-on-psalm-31/.

Fringer, Rob A., and Jeff K. Lane. *Theology of Luck: Fate, Chaos, and Faith*. Kansas City, MO: Beacon Hill, 2015.

Greenberg, Sanford D. *Hello Darkness, My Old Friend: How Daring Dreams and Unyielding Friendship Turned One Man's Blindness into an Extraordinary Vision for Life*. New York: Posthill, 2020.

Gregory the Great. "Homily 8: Now When Jesus Was Born." In *Forty Gospel Homilies*, translated by Dom David Hurst, 54–61. Kalamazoo, MI: Cistercian, 2009.

Gross, Bobby. *Living the Christian Year: Time to Inhabit the Story of God*. Downers Grove, IL: InterVarsity, 2009.

Hahn, Scott. *A Father Who Keeps His Promises*. Cincinnati, OH: Franciscan Media, 1998.

———. *The Fourth Cup: Unveiling the Mystery of the Last Supper and the Cross*. New York: Image, 2018.

———. *Reasons to Believe: How to Understand, Explain, and Defend the Catholic Faith*. New York: Doubleday, 2007.

Haidt, Jonathan. "Why the Past 10 Years of American Life Have Been Uniquely Stupid." *The Atlantic*, April 11, 2022. https://www.theatlantic.com/magazine/archive/2022/05/social-media-democracy-trust-babel/629369/.

Hayford, Jack. *Pursuing the Will of God: Reflections and Meditations on the Life of Abraham*. Sisters, OR: Multnomah, 1997.

Heady, Chene. *Numbering My Days: How the Liturgical Calendar Rearranged My Life*. San Francisco: Ignatius, 2016.

Hello, Ernest. *Studies in Saintship*. London: Methuen, 1903.

Henrich, Sarah. "First Sunday in Lent." *Working Preacher* (blog), February 26, 2012. https://www.workingpreacher.org/commentaries/revised-common-lectionary/first-sunday-in-lent-2/commentary-on-mark-19-15.

Howard, Thomas. *Evangelical Is Not Enough: Worship of God in Liturgy and Sacrament*. Nashville, TN: Nelson, 1984.

Hying, Donald J. "Fully Entering Into the Triduum." *Simply Catholic* (blog), n.d. http://www.simplycatholic.com/how-to-enter-fully-into-the-triduum-this-week.

Ireton, K. C. *The Circle of Seasons: Meeting God in the Church Year*. Edmonds, WA: Mason Lewis, 2018.

John Paul II, Pope. *Salvifici Doloris*. https://www.vatican.va/content/john-paul-ii/en/apost_letters/1984/documents/hf_jp-ii_apl_11021984_salvifici-doloris.html.

Kreeft, Peter. *I Burned for Your Peace: Augustine's Confessions Unpacked*. San Francisco: Ignatius, 2016.

LaCugna, Catherine Mowry. "Making the Most of Trinity Sunday." In *Between Memory and Hope: Readings on the Liturgical Year*, edited by Maxwell E. Johnson, 247–64. Collegeville, MN: The Liturgical, 2000.

LeClerc, Diane, and Brent Peterson. *The Backside of the Cross: An Atonement Theology for the Abused and Abandoned*. Eugene, OR: Cascade, 2022.

L'Engle, Madeline. *The Irrational Season*. New York: Seabury, 1977.

Levertov, Denise. *The Stream and the Sapphire: Selected Poems on Religious Themes*. New York: New Directions, 1997.

Lewis, C. S. *A Grief Observed*. New York: HarperCollins, 2002.

The Liturgy of the Hours according to the Roman Rite. English Translation prepared by the International Commission on English in the Liturgy. 4 vols. New York: Catholic Book, 1975.

"The Lord's Descent into Hell." https://www.vatican.va/spirit/documents/spirit_20010414_omelia-sabato-santo_en.html.

Luther, Martin. "Easter Eve." In *The Complete Sermons of Martin Luther*, edited by Eugene F. A. Klug, translated by Eugene F. A. Klug et al., 5:476–89. 7 vols. Grand Rapids: Baker, 2000.

Madrid, Patrick. "Any Friend of God Is a Friend of Mine." *Catholic Answers* (blog), May 1, 2009. https://www.catholic.com/magazine/print-edition/any-friend-of-god-is-a-friend-of-mine.

Marr, Ryan. *John Henry Newman*. Boston: Pauline Books and Media, 2019.

Martinez, Luis M. *When God Is Silent: Finding Spiritual Peace amid the Storms of Life*. Manchester, NH: Sophia Institute, 2014.

————. *Worshiping a Hidden God: Unlocking the Secrets of the Interior Life*. Manchester, NH: Sophia Institute, 2014.

Maximus of Turin, Saint. "Sermon 100." In *The Liturgy of the Hours*, 1:612–13. 4 vols. New York: Catholic Book, 1975.

Mendenhall, Laura. "Led from Behind." *Lectionary Homiletics* 20 (2009) 38–39.

Millay, Edna St. Vincent. *Collected Sonnets*. Rev. exp. ed. New York: Harper Perennial, 1988.

Moore, Gerard. *Earth Unites with Heaven: An Introduction to the Liturgical Year*. Eugene, OR: Wipf & Stock, 2014.

Newman, John Henry. "The Pillar of the Cloud." https://newmanreader.org/works/verses/verse90.html.

Nicholson, D. H. S., and A. H. E. Lee, eds. *The Oxford Book of English Mystical Verse*. Classic repr. ed. London: Forgotten, 2015.

Oden, Thomas C,. and Christopher A. Hall, eds. *Ancient Christian Commentary on Scripture: New Testament*. Ancient Christian Commentary. Downers Grove, IL: InterVarsity, 1998.

Oord, Thomas Jay. *God Can't: How to Believe in God after Tragedy, Abuse and Other Evils*. N.p.: Sacrasage, 2019.

————. *The Uncontrolling Love of God: An Open and Relational Account of Providence*. Downers Grove, IL: InterVarsity, 2015.

Pakaluk, Michael. "Doing Justice to St. Joseph." *The Catholic Thing* (blog), December 22, 2020. https://www.thecatholicthing.org/2020/12/22/doing-justice-to-st-joseph/.

Papandrea, James L. *Reading the Church Fathers: A History of the Early Church and the Development of Doctrine*. Manchester, NH: Sophia Institute, 2022.

Paul VI, Pope. *Evangelii Nuntiandi*. https://www.vatican.va/content/paul-vi/en/apost_exhortations/documents/hf_p-vi_exh_19751208_evangelii-nuntiandi.html.

Percy, Walker. *Signposts in a Strange Land*. New York: Picador, 1991.

Peterson, Eugene. *The Pastor: A Memoir*. New York: HarperCollins, 2011.

Pitre, Brant. *Jesus the Bridegroom: The Greatest Love Story Ever Told*. New York: Image, 2014.

Pius XI, Pope. *Quas Primas*. https://www.vatican.va/content/pius-xi/encyclicals/documents/hf_p-xi_enc_11121925_quas-primas.html.

Posey, Minnie H. *The Poems of Alexander Lawrence Posey*. Topeka, KS: Crane, 1910.

Postman, Neil. *Amusing Ourselves to Death: Public Discourse in the Age of Show Business*. New York: Penguin, 1985.

Pressfield, Steven. *The War of Art: Break Through the Blocks and Win Your Inner Creative Battles*. New York: Warner, 2002.

Rosetti, William Michael. *The Poetical Works of Christina Georgina Rosetti*. London: Macmillan, 1904.

Sarah, Cardinal Robert. *The Power of Silence: Against the Dictatorship of Noise*. San Francisco: Ignatius, 2017.

Sayers, Dorothy L. *The Mind of the Maker*. New York: Harcourt Brace, 1941.

Scanlon, Michael. *What Does God Want: A Practical Guide to Making Decisions*. Manchester, NH: Sophia Institute, 2018.

Schall, James V. *The Reason for the Seasons: Why Christians Celebrate What and When They Do*. Manchester, NH: Sophia Institute, 2018.

Schneider, Athanasius. "Bishop Athanasius Schneider: 'The Gift of Filial Adoption.'" *Catholicism.org*, February 11, 2019. https://catholicism.org/bishop-athanasius-schneider-the-gift-of-filial-adoption.html.

Slim, Hugo. *A Feast of Festivals: Celebrating the Spiritual Seasons of the Year.* London: Marshall Pickering, 1996.

Snell, R. J., and Robert P. George. *Mind, Heart, and Soul: Intellectuals and the Path to Rome.* Charlotte, NC: Tan, 2018.

Stanley, Charles. *Waiting on God: Strength for Today and Hope for Tomorrow.* New York: Howard, 2015.

Stookey, Laurence Hull. *Calendar: Christ's Time for the Church.* Nashville, TN: Abingdon, 1996.

Sumerau, Stacey. "Discerning Vocation: Advice I Would Give My Younger Self." *Catholic Exchange* (blog), April 14, 2022. https://catholicexchange.com/discerning-vocation-advice-i-would-give-my-younger-self/.

Talley, Thomas J. *The Origins of the Liturgical Year.* Collegeville, MN: The Liturgical, 1986.

Tertullian. *The Apology.* Savage, MN: Lighthouse Christian, 2015.

Webber, Robert E. *Ancient-Future Time: Forming Spirituality through the Christian Year.* Grand Rapids: Baker, 2004.

———, ed. *The Complete Library of Christian Worship.* Nashville, TN: Star Song, 1994.

Whalen, Michael D. *Seasons and Feasts of the Church Year: An Introduction.* Eugene, OR: Wipf & Stock, 1993.

White, Thomas Joseph. *The Light of Christ: An Introduction to Catholicism.* Washington, DC: The Catholic University of America Press, 2017.

Wiesel, Elie. *Night.* New York: Bantam, 1983.

Wilson, Paul Scott. *God Sense: Reading the Bible for Preaching.* Nashville, TN: Abingdon, 2001.

Willard, Dallas. *Hearing God: Developing a Conversational Relationship with God.* Updated and Expanded. Downers Grove, IL: Intervarsity, 2012.

Wright, Wendy M. *The Rising: Living the Mysteries of Lent, Easter, and Pentecost.* Nashville, TN: Upper Room, 1994.

———. *The Time Between: Cycles and Rhythms in Ordinary Time.* Nashville, TN: Upper Room, 1999.

Yancey, Phillip. *Disappointment with God: Three Questions No One Asks Aloud.* Grand Rapids: Zondervan, 1988.

Ybarra, Erick. *Melchizedek and the Last Supper: Biblical and Patristic Evidence for the Sacrifice of the Mass.* N.p.: Classical Christian Thought, 2022.

"Year of Mercy Prayer." https://www.usccb.org/beliefs-and-teachings/how-we-teach/new-evangelization/jubilee-of-mercy/year-of-mercy-prayer.

Young, William Paul. *The Shack: Where Tragedy Confronts Eternity.* Los Angeles: Windblown Media, 2008.

Made in the USA
Las Vegas, NV
07 November 2023